From an Oak to His Acorns

Essential Lessons for Life

Douglas A. Kretkowski

Cover and book design by Douglas A. Kretkowski

Front cover photograph © Ralph Loesche. Licensed via iStockphoto.com.
Back cover photograph © Ewa Brozek. Licensed via iStockphoto.com.
Dedication photograph © Douglas A. Kretkowski, enhanced by A. Peraza
Spine art © Douglas A. Kretkowski

ISBN: 978-0-578-01443-2

Visit us on the web at www.FromAnOak.com for special bonuses and offers.

To my beautiful wife,
for giving life to our little angels and
nurturing their minds, bodies, and spirits every day.

Hannah and Andrew, thank you
for all the soul-touching memories, past, present, and future.

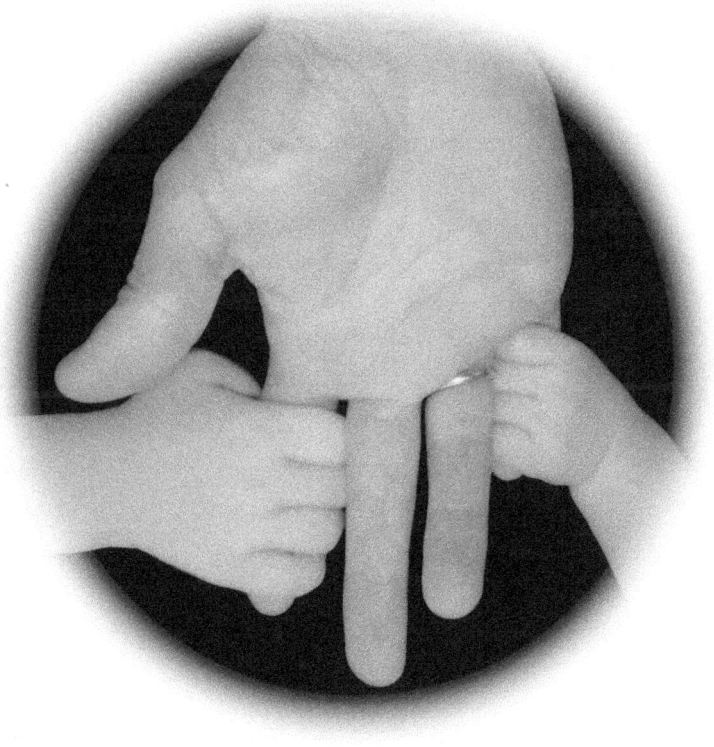

I am you and you are me,
follow my guidance and you will see.

Contents

Brief Note to Fellow Parents

It is every parent's natural responsibility to provide their children with all the necessary components for a safe, successful, happy, and healthy life. Hopefully, with the proper foundation, our children will do even better than us in life. However, times are not what they used to be. Over the last couple of decades, all aspects of life have accelerated at an exponential rate compared to yesteryear. Between the high cost of living (which has forced many parents to work), even higher divorce rates and technology fueling the speed of everything, there is an even greater need for our children to have a strong foundation comprised of basic building blocks.

Herein lies the purpose of this book. However, simply possessing a copy will not guarantee a strong life for your child. As parents, we need to continually carve out consistent blocks of time to review past lessons and to tackle new topics. We also need to take full responsibility for our children and their actions. This holds true for everything, from their usage of the Internet to how they behave in public. Whether you are simply checking homework or helping your children select a profession, you need to be there to support them. There are no shortcuts or easy ways out when it comes to our children and their future.

There is no minimum or maximum age for which these lessons apply. In fact, your first goal as a parent is to establish a routine with your newborn. Furthermore, do not limit the scope of your discussions to the topics or samples found in this book. Integrate real life and personal examples to help solidify the principles and lessons. Lastly, keep in mind that the lessons are just as much for us parents as they are for our children.

Just as life's building blocks are relatively straightforward, so too is the design of this book. However, unlike life, this guide is constrained to a linear

format. In general, the topics begin with the fundamentals critical to your child's core. The discussions continue to spiral outward like a conch shell towards concepts that affect others, ranging from family to the rest of society.

In nearly all lessons, you will be presented with a topic, a brief description, whether to avoid or engage it, benefits and/or consequences as well as practical examples. Each of the life lessons and characteristics were selected as an important factor or influence in the "success" of your child's life. While no single book could possibly capture all of the facets of what they may encounter in life, this guide highlights key elements that can be combined or used singularly to your child's advantage.

Parents, and parents-to-be, I ask only a few things of you. Hopefully, you noticed how the word "parents" is plural. This was not done by accident or haphazardly. Unless there are extenuating circumstances, both mothers and fathers need to be fully engaged in the raising of their children. Do you think it is a coincidence that it takes two people to have a baby in the first place? Believe me, nature knows much better than we do. Forcing or allowing all the responsibility to fall onto one parent robs our children by only giving them half of what they need to be prepared for life. Complete neglect of your child is a surefire recipe for disaster.

First I ask that you protect your children, not only from the obvious, but from the little distractions in daily life. Whether it is to answer a phone that is in another room while your baby is in the bathtub or trying to beat a yellow traffic light, always think about how your actions may affect your child before you carry them out. In our children's minds, our actions speak just as loudly as our words. Secondly, your children are your number one priority in life. Spend as much time with them as you can, have meaningful conversations and enjoy their company. Try starting off a daily conversation

with a simple question, "Did you meet anyone new today?" See how you can take an interest in their lives while protecting them at the same time. Before you know it, our children will turn into adults and move on with their own lives. We have so little time to positively influence our children; *both* parents need to make the most of it while we have the chance. Therefore, every night hug them tight, tell them that you love them and how proud they make you. If you ever find yourself at your mental or physical end, just take a few minutes to watch your child as they sleep. Notice how peaceful, perfect, and full of potential they are. If that is not enough to recharge you, I do not know what is. However, if you ever feel yourself going over the edge and potentially endangering the health or well-being of your child, place them in the care of a responsible adult and remove yourself from the situation immediately. There is no good reason or excuse in the world why a child should ever be suffocated, drowned, poisoned, or otherwise injured at the hands of their parent or guardian. If worse comes to worst, dial 9-1-1 and report yourself to the police before you lift a single harmful finger.

Finally, during the process of writing this book, the teacher became the proverbial student. After thinking I was done creating all the lessons, I suddenly came to the realization that the same qualities and traits that were deficient in my own life were also blatantly missing from the book. This clearly proves several things to be very true. First, no one is perfect and knows everything. Secondly, a hundred thousand textbooks cannot replace firsthand experience; you will never know what something is like until it touches you personally. Thirdly, nothing in life truly comes to an end; even with the death of others we continue to learn. Lastly, you cannot always see the trees through your own forest; therefore, you need trustful people in your life to constructively point out your imperfections. With all that said, I invite and encourage you as both an individual and a parent to take on the challenge

3

of writing your own lessons for life. You do not have to be the best writer or go so far as publishing the work, but I guarantee the exercise will not only help improve and mold your future generations, it will also assist you in refining and enhancing your own life.

Introduction

Hannah and Andrew, I have two primary responsibilities when it comes to you. First and foremost is to ensure your physical, emotional, and mental health and safety. The second is to provide you with all the basic concepts and lessons in order to prepare you for the world that lies ahead. While I wish I could protect you forever, and provide you with the solution to every problem or situation you may face, that is simply not how life works. However, I can promise that I will do my very best to expose you to all the fundamental building blocks, so you can tackle any situation that may cross your path. Rest assured, all that you are about to learn is based on my personal knowledge and firsthand experiences; this is not simply information copied from some theoretical textbooks, or questionable web sites. Also, take comfort in knowing that these lessons are fit for the real world. Most will not cost you any time or money, and those that do require only a small investment that will add to the overall value.

You may hear other parents say that they just want the best for their children. While I want nothing more than for you to have the very best, I may not be able to provide you with the finest of everything in the materialistic sense. This is not for lack of trying, but to be honest, even those who have all the Earthly possessions they could ever want may not have what truly matters – happiness. As your father, I will do everything in my power to make sure that happiness reigns supreme throughout your life.

Always know that no matter how things turn out, or what bumps you encounter on your journey, I will always love you, and be there to help guide you. I may not always be with you in the physical sense, but you should always count on my words to be at your core. As a refresher, review my guidance numerous times during the course of your life, especially at major milestones, such as marriage or at the beginning of a new career. Do not be surprised if you start to appreciate different perspectives throughout your voyage in life; you will continuously evolve, just as all living creatures do. Furthermore, just as important as following my guidance is the timing in which you do. Do not wait until it is too late, and put your health, safety, emotions, career or finances at risk or in ruins. You may not always fully understand or appreciate my recommendations and lessons at the time; just keep in mind that I have the advantage of many years of real life experience and education.

Hannah and Andrew, the only thing I ask in return is that you love and protect each other, no matter what adversities or situations you face, whether separate or together. Prove the saying that blood is thicker than water by always looking out for each other, since I cannot, and may not, always physically be there for each of you. Never hurt each other with words or actions, but continually build on your love and trust for each other. If the opportunity presents itself in the future, take these lessons to the next level with your own children, to continually feed our legacy.

Hannah, as a big sister, you have some additional responsibilities. Being the older sibling, you will be asked to look out for your little brother Andrew. Put your extra few years of knowledge and experience to good use, and help guide him, both while you are children and grown adults. Do not be surprised if he comes to you for help and advice, or seeks your confidence. Your parents will always try to protect and aid Andrew in this Earthly realm, however, you are our "second-in-command" when it comes to your little brother.

Personal Traits

Anyone can be polite to a king.
It takes a gentleman to be polite to a beggar.
- Unknown

Responsibility

Responsibility, in all forms, is extremely important in life. For every action you take or possession you own, there is an element of responsibility. You can be responsible for a task, a situation, and even a life. Parents are responsible for their children's actions and for raising them properly. Doctors are responsible for his or her actions with their patients. You must take responsibility and accountability for your own actions and those things that are in your control. There is no excuse for being irresponsible since it could prove to have enormous repercussions. Never take on more than you can handle and do not be shy or feel ashamed for asking for help or saying something is too much to handle on your own.

Focus and Direction

There are two essential components required for a successful transition into adulthood. The first element is focus. You must remain focused on your schoolwork, grades, and goals and avoid extraneous distractions whenever and however possible. You can easily fall into the wrong crowd, become distracted by trends, or sidetracked by popular items of the day. You can also lose focus by being involved in too many extracurricular activities. It is better to concentrate on one or two activities at most and do them well rather than take a shotgun approach and do a large number of them fairly or poorly.

Direction is just as important as focus. You may have your blinders on and working on all cylinders; however, if you are headed in the wrong direction, it can produce anything from wasted to disastrous results. You are entitled to a reasonable quantity and quality of direction from your parents/guardians, teachers, guidance counselors, and mentors. Unfortunately, all too often in this day and age, adults become enthralled in the typically meaningless trials and tribulations of daily life. However, that is no excuse for supplying you with little or inadequate direction and guidance. If, for whatever reason, you feel you are not receiving proper direction, you owe it to yourself to speak up and ask for it or find it from other/better sources. Your childhood years set the stage for the rest of your life, so do not treat them lightly or let them pass you by without setting both goals and executable plans. Moreover, just because your higher education is behind you that does not mean that you can coast the rest of the way through life. From your daily activities to your finances, career, and beyond, it is critical that you remain focused and dedicated in all aspects of life if you wish to succeed.

Independence

Having a strong sense of independence is a great quality to possess. Being able to work and function on your own is just as important as being an integral member of a team. More often than not, you will be facing situations without the aid or benefit of others, so you need to develop the skills to tackle any situation, long or short term, on your own. Do not be afraid to face situations by yourself. I guarantee that as soon as you successfully overcome one challenge, you will be excited to take on the next one. Do not look at a challenge as a burden but rather as an opportunity to better yourself. Just think, if you sat on the couch and did nothing for the next fifty years, you would not learn, grow strong, or contribute positively to society. Therefore, start off with small tasks on your own and work your way up to bigger and more complex adventures. Before you know it, you will have the confidence to always believe in yourself and trust your own judgment.

There will be many times in life when you will need to depend on your sense of independence. They can be as simple as taking a test to surviving an emergency situation on your own. The death of a spouse can be a great test of your independence, especially after many years of relying on each other physically and emotionally. Do not let an emergency or stressful event be the first time your skills are put to the test.

However, being too independent can have adverse effects on everything from personal relationships to your career. As the saying goes, no man is an island. Do not be stubborn and try to do everything on your own. It will not only be easier to let others in to help you, but cooperation is how societies advance.

Self-Reliance

Having the confidence in yourself to tackle any challenge that comes your way is essential. One of the most successful and famous believers in self-reliance was Benjamin Franklin. I highly recommend that you read his autobiography for a firsthand account of his inspirational experiences. No matter how many friends, co-workers, or relatives you may have, you ultimately need to be able to rely on yourself. Whether it is an emergency situation or everyday life, you cannot always count on others being available. This is not to say that you should reject offers of assistance from others or be stubborn either. Just take comfort in knowing that you can stand on your own two feet if a situation arises.

Honesty

When "they" say honesty is the best policy, they are 100% correct. Whether it is in a relationship or in school, in business or in a home environment, there is no shame in being honest. Chances are that one lie will lead to another lie, which will lead to even bigger lies. However, it is never too late to come out and tell the truth. As with any other bad habit such as stealing, the truth will come out at one point or another. Do not waste time and energy trying to cover up one story with another story. It is best for the sake of your integrity, not to mention your stress levels, to stay on the "straight and narrow path," even if it is a more difficult road to travel.

Pride

You should always take pride in everything you do. At a minimum, it will translate into higher quality which will help fuel everything from your reputation to your self-confidence. You should also take pride in your surroundings, whether it is your room, apartment, house, property, city, state, country, or most importantly, the environment in general. If everyone took even a little bit more pride in what they do and where they live and work, we could instantly make our world a better place.

Loyalty

On the surface, the topic of loyalty would appear to be a quick and easy one. Your allegiance should start with your family and extend to your friends, school, company, and country. However, there will probably be more than one occasion throughout your life when your loyalty is tested. You may find yourself having to make a difficult decision between two or more choices; the proper decision should always be on the side of what is ethically and morally correct. Your first loyalty should be to yourself and your integrity. Otherwise, you will find yourself supporting or defending a cause that is not just. Think carefully about your decision and remember to listen to what your gut tells you no matter who is involved or how awkward the situation.

Cooperation

Cooperation, at the very least, will make your life easier and less stressful. Why waste your time, and the time of others, by being stubborn for no good reason. Working in harmony with others will not only help you in that one situation, but it could make life easier when the next challenge comes along. Keep in mind that you should not turn into a pushover either. Do not allow people to simply dump their tasks on you because they know you will do them. Cooperation is a lifelong used and needed quality since you cannot live as an island.

Tolerance

Tolerance is a quality that needs to be developed since it is not innately a part of you. Not everyone thinks and acts as you do, so if you are unable to accept these differences in life, you should at least tolerate them. Learn to have patience for other people's beliefs, methods, and backgrounds. Instead of viewing differences as a negative quality, think of them in a positive light. There are a wealth of benefits in learning and understanding what makes people different from one another. You may surprise yourself when you start appreciating, adopting, and applying the things you learn from other cultures, religions, and heritages. Just think how boring life would be if everyone and everything were the same.

Quality

The quality of your work is a standalone testament to your character. It can, therefore, work in your favor or against you if it is poor and inadequate.

You should always make a conscious effort to produce quality products and services in everything you do, regardless of size or importance. Since you cannot always be around in person to explain the circumstances of the end result, you will need to let your attention to detail speak for itself. Do not rush or take shortcuts if it will affect the final outcome. Take your time and do not be afraid or get frustrated if you have to repeat something over and over again, or even start from scratch. You may need to step away from what you are doing for a minute, hour, day, week, or year to regain your composure and self-confidence. Just keep in mind that nothing worthwhile in life comes quickly or with great ease.

Confidence

Having confidence is almost as important as the air you breathe. Without it, you can quickly and easily defeat yourself; having a high level of confidence allows little to stand in your mental or physical way. When you come across a new or different situation, you may not have the exact skill set to tackle the challenge, but if you have confidence in yourself, you can quickly get to the solution. Your confidence level is also as apparent as the color of the shirt you are wearing. In fact, it can be seen by others to be either a "turn on" just as much and quickly as a "turn off." You also should not fool yourself into having false confidence which can easily get you into a jam. Lastly, exuding too much confidence in yourself may come across to others poorly, thereby making yourself appear as a "know-it-all."

Determination and Fortitude

The strength of your determination is one of the only limiting factors in how successful you can be in life. Having the fortitude to get through any situation or challenge is paramount. Never let yourself waver, and never doubt your capabilities. As soon as hesitation enters the picture, you will instantly begin to fail. Enhance your determination and confidence levels by conquering small challenges first, and never let a small bump in the road completely derail you. While sometimes bad, unfortunate, or unfavorable things happen to good people, never let it discourage, deter, deject, or demoralize you in any way; find the positive and come back even stronger than before.

Unless you will suffer significant or permanent physical, emotional or financial hardship, you should never quit or give up on something partway through. Having a defeatist attitude will surely not only adversely affect the current challenge but future efforts as well. Always try to maintain a positive outlook and attitude since you never know when you may make a breakthrough, have a change of luck, or find new opportunities.

You cannot get far in anything you do in life if you do not follow it through. Whether swinging a baseball bat or creating an invention, you will always fall short if you do not see things through to the end. Loose ends can create everything from disorganization to disappointment when you look back at your life. Remember, unless you are going to give a hundred percent, do not bother wasting your time, energy, and money in the first place.

Persistence

Persistence is a very important trait to have, but you must know the limits to which it should be used when it is applied. Persistence is crucial when it comes to activities such as studying, tackling new challenges, and anything relating to your health or that of a loved one. However, in certain situations, persistence can work against you. You need to throttle the intensity and duration of your persistence, especially when a task requires the assistance of others. You should be mindful that while you may get through

13

the current situation, you might require the assistance of that same person or group in the future. If you are perceived as too pushy, it may negatively affect the process or outcome the next time you need help. As the saying goes, learn to pick your battles.

Perfection

Perfection is a funny concept since it really does not exist; no one person or object can ever truly be perfect. However, perfection should be seen as the ultimate goal in everything you do. In some cases you may get a perfect score on a test, and that is exactly what you should strive towards. That is not to say that less than perfect is intolerable. More often than not, you may fall just short of a hundred percent, and that is normal and acceptable as long as you learn from your mistakes and try to do better the next time.

Perfection not only relates to actions but to environments and material items as well. You may think that someone has the perfect life or the perfect house, but that may not always be the case when you look beneath the surface. Perfection is something that you define for yourself. Furthermore, be careful not to force your standards, beliefs, and opinions on others.

Diligence

You should always be diligent in your efforts, regardless of significance. No matter who the request is from, including yourself, or the degree of difficultly, you should always give the effort your full attention and devotion. This ethic will reflect in your reputation, for both better and worse. If you are not able to complete a task for any reason, do not wait until the last minute or after the fact to speak up. There is no shame in saying that you cannot do or figure something out. Always seek help from a reliable source if you do need assistance.

14

Humility/Humbleness

Humility and humbleness show that you respect your place the world. Keeping a modest view of yourself will help you more in life than all the "kissing up" ever could. No one in any environment enjoys being around someone that is egotistical or full of themselves. The quality of your reputation will greatly diminish if you do not exercise a reasonable amount of humility and humbleness.

Moderation

Moderation is one of the most important concepts in life to master. It applies to everything you should and should not do in life. Even things that are normally good for you, like exercise, could have damaging effects if done in excess. Whether it is something good or bad, it should always be carefully balanced.

Personal Limitations

While you should always strive for lofty goals, you also need to be a realist at a point. We all are born with massive potential, but as situations evolve, so do our personal limitations. You should always give your goals and challenges one hundred percent devotion and attention. However, if you find the situation degenerating beyond your control, you may need to re-evaluate your intentions. This is not always easy to accept, but you must be honest with yourself. Do not view it as a failure or a defeat but rather the end to a challenge. It could be for physical reasons, such as your age factoring into your reaction time when driving a car, or it could be as a result of reaching the limit of your mental abilities on a subject. If you are not able to tackle the situation from multiple angles, have the integrity to end it on your own terms. Never allow yourself or someone else to be harmed as a result of your unsafe actions. If a "one-off" situation requires the aid of someone else, do not be ashamed or afraid to ask for help.

Tone

It is very important to watch your tone when you are speaking and writing. It is the verbal equivalent of body language, which can either work in your favor or against you. You can easily say the same sentence in two different tones and portray two completely different meanings. More important than your verbal tone is your written tone. The reason is that your words have to stand on their own merit and can often be open to misinterpretation by the reader. Be very deliberate and clear in your tone, and you should not have any issues. If there is a miscommunication, quickly provide an explanation or clarify your intent before it leads to a potential conflict.

Cursing/Swearing

There is absolutely no need to ever be vulgar. Cursing or swearing is not something that is just for adults either. You can be the chief executive officer of an international company and still sound classless if you curse verbally or in writing. Consider cursing equal to physically assaulting someone; avoid it at all costs to save your reputation.

Thick Skin

For most of us, life is not exactly a walk in the park for one reason or another. Even the rich and famous have their own set of challenges, and everyone is open to potential health issues. There is always going to be small stresses associated with everyday life. On top of that, there could be external forces nipping at you, and you need to have a thick skin to ward them off. Like water rolling off a duck's back, do not even let insignificant things into your world. Whether it is a small verbal comment or a minor medical issue, you need to put things in perspective. Save your stress, worries, and energy for the bigger battles in life and do not let the little ones eat away at you.

Failure

Failure is as much a part of life as success, and sometimes it happens more often than we would like. Failure comes in numerous flavors but can be broken up into three main categories: something that you had complete control over, something that you had no control over, and lastly, a blend of control. Do not worry about the things in life that you cannot control; there are more situations in life that you can control than you realize. For the things that you can control or have partial influence over, as long as you tried your best and acted with integrity, professionalism, and all the other positive qualities that you have been taught, then do not stress over the failure. We are all human and subject to fail, and, in fact, we are not alone. Both animals and plants may fail in things they do too, so know that you are in good company. The key to it all is to learn from the failure and try not to let it happen again. You can learn volumes from other people's failures as well, so always be observant. Just get back up on the horse again and give it your all a second, third, or fourth time. Ironically, you may find that after you have successfully completed the challenge, that it was not that hard after all, but in all cases, the natural high will raise your confidence level for the next challenge.

On the other hand, be aware of situations where you are being set up to fail. In this case, it is that much more important to rely on your lessons and experience to overcome the challenge. However, most of the time it is more a feeling than a reality.

17

Attire

The type of clothes that you wear, and how you wear them, has a huge impact on your appearance. Make sure that you always look decent and presentable. Ensure that your clothes are not too small, tight, large, or baggy. Just as important as the type of clothes you wear is the condition they are in. You could have spent thousands of dollars on your clothes, but if they are ripped, tattered, or stained, you might as well be wearing the clothes of a homeless person. In addition, never leave the house wearing wrinkled clothes; it only takes a few minutes to iron them to avoid looking like an unmade bed in public. A quick piece of advice is to always wash/dry-clean all parts of a multi-piece outfit, such as a dress suit, together even if only one of them is soiled. Otherwise, the outfit will noticeably develop different shades of color if one component is cleaned more often than the other.

Always make sure that your outfit matches the occasion or event. For example, if your work dress code calls for business casual, do not wear a T-shirt and jeans. Furthermore, what you wear when you are fourteen years old is not the same as what you should where when you are forty years old. Lastly, you do not have to spend hundreds of dollars or be on the bleeding edge of fashion to look good. Keep in mind that your reputation can also be greatly affected, both in a positive and negative sense, by the clothes you choose to wear.

Appearances

As unfair as it may be, people judge books by their covers. Be mindful of your outward appearance since it is the very first physical impression someone will have of you. If you appear to be dishevel and sloppy, you may be seen and treated as if you are even if you are not. Now this does not mean that you need to be in a three-piece suit or a ballroom gown all the time, but you should take pride in your appearance. We sometimes forget just how often we are judged by people, and starting off with a strike against you will never make it any easier.

Reputation

More important than your appearance is your reputation. Your reputation is a non-tangible trait that is a reflection of all your qualities in one. Your reputation often precedes you so be careful not to start off a new relationship with two strikes already against yourself.

Just like any living organism, you must continually feed and maintain your reputation or it will perish. If your reputation is attacked or maligned, you should immediately repair it, whether you are at fault or not. Always clear the air with facts and keep your emotions in check, especially your anger.

Eye Contact

Maintaining strong eye contact with someone is just as important as the content of your conversation. Focusing on a person's eyes tells them that you respect their time and are listening to them with your full attention. Whether you are with a person one-on-one or a group of people, there is no reason to look down or become distracted by external events and objects. Eye contact is equally important for the person speaking as well as those who are listening. Talking to someone while looking down can imply that you are not confident or that you are unprepared. Lastly, never allow yourself to focus your attention on anything but a person's eyes; looking or staring at other body parts is extremely rude, disrespectful, and a sign of immaturity.

Natural Order

Just as the animal kingdom has a "pecking order", so does society. It is customary and polite to allow women to be first. This holds true from opening a door to serving a lady first during a meal. Next, you should give your attention to older people; they deserve your respect in anything and everything. In the academic and business worlds, the natural order is known as "seniority". A person who has more years of experience within the same level or category has earned the right to come before others. In addition, those of a higher rank, regardless of your opinion of them, have the right to be at the top of the order. Lastly, in times of emergency, women, children, and the elderly should be the first to receive attention.

Manners

Good manners never go out of style and are an outward display of respect. You should always be considerate and polite no matter the situation. Children are a reflection on their parents, and this holds especially true when it comes to manners. It does not take much additional energy or effort to say "please," "thank you," "bless you," or to hold a door open for someone. Furthermore, never be impolite and ask questions such as how old someone is or how much money they make. As always, treat others as you would like to be treated; lead and learn by example.

Andrew, even if you cannot single-handedly revive chivalry, always try to be a gentlemen and prove that it is not completely dead. Unfortunately, chivalry has become a lost art for no go reason. However, that does not mean that you should lead a discourteous lifestyle with a lack of respect for those around you; honor women, children, and strangers alike.

Class

Having class is another one of those qualities that really cannot be taught. Having class or being classy has nothing to do with the amount of money you have, your age or any other external factor; it is how you carry yourself. You can be wearing a potato sack and still have class. Try to remember your manners and treat/act towards others how you yourself would like to be treated. Respect is a key ingredient when it comes to class. Lastly, do not take class too far because you may be seen as someone who is "stuck up."

Helping Others

Always take the opportunity to help others since it usually requires little additional effort. Opening a door for someone or helping them pick up a dropped item is a simple yet powerful way to make this truly a kinder, gentler world. Be polite to strangers and friends alike since it is a small world and you never know who you may bump into or who is related/friends with someone else you know.

Compassion

You should always have compassion for others since you never know when you or someone you love may be in their situation. Do what you can to help alleviate their burden or reduce their sadness. It does not have to be anything elaborate or expensive; sometimes a simple hug or just sitting with the person quietly can be the best medicine. As always, treat others as you would like to be treated.

Privacy

The issue of privacy is very complex and has many levels of importance, however, it can be broken down into two main categories. The first area of concern is your personal privacy. This includes everything from keeping personal issues to yourself to protecting your identity. Every aspect of your life can be impacted by personal privacy, especially when it comes to your physical, medical, financial, and career security, and the safety of your reputation. Some types of data, Social Security numbers for example, are dangerous enough by themselves, but when you couple two or more pieces of information, such as name and telephone number, you cross into the area known as "personally identifiable information." Always take a moment to stop and review matters before you release personal information, especially when it is not face-to-face. Between e-mails, transactional web sites, blogging, and social networks, the Internet is a great example for information mis-sharing. Take into consideration not only the primary recipient of the information but also those entities that may inherit or purchase your information, as in the case of mailing or other distributed lists. In addition, privacy transverses all media, including verbal and written communication both in electronic format as well as hardcopy. Always be sure to secure all legal documents from theft, prying eyes or unintentional viewing. Be sure to completely destroy any old paper-based documents by shredding at a minimum. Furthermore, do not forget to physically destroy old cards such credit and debit/ATM cards as well as any laminated card that you may typically carry around in your wallet or purse.

The second type of privacy you need to concern yourself with is that of others. Whether you are privy to confidential information, a secret, or otherwise have access to sensitive information, it is your ethical duty to respect and protect it just the same as if it were your own information. Never gossip, share or distribute private information with others, and when you do have legitimate reasons for distributing data, be sure to double-check the recipients to prevent accidents from occurring. Mishandling private information can lead to anything from broken relationships between friends to being fired by your employer. Furthermore, you can easily find yourself in legal hot water if you allow or are a part of information misuse. Remember, loose lips sink ships!

Emotions

"When I repress my emotion my stomach keeps score."
— *John Enoch Powell, British statesman*

Perspective

Viewing people, places, objects, and methods from all different angles is a great way to better understand them, as well as potentially improve them. Since no two people think identically alike, you should always consider what other people have to say. This does not mean that you should follow them exactly, but you may want to consider adopting one or two aspects of their rationalization or actions.

Looking at a physical object turned 30, 45, 90, or 180 degrees can have a huge impact. If possible, you should even go so far as to turn the object inside out. You may be able to improve the efficiency of an existing product or process by taking such simple actions. Not to date myself, but the capacity of videocassette recorder (VCR) tapes was greatly improved by recording the data at an angle rather than at 90 degrees. Let your imagination take a front seat and logic a back seat at some point in all your evaluations.

Happiness

Being happy has more benefits, for both yourself and others, than you probably realize. Happiness means less stress, which leads to lower levels of physical strain on your body. Happiness, like a negative attitude, can also be contagious. Having a happy disposition improves your reputation and outlook on life. Happiness is not proportionate to how much money you make or how many material possessions you own. In fact, I would argue that absolute true happiness is devoid of any material objects and only comes from the inner peace of relationships between friends, family, nature, and yes, yourself. In fact, before you can be happy with anyone else in your life, you have to be happy and at peace with yourself first. You make your own happiness just as you make your own misery, and no one can make you happy other than yourself. Find joy and happiness in the little things in life. Realize that no matter how bad the situation may seem, there is always someone less fortunate or in a worse position than you. Chances are things are not as bad as you are making them out to be, and you should try to pull yourself out of it before it leads to depression. Life is what you make of it.

Love

I am smart enough to realize that giving guidance on love is nearly impossible. During the course of your life, you will love many people and, hopefully, it all begins with your parents. Your parents will always love you no matter what happens in this Earthly world. Love is unconditional and timeless; its bonds are unbreakable. Having your heart broken can be more emotionally painful than the worst physical injury. Never be afraid to love, in fact, *love* love.

The only practical advice I can impart is not to let love hurt you. Be careful not to confuse love with lust or some other emotion. Do not let it blind you to the extent that it causes significant physical or mental harm as in the case of an abusive relationship.

Passion

The power of being passionate about the things you do and how you live your life is extremely underestimated. Passion drives you naturally by releasing adrenaline and endorphins into your bloodstream, and it allows little to stand in the way of your goals and dreams. You do not have to be passionate about everything you do, but you should have at least one passion in life such as your family, relationships, sports, career, music, art, or a hobby. Let a little excitement shine on your world and avoid wandering through life aimlessly like a piece of driftwood. However, keep in mind that passion, like many emotions, can be a double-edged sword. Always make sure that you direct your passionate energy towards positive causes and never for purposes of evil or negative acts and behavior.

Appreciation

You should always show your appreciation towards people for their efforts, especially when they are specifically for you. Also, do not forget about those folks whose efforts are performed "behind the scenes"; chances are their hard work is even more vital when compared to efforts that are in plain sight. It does not require an expensive thank you gift, and it can be as simple as a few kind words or a handwritten note. Unfortunately, few people in this hectic world we live in take the time to show their appreciation of others. If only a small percentage of people started to show a little more appreciation towards others, it would have a significant impact on our society.

Chances are, you can improve upon your appreciation of life as well. Too often we are focused on completing the task at hand or getting to the next one rather than pausing to appreciate all that we have. We should all take stock of our friends and family as well as the community, country, and world we all share. Appreciate your body by eating properly, exercising regularly and taking care of medical problems before they become major issues. Life is what you make of it, so why not make it an enjoyable journey?

Expectations/Disappointment

Disappointment is a natural part of expectation. However, when you know it is coming, you can limit the effects of disappointment very easily. Simply set your expectations to a low or zero level, and if anything better occurs, it can be viewed as a bonus or an extra. This is not to say that you should always have low expectations and constantly accept disappointment either. When you do have an influence over a situation, stay positive and try your very best. The last thing you want to do is look back and feel that things could have turned out differently had you only given it more. When you are faced with a disappointing event or experience, try to learn what you can from it in order to limit its current and any re-occurring effects. Try to find the positive in every seemingly negative experience.

Fear and Apprehension

While fear and apprehension may appear to be one and the same, they are actually very different. Often when we are confronted with a new situation or environment, we may be hesitant about it but not fearful of it. That is what is known as "apprehension." It is perfectly normal to fear certain things, but you should try at least once to overcome the fear. Fears can range from something as simple as a picture of a snake to a fear of death. Take small steps to break down the fear little by little. Try to find someone that has or had the same fear so you can get past it together. Lastly, do not ever let your fears overpower or cripple you mentally or physically.

When you do start off on a new or unfamiliar path, you should try and "cut your teeth" first. You can do this by either tackling a smaller representative component or practicing your actions before committing to the full-blown version or using real/valuable items. For example, if you are about to use a new power tool for the first time, you may want to cut your teeth using a scrap or smaller section of wood before potentially ruining the costly or whole piece respectively. This practice applies to non-physical items and skills equally. On a related note, you may want to "test the waters" before committing your time, money, and devotion to a matter. Always make sure that you are using precious resources wisely.

Overwhelmed

During the course of your life, you will more than likely become overwhelmed a number of times. Unfortunately, it can affect anyone at anytime and at any age; no one is immune to it. There are actually two versions of this emotion, both of which can have a large range in magnitude and substance. On the one hand, you may feel overwhelmed, and on the other, you may actually be overwhelmed. Either way, you need to pause, evaluate the situation and take the appropriate action before stress builds up and wears you down physically and mentally. Hopefully, you get the sense of being overwhelmed before you actually become overwhelmed. If you do start to feel yourself heading in that direction, you first need to stop everything and step away from all the situations to clear your mind. Next, take inventory of all the emotions, tasks, and other items that are taxing you. As you go through them, evaluate each and determine if you should allow it to concern you either at all or at the present time. Sometimes things may just seem bigger or more important than they really are. Once you have gone through the list of items and are left with only the ones that are truly important, you now need to prioritize each. As soon as you can place all of the burdens in an orderly, concise list, you are guaranteed to at least feel better about the situation, even though nothing has actually changed. Then, simply and calmly tackle each challenge, chipping away at the larger ones until they become manageable.

If you are overwhelmed by the number of actual tasks or pressures on your life, follow the steps above. However, as difficult as it may be, you may need to cut back on some of your commitments. This may be easier said than done, especially if you let your pride get in the way. Sometimes we have a hard time saying "No" to people, and it winds up burying us to the point that nothing gets done successfully. Multitasking is a great method to accomplish several jobs at one time, but it is also a perfect example of how doing too many things at once can lead to all around reduced/poor quality. If reducing your responsibilities is not an option, then you will need to either come to a compromise with the other people you are working with or figure out a better way to cope with or attack the issues.

Frustration

Frustration is as human as making mistakes, it just happens. Frustration is the precursor to anger and therefore needs to be regulated before it gets out of control. Think of frustration as a relief valve that releases stress and pressure when a certain point is reached. It is perfectly acceptable to get frustrated every once in a while. However, constant frustration could lead to bigger and worse issues, including stress which causes physical damage to your body. Try to vent your frustration to a trusted friend, colleague, or relative. However, be sure that you do not turn into a constant complainer or allow a rant to work against you in the future.

Rage

Rage is an extremely volatile emotion that can cause serious physical and emotional destruction at an alarming rate. Regardless of the causes or sources, you should never let a matter flash over into rage. Try to vent your frustrations before they explode into larger issues; take a step back or physically move away from the situation to get some "fresh air." Never couple your rage with other activities such as drinking or driving, which can prove to have fatal consequences. If you are faced with someone in an enraged state, one of the most effective options is to remove yourself from their environment until they have cooled off. Logic is often thrown out of the window when dealing with an enraged person. You may also need to physically protect yourself and others under your care from their line of fire. Lastly, never let yourself become abusive towards others or a victim of abuse. If you need help, in either case, seek outside assistance from friends, relatives, counselors, or medical professionals.

Hate

Hate is an ugly four-letter word that should not be part of your vocabulary. Nothing good can come of hatred, and it is usually a sign of ignorance. Ensure that you have a full understanding of the matter and, if not, educate yourself. Do not rely on the advice or experience of others in the formulation of your own opinion. Furthermore, do not condemn the whole based on the actions or results of a few. This especially holds true for cultures, religions, races, and ethic backgrounds. If you do have to hate, keep it to yourself and never spread it to others.

Depression

Depression is very much like stress, and some may say that it is an extreme form of stress. Like stress, depression can weaken your immune system in obvious ways as well as subconsciously. Unlike stress, depression is not always as apparent to those around you, therefore making it more dangerous. It is perfectly normal to feel like you are on the Hindenburg, which is moored to the Titanic, every once in a while, but constant depression requires immediate attention. Depression can take many forms and levels of severity. If you are feeling depressed for whatever reason, seek help from someone you trust. It can be a friend, relative, or professional. The important point is that you let someone in to help you get yourself out of the depression. The solutions can be very simple or could require medication. Obviously, the less invasive solutions should be tried first since medication may only mask the real problem. Never let depression lead to a suicide attempt. Nothing in this world is worth giving back the precious gift of life.

Positive Traits

"Adopt the pace of nature; her secret is patience."
– Ralph Waldo Emerson

Common Sense

Unfortunately, common sense is not exactly as common as it could be. Too often you will notice people making decisions that leave you scratching your head asking, "Now why in the world would they do that?" Common sense cannot be taught and, for some reason, seems to be covered in Teflon® so it never quite sticks to some people. The concept is actually very simple, and there is a quick and easy way to test for it. Whatever the issue is, say it out loud. If it sounds like it makes sense, then maybe it does. However, if you say to yourself "That just does not sound right," then it probably does not fit the definition of common sense. If you are still confused, try asking someone whose opinion you value and trust to evaluate the topic or issue.

Respect – People

Respect for each other is one of the basic principles that separates us from the animal world. It allows us to live and work in productive, cooperative societies. Granted it does not always work out that way, hence wars, genocide, and various other conflicts. When it comes to respect, you need to start with yourself and work your way outward. If you do not have respect for yourself, you can never have it for anyone or anything else. Next you should respect your parents as long as they do not physically, emotionally or mentally harm you. You may not always like it, but you should always respect them regardless. Your respect should then spiral outward to your significant other, family, neighbors, class, or workmates and all the way to strangers. You should actually treat strangers with more respect and never let the fact that someone is related to you give them license to treat you poorly. Always have respect for the mentally and physically challenged as well; never poke fun, stare, look down on or treat them any differently. No matter who you are or what you are doing, it begins and ends with common courtesy. It is the minimum sign of respect, and you should always keep it in the forefront of everything you do.

There is never a good reason to disrespect someone else unless they have physically or mentally harmed you or a loved one. Furthermore, there is never a good reason for taking advantage of someone else. Appreciate your elders as they may have contributed to your life without you even knowing it, as in the case of war veterans. Keep an open mind, and you may even learn a thing or two from your elders since they have experienced much more of life than you. Finally, have respect for those less fortunate than you and respect people for their differences regardless of age, wealth, race, gender, sexual orientation, religion, background, or abilities.

Respect – Laws/Rules

As a general practice, you should obey and respect laws and rules. Laws and rules are typically established for a good reason such as public safety. Therefore, you should obey the laws of the land, whether at a government level or those for a simple board game. Keep in mind that laws and rules can, and often do, vary by region or country. No matter how petty or at what age, never commit or be associated with a crime. Trust me, it will follow you around and haunt you for life.

On the other hand, obeying laws and rules should not be done blindly. Understand why you are supposed to do or not do things. Since laws and rules are created by us humans, there is a chance that they could be flawed or even outdated. Many rules are established for the greater good of society, which may or may not be best. Challenge them in appropriate ways and not through counteractive means such as violence. Consult with others to get their opinions and gather facts about the situation before you take action.

Respect – Animals

Just as you should respect nature, you should also respect her children (better know as animals). As advanced as we think we are, there is a thing or two that we can learn from animals. You should never abuse or harm an animal unless it is considered a pest. Rather than killing a spider, collect it and put it outside. Fearing an animal is usually nothing more than having a poor understanding of it. Overcome the issue by safely interacting with an animal you fear. You do not have to fall in love with it, but you should at least try to gain a better insight. The other key component to respecting an animal is respecting its territory. This includes where it lives, roams, and migrates. For your safety, and that of the animal, do not automatically assume that it is friendly. Never approach an animal with aggression, and always get the owner's approval before you pet or interact with it. Lastly, never interact with a wild animal.

If, for any reason, you are unable to care for a pet, you should bring it to a no-kill shelter or contact your local animal control center. Never set loose a domestic or wild animal. Respect the land that they owned far before we humans came along, and do not think that you have rights to it over them.

Respect – Environment/Nature

Respect your surroundings and the global environment equally. Never intentionally harm or destroy nature physically or by supporting efforts that may cause harm to the environment. The impacts you have on the world range from the type of vehicle you drive to the lifestyle you lead. Do not be afraid to correct or show others how they can lessen their impact on the environment. Start by supporting conservation and recycling efforts, and never litter or dump materials that can be toxic to the environment. The Earth was here long before you; its condition should continue to improve long after you return to it.

Positive Attitude

Maintaining a positive attitude is a key factor in almost every aspect of life. It helps reduce stress, combat depression and is half the battle when facing a new challenge. Just as important as the direction of your attitude is how flexible it is. Environments, situations, goals, people, and needs change constantly throughout life; you cannot realistically succeed or survive in life with a rigid or singular attitude. Your attitude can also have a large impact on how people perceive you. No one likes to be around a person who is always negative. This holds true for everything from friendships to work environments to family and relationships. No matter how old or set in your ways you are, it is never too late to start changing your attitude.

Discretion

Unfortunately, discretion is a skill that is usually developed over time and through experience. A high level of discretion is a sign of maturity and affects everything from an argument with a family member to alerting someone of an embarrassing situation. While it may be difficult to suppress acting upon your initial reaction, you need to dig deep and be bigger than the situation. No matter how big or small, bursting out can adversely and permanently affect your reputation. Never put anything negative in writing or on audio or video media either. You may find it helpful to put your reaction down on paper or electronically (for your eyes only) and place it aside until your initial emotions have cooled and you are more relaxed. Do not immediately send or act inappropriately. People can go a lifetime without being able to control their tempers and feelings of revenge, but there is a right time, place, and way to express your feelings in a mature manner. Be smarter and classer than someone who just shoots from the hip.

Patience

Patience is not something that you are born with but instead needs to be self-taught. It requires great practice and discipline to perfect as a skill. You should learn to be patient with yourself and others. You need to keep in mind that you are not always the focus of everyone or deserving of immediate attention. Many things in life are out of your control and the control of others around you, so you need to learn to wait calmly. Everything will happen in due time and is often worth the extra wait.

Natural Curiosity

Having a natural curiosity for the world around you will lead to power. Take the time to understand the who, what, where, when, why, and how of everything you interact with. Armed with the information, reasoning, and history, you will organically enhance your observation skills, supplement your education and allow better associations, connections, and decisions to come your way. For example, I have used canola oil for decades and only recently said to myself, "What in the world is a canola?" Actually there is no such thing as a canola; it stands for "Canadian oil, low acid" and it is made from rapeseed oil. Do not just think outside of the box, think about what the box is made of, how big it is, and why there is even one in the first place. Open your mind and your world will automatically expand and flourish.

Drive and Ambition

Just as no two people's fingerprints are identical (including twins), the same holds true when it comes to their personal drive and ambition. Some folks have a natural burning desire that fuels their passion for a particular interest or a wide variety of items, including life itself. Unfortunately, the natural form of drive and ambition is rather rare and not something that can be taught or learned. However, that does not mean that you cannot become inspired by someone or jumpstarted by an event. Frankly, being a couch potato can affect everything from your career to your relationships; even your health could be at risk if you have little motivation to exercise or eat properly. Constantly try to develop, maintain, and enhance your level of ambition and internal drive. Never let monotony, a string of unsuccessful attempts, a minor bump in the road, a major setback, or exhaustion extinguish your own desire, and always have words of encouragement for anyone who may be facing a difficult time or may be just in need of a quick boost.

Encouragement

Encouragement is one of the few things in life that is very valuable but does not cost you anything. Too often there is a general lack of encouragement between family, friends, and colleagues. It only takes a moment to offer a few words of support to encourage someone. Just think back to the times when someone encouraged you and how good it made you feel that someone appreciated your efforts and supported your situation or goals. Think of encouragement as a random act of kindness that should be committed on a daily basis.

Sharing

Sharing is one of the very first social skills that you learn as a person. It is also one that carries on throughout your entire life and impacts many other basic principles such as teamwork and cooperation. Sharing can take on any form and is important regardless of quantity or financial worth. Other than materialistic items, you can share your time by volunteering or helping out with less formal causes. You can make a positive impact on someone's day by just sharing a happy story or experience.

Believe it or not, sharing can be something unfavorable as well. Having a negative attitude or constantly complaining are ways that you can spread negative energy. It could adversely affect your own reputation and undermine your professionalism. Try to surround yourself with as many positive people in life as you can while keeping negative forces at arm's length.

Kindness

There is no reason to be rude to others. This applies not only to family, friends, and co-workers but perfect strangers as well. Kindness takes little to no effort but has exponential dividends. Be kind to animals as well since they will provide you with endless love, affection, and loyalty. Kindness shows that you respect society, and it goes hand-in-hand with politeness. However, do not allow people to confuse your kindness for stupidity. Set a good example to others by being kind, and hopefully it will become contagious.

Dedication

Be dedicated to everything you do no matter how large or small. Whether it is an object, goal, product, or service, the more dedication you put into something, the better it will turn out. Your dedication will lead to a favorable reputation and enhance your leadership qualities. You should always put a hundred percent into everything you do.

Reliability

Being reliable is a trait that helps you in countless ways. It will not only enhance your own performance and quality but will help build your reputation. Reliability includes doing things right the first time, being organized, and highly accurate. Sloppy, disorganized work will surely lead to inconsistencies. Also, make sure that you are always on time. Constantly being late is not only a bad habit to fall into, but it is also a negative mark against you right off the bat.

Accountability

Accountability is a very significant, yet often disregarded quality. Simply stated, accountability is taking responsibility for your actions, good or bad. Every situation or event should hold at least one person accountable. Whether or not the person actually claims responsibility for their actions is, unfortunately, another story. However, for your own integrity and responsibility, you should hold yourself accountable regardless of the issue's magnitude. Doing anything less would only fool yourself, raise your stress levels and turn you into a liar. When the truth does surface, and it will, your reputation will quickly plummet. Lastly, in cases when you absolutely should have known better, save yourself and everyone involved the embarrassment by not pleading ignorance.

There are two phrases that you should always keep in mind no matter where you are, what you are doing, or who you are interfacing with. The first is to never bite the hand that feeds you. While it may be tempting or easy to slip into a rant, always keep in mind the bigger picture, and how one little action can ruin everything. The second saying is to never poop where you eat. As you can easily tell, this one is very basic in nature and applies to everyone from animals to humans. Basically, it is telling you not to combine a good thing with a bad thing. For example, never jeopardize your association with an organization or institution by doing something inappropriate. This commonly occurs in schools and in the workplace, so if you have to fulfill a need, just make sure that you do not do it in the same environment that can cause you to be expelled from school or fired from a job.

Integrity

Integrity is a combination of several qualities wrapped into one. It is comprised of reputation, pride, fortitude, quality, and many other inward and outward components. Someone with strong integrity also has strong moral and ethical standards. You should never compromise your integrity by, for example, getting involved with illegal matters, keeping a lost item without first seeking out its rightful owner, or accepting bribes in return for special consideration or favors. One easy trick to ensure you consistently act with integrity is to pretend that you are always on video and audiotape. Your integrity is something that can only be taken away from you by you. No matter how good or bad something turns out, if you do it with integrity, you are giving the effort nothing less than your all.

Organization

Being organized helps you become successful. Disorganization leads to wasted time and money and is a poor reflection on your overall appearance and reputation. You do not need to be obsessive-compulsive, but you should have a high standard of organization in everything you do and own. Organization easily improves your other qualities with no additional effort. Taking a small amount of time upfront will undoubtedly have long-lasting, positive effects in the future.

An essential component of organization is documentation. Documentation can vary in many degrees, but at a minimum, it is a time saver. Furthermore, it is a skill that benefits you at home, work, and everywhere in between. For example, you should develop procedures for your major and minor tasks at work. This way you are covered in the event of an emergency, if you are out on vacation or if someone needs to fill in for you during an extended period of time. In addition, they can be very useful when you need to transition your responsibilities to another person due to any type of job change. Documentation can also help you when it comes to legal matters. Having all the facts with the appropriate dates and supporting paperwork can mean the difference between a successful or unsuccessful defense and offense. In the home, aside from orderly financial matters, something as simple as writing the date on the freezer bag will help you determine if the food is still fresh and good to eat. To help in daily matters, as well as emergency situations such as identity theft, you should maintain a copy of all your account numbers, passwords, and important phone numbers in one central, organized document. For security reasons, the information should reside in a password-protected file on a home computer, with regular back-ups locked in a home safe. Never e-mail the file or leave hardcopies lying around. Lastly, almost as important as the documentation itself is maintaining it. If the facts, figures, and procedures are out of date or inaccurate, it can be worse than not having anything at all. Try to review and update your documentation at the time the change happens, or at least on a regular basis such as quarterly or annually.

Innovation

While necessity may be the mother of invention, it should not be the only means to innovation. Your innovation does not need to be Noble Peace Prize winning and can be as small as an improvement to your personal routine. Never be shy to voice your idea, and if you have any doubts, first run the concept by someone whose opinion you trust. Just like when it comes to a question, the only dumb idea is the one never given a proper opportunity. Avoid falling into a mental rut of performing the same actions and tasks over and over again. Challenge both sides of your brain by creating new ideas and synergies, big and small. Something innovative does not always need to be a completely new product or method either; it can be an improvement on an old or existing product or process. Even if you do not make a cent on the innovation, it will hopefully be a fun experience and lead to other ideas that can be applied in the future.

Anticipating

Rather than approaching life as a bump on a log, you should always be proactive and anticipate future events as well as people's next move, including your own. This skill can and should be used every minute of your day; it can have a huge impact on every aspect of your life, including your safety, health, and financial well-being. Ranging from weather conditions to someone's driving behavior, you need to consciously recognize potential warning signs and act on them appropriately. For example, if you look through someone's back window while traveling down the road and the driver is leaning over to search or pick up something from the floor, they may be headed for an accident. In this case, simply give yourself a safety cushion by changing lanes and/or reducing your speed. Use your pattern recognition and observation skills to get ahead on an event before it unfolds and becomes an issue. Half of the time, you can probably avoid problems just by sidestepping them, whereas the other half of the time, you may be able to advance your position just by looking, thinking, and taking action. Remember though, sometimes the best action to take is no action at all.

Being Prepared

Being prepared is always a good idea and helps you become more organized automatically. Now this is not to say that you need to go overboard and be obsessive-compulsive, but a little planning can go a long way. The concept does not only have to apply to large events or tasks, such as a project, since more often, it is the little things that add up. Preparation can also play a role in safety, such as in the case with emergency procedures and planning. However, before you start working on any size project, you should take the time to put together a project plan, complete with milestones and timelines. Without question it will save you time, money, energy and frustration. The plan does not have to be written using Microsoft® Project, however, it should be complete, concise and orderly. Preparation, at a minimum, leads to convenience later.

Double-Check Everything/Everyone

Not to turn you into a paranoid person, but it is always a good idea to double-check both yourself and others. It can be something small like a measurement, but the more significant it is, the more important it is to double-check. While you may think that you can trust the source or that you are a hundred percent correct, it usually only takes a few seconds to confirm. A simple check of the order of magnitude (1, 10, 100, 1000, 10000, etc.) is a quick and reliable barometer to nearly any situation. Furthermore, just because something has been generated automatically, such as a bank statement or transaction, that does not mean it is a hundred percent error proof either. Computer-generated items are programmed by humans who, as we all know, are not perfect. In addition, the error could have been introduced through the initial input by a person or the failure or accidental rerun of an automated task or program. Needless to say, it can take much more time and money to fix something the longer the issue lingers. This is why it is so critical that you receive either a receipt or confirmation with every transaction. Lastly, do not take insult to someone who is double-checking you. It is not that they have a lack of trust or think you are incompetent, but we are all only human, and everyone is susceptible to making mistakes.

Hospitality

Being a good host or hostess is a very important trait for several reasons. It is your social appearance, reputation, and manners all rolled into one. Whether it is a home-delivery person or a dinner party with important business clients, you should be cordial to everyone who is a guest in your home. At a minimum, you should offer your guest a beverage and treat them with respect no matter who they are or the reason for their visit. If people are going to be staying for more than a couple of hours, you should also offer them a light snack. On the other hand, your guests may have been invited for a full meal. In either case, you should always make sure that you have some extra food available that can be quickly prepared.

When you are invited to someone's home, you should never show up empty-handed. You do not have to spend a million dollars, but something as simple as a dessert (homemade or store bought) or a bottle of wine is always a very nice gesture. Even better, convert your observation skills into meaningful actions by selecting something that relates specifically to your host or something that has a personal meaning. Furthermore, there may be occasions, such as a housewarming, which call for a special gift. Again, the dollar amount is not as important as the gesture. A houseplant or gift card to a home improvement store is always very much appreciated. Lastly, as a guest you should always be respectful, polite, and openly thankful for your host's generosity.

Just because you are someone's guest, that does not mean that you should act or expect to be treated like the King or Queen of England. Always at least offer to assist your host, especially when meals are being served or as the event is winding down and it is time to clean up.

The condition of your home is a direct reflection on you. A home does not have to be the traditional single-family house; it can be as simple as your room or apartment. Like your appearance, the first impression that your home presents can change people's perceptions for both the better as well as the worse. Be sure to keep your space, big or small, neat and orderly at all times.

Patriotism

Patriotism by definition is pride in and loyalty towards one's country. While this is an extremely important factor in the success of your country, it can also have negative impacts. Patriotism should be felt and expressed in moderation. Extreme cases of patriotism can easily slip into fanaticism, which can lead to conflict, war, terrorism, and death. You can honor your country in many ways, and some are more costly than others. It can be as significant as serving in the armed forces or as simple as flying a flag or purchasing goods made in your country. As with many of the other qualities, traits, and lessons mentioned throughout this book, you should do your fair share towards the greater good, in this case, your country.

Bravery

Bravery does not need to come in the form of grand heroic acts such as rescuing a baby from a burning building. It can be relatively simple action that few people even notice. For example, having the courage to sit and have lunch with a person that everyone else is shunning for no good reason is a small act of bravery. On a personal scale, there is bravery in admitting to yourself that you have a problem with drugs or alcohol, or that it is time to stop trying something that you just do not seem to be able to get the hang of. Ultimate bravery comes in the form of selfishly risking your life for the safety of others such as in the case of the armed forces, police officers, and firefighters. Never fear the unknown or lack the courage to tackle a challenge regardless of its size or complexity.

Heroism

It is nearly impossible to define what a hero is since there are almost infinite possibilities. Heroes can be young, old, rich, poor, intellectual, or unskilled. The heroic action can also vary in degree from simply helping a person to saving a life. The common element in every hero is that their attitude and/or actions are greatly valued by the admirer or recipient. You should not go through life trying to be a hero, but you should be a positive, kind, and helpful person every day. If the opportunity to rise to an occasion is meant to happen, it will on its own; just always be aware of your surroundings and keep your eyes and ears open at all times.

Leadership

Elements of leadership can be taught, but it is one of those qualities that must be brought to the surface (and remain there) in order to take full advantage of it. That is not to say that you cannot rise to an occasion but being a good leader means consistency. Do not shy away from accepting a new challenge or raising your hand when a volunteer is requested. Surround yourself with quality minds and select mentors and role models with great care. Build up your leadership skills and confidence little by little, and before you know it, you too will be the best in the class.

Volunteering

Granted, life in general is pretty hectic, but volunteering should be as important of a component as eating or sleeping. Volunteering can take many forms and should not be seen as a burden. It does not have to be a daily effort and can be as infrequent as once a month or once a year. The point is that you should make time to help others in need or that are less fortunate than you. Furthermore, you can volunteer at any age, and it does not need to be part of a traditional organization. It can be as simple as sitting with an elderly person for an hour, or as noble as being a volunteer firefighter. Increased volunteering would have a dramatic and immediate effect on the quality of our society.

Donating Blood and Organs

Assuming you meet the requirements, donating blood is one of the easiest and most valuable actions you can perform that will benefit all of society. It is especially important if you have one of the versatile or rare blood types. There is always a shortage of blood and other blood products for no good reason. Therefore, take the thirty minutes every couple of months to give the gift of life. In general the requirements are easy to meet. In order to qualify as a donor, you usually need to be over 110 pounds, in good overall health with a clean medical history, not had changes to your body, including tattoos, piercing, and surgeries and have mainly remained in the United States for the past few years. Furthermore, if there is a significant problem with your blood, you will be notified by the blood center, so think of it as a free mini checkup.

Another noble action you can take after you leave this world is donating some or all of your organs. While this practice is surrounded by unwarranted stigmatisms, it is a personal choice. However, the benefits for the people on organ waiting lists are immediate and literally life saving. Even if you donate just one organ, it would deeply touch the life of another person and their family. Just think how appreciative you would be if you or someone you loved received a life-saving organ.

Negative Traits

"To do no evil is good, to intend none better."
– *Claudius, Roman Emperor*

Cheating

Whether you are cheating on an exam or a boyfriend/girlfriend, it is unacceptable on any scale. You are merely avoiding the real issue or doing an injustice to yourself by not learning what you need to. You may think that you are getting over on people or getting away with something, but chances are it will catch up with you. Think of the embarrassment and potential hurt you are inflicting on yourself and others with your deceitful actions. Taking the easy way out may cost you more, if not everything, in the future, so think twice about your actions before it is too late.

Stealing

Stealing, as evident in every religion and culture, is never acceptable. You may think that you are getting away with it at the time, but your thieving ways will catch up with you. Furthermore, if you think you can trust someone else to either help you or let them in on your actions, you are dead wrong. Considering the high-tech world we live in today, chances are you will be caught on someone's video camera or cell phone. The last thing you want is your image played over and over again on the Internet or plastered on the front page of the morning newspaper.

Traditional stealing, such as shoplifting, as well as frivolous lawsuits and insurance claims hurt everyone equally with higher prices for goods and services. There is absolutely no need to contribute to the problem since prices skyrocket on their own by epidemic proportions under the best of conditions.

Complaining

Simply put, no one likes a person who complains all the time. It implies that you have a negative attitude, and it can easily damage your reputation. Worse than just affecting yourself, complaining can become contagious to those around you. In the workplace, this behavior can cause an issue with superiors which can lead to unfavorable repercussions, including termination. With friends and family, you may find that they insulate themselves or limit their exposure to you if you constantly complain.

If you find yourself in a negative atmosphere, try to limit your contact with the person. Depending on your relationship, you may want to make an attempt to help them find the root cause of their issue. Just be careful with your approach since it may be perceived by the other person as being hostile or confrontational.

Tardiness

You should always plan ahead and be on time regardless of the event. There are few excuses for being tardy and, if it becomes chronic, it could negatively affect your reputation. Whether walking in late to a formal occasion or holding up the daily family dinner, being late is just plain rude. Respect the time that others have set aside for you as you would expect in return.

Procrastination

No good can come of procrastinating. If anything, it usually makes the situation worse. Take the time to complete the task upfront so that you have enough time to double-check your work later. Furthermore, you never know when deadlines may be moved up, unforeseen events may occur, or timeframes may become accelerated. If you wait until the last minute, chances are you will make mistakes and the overall quality will suffer. Keeping yourself and your surroundings organized is half the battle when it comes to procrastination. Procrastinating will also increase your stress level which, as we all know, is no good for your immune system. As they say, haste makes waste.

Enabling

Being an enabler is a subtle yet powerful trait that benefits no one. When you enable someone, either consciously or subconsciously, you repeatedly do an injustice to yourself as well as fuel a bad habit or negative trait in someone else. Enabling can take on many forms and degrees of importance; however, the practice should be diagnosed and discontinued as soon as possible in all cases. For example, if you feel sorry for someone and continuously provide them with money and they just turn around and spend it on gambling, drugs, or alcohol, you are helping fuel their addiction. Furthermore, enabling does not have to be in the form of physical items such as money. Perhaps you always take care of things around the house while the other person contributes nothing. In this case, you are mainly hurting yourself, but at the same time you are also eroding your relationship by allowing it to continue. Do not let anyone take advantage of you because you either have the means or the knowledge. Apply your pattern recognition skills on yourself and others to make sure nothing gets out of control or turns into a bad habit.

Greed

Greed, one of the seven deadly sins, is a fruitless trait. Greed for material goods or money will always lead to no good. Needless to say, having all the money or possessions in the world will not make you truly happy either. Do not waste your time or money on "get rich quick" schemes since they almost never pay off. There is no replacement for good, old-fashioned hard work. As Aesop told us, slow and steady wins the race.

Jealousy

Jealously is an emotion that can be minor or major. In either case, it is not a favorable quality since it does not bode well for your personal composition or external character. While we will all get jealous of someone or something during the course of our life, it can cause unnecessary stress which will only hurt yourself. Instead, use your jealously as motivational fuel to achieve higher goals and to better your mind, body, and spirit.

When you do feel yourself getting jealous of someone else, stop and think of the bigger picture. You do not always know all the details behind someone's life and while one event may have been in their favor, what is the overall context? Take stock of the positive things in your own life and realize that no one is better than anyone else. Life is a series of ups and downs, so celebrate with the fortunate person on their new gain instead of wasting time and energy being jealous.

Anger

Anger, like jealously, is another negative emotion that you should try to keep under control and to a minimum. Anger quickly leads to stress, which weakens your immune system. Anger can also take a destructive path, not only in a physical capacity but also in a mental sense.

The first lesson to learn about anger is not let yourself get to the point of being angry. Learn to be like a duck with water and simply let problems roll off your back. Maintaining a calm demeanor helps keep your blood pressure from becoming elevated and allows you to tackle the issue with a clear mind. Like a very wise fortune cookie once told me, the remedy for anger is delay. Assuming you cannot contain your anger, try putting it on hold. For example, before sending a nasty e-mail to someone, save it as a draft first and revisit it a few hours or days later. Give yourself time to relax and gather your thoughts before you do something that you will regret later. Lastly, remember that violence is never a wise option or solution.

Sexual Harassment

As far as we think we have progressed as a society, sexual harassment continues to run nearly as rampant as the Black Plague once did. Sexual harassment is disrespectful, rude, unnecessary, and against the law. Furthermore, it is a two-way street that not only targets women but men as well. You should never harass anyone, in any manner, not to mention sexually. This also holds true regardless of a person's sexual orientation. There is simply no need or good reason for it to occur, and you should also stay clear of any environment that fosters that type of behavior. Guilt by association can easily occur, and you do not need to a part of any trouble. Keep any vulgar comments to yourself and try to change your general way of thinking before it gets you in hot water.

Spite

Never let yourself get to the point where your actions are driven by spite. Being spiteful is a non-productive emotion that can lead to additional and more severe emotional and/or physical harm. Spite can also damage your reputation. Be the better person and walk away from the negative environment to focus on the positive aspects of your life. Ensure that you learn lessons from the bad experience so as not to let the feelings surface again in the future.

Grudges

Holding a grudge or wishing any ill will towards someone is as futile as raking leaves in a tornado. You are only hurting yourself, for no good reason, by adding extra stress to your life. Trust me, the other person will probably not be losing any sleep over your grudge, assuming they are even aware of it. Begrudging someone is a complete waste of your time and energy. Instead, you should focus on your own life and only wish the best upon your fellow human beings.

Stereotyping

Stereotyping is when you classify or label all people of a particular group based on a characterization of a few people. The characterization may or may not even be true. For example, saying that all Middle Eastern people are terrorists is a stereotype. Although some terrorist are of Middle Eastern descent, this does not mean that all Middle Eastern people are terrorists. Just remember people like Timothy McVeigh, a red-blooded American who killed dozens of innocent men, women, and children in Oklahoma. Stereotypes adversely affect relations between races, cultures, genders, and nationalities, and they should never be used to judge people on an individual basis or as a whole. When you exercise this evil practice, you not only offend the group, but it is completely hurtful and spiteful on a personal level.

Racism

Racism is always a controversial topic. Unfortunately, no matter how much we think we have advanced as a society or educate our young, the ugly head of racism continues to surface. It is never acceptable to hate or poke fun at another race regardless of the context. It does not matter which type of circles you travel in, your age or race, racist comments hurt everyone and sets all positive efforts back numerous steps. If we can somehow accept each other at the higher level as human beings, we can keep racism at bay. Tolerance and turning a blind or colorblind eye are not viable solutions either. Until we unite and act as one species, we should not sweep the effects of racism under the rug and pretend they are nonexistent.

If you find yourself in either a temporary or long-term racist environment, you should immediately separate from it. Racism feeds on hate and is born of a lack of understanding and education of other cultures. Never take part in any situation that denounces another race, culture or heritage.

Sexism

Just as racism is absolutely unacceptable, so too is sexism. One gender can never be better than the other. Believing otherwise is usually a huge sign of ignorance. While some men may think they are the stronger gender, I highly doubt we would be able to weather the challenges of pregnancy for even just a couple of days, not to mention forty-plus weeks. Furthermore, not all men are insensitive, lazy, and crude. Live life in moderation and you will have no problems.

Religious Intolerance

Just like racism and sexism, being intolerant (or worse) of a religion is inexcusable. Major events such as the Crusades and World War II have caused the deaths of millions of people, all thanks to religion. However, scores of people continue to needlessly die on a daily basis thanks to religious intolerance. Just as people come in all colors, shapes, and sizes, they also hold various religious beliefs. None is better or worse than another, and all should be respected equally. Given the global world we live in today, there are many people, especially children, who are from mixed religious backgrounds. Take the time to learn the similarities and differences between religions; you may be surprised to find out just how few differences there really are. Never become ignorant and stick your head in the sand or raise a fist in the air when it comes to religious beliefs. Join a friend in visiting a church, temple, mosque or attend a religious event to learn firsthand and dispel any myths or misconceptions.

Intimidation

Under normal circumstances, intimidation is not a positive quality. You should never try to make yourself sound or appear more important than you really are or threaten others with physical intimidation. The only viable scenario in which it is acceptable to try and be intimidating is when you are threatened or on the defensive. Self-defense situations give you the right to do whatever you need to do in order to protect yourself or someone else in harm's way.

Taking Credit

You should never claim credit for someone else's efforts, no matter how big or small. It really is no different than stealing and, in the case of copy-written material, taking false credit can even be against the law. If someone mistakenly gives you credit or praise for work that is not your own, you should immediately and publicly correct them. Otherwise, you can do serious damage to your reputation and career once the truth does come to light. Just think how you would feel if someone took credit for your hard work.

On the other hand, you should be humble when it comes to taking credit for your work. You can easily put yourself in a bad light if you are loud, obnoxious and persistent when accepting credit for your efforts. Instead, you should be quietly thankful and appreciative to those praising you and use it as motivation in future efforts.

Crying Wolf

Asking for assistance is never something you should hesitate in doing, however, false cries for help are not acceptable. Whether it is a request to a friend or a call to 9-1-1, you should never mislead anyone. Abuse of a friend, relative or colleague will lead to lack of trust in the future as well as cause damage to your reputation. False reports to agencies wastes time and money by pulling resources off real issues to pursue your claim. If you really do need help, be open and upfront about the nature and severity of the issue. Otherwise refrain from fabricating a situation out of nothing.

Health

"The first wealth is health."
– Ralph Waldo Emerson

Health

Your health is all you need in life because without it, nothing else matters very much. Regardless of how much money you have or how famous you get, everyone's health is at potential risk. Take the time to eat a balanced diet, exercise and take United States Pharmacopoeia (USP) verified supplements such as vitamins and minerals. If you are on medication, even for a short time, be sure to take it all, in the correct dosage and at the right times. Conversely, you should avoid excessive or unnecessary medications since your body can become immune to their beneficial affects, especially in the common case of antibiotics. Speaking of medication, do you have a difficult time swallowing even small pills? Instead of throwing your head back, lean forward while bowing your head slightly. As counterintuitive as it may seem, it will actually open up the passage and allow you to easily swallow the largest of pills. Furthermore, if you require testing to monitor your affliction, make sure that you perform or have it performed religiously. Follow up on all appointments, even if they are routine. Ask as many questions of your healthcare professional as necessary to make you feel comfortable and knowledgeable. If you are still not satisfied, never be afraid to seek a second professional opinion.

Limit your exposure to dangerous conditions. This does not have to be a hazardous chemical, as would be found in a workplace, but it could be as common as exposure to the sun. From your scalp to the top of your feet, be sure to protect your entire body from the dangers of the sun. Even your lips and eyes could be damaged by the ultraviolet (UV) rays of the sun, so make sure that you protect yourself appropriately. Many products, including lip balm and contact lenses, come with UV protection included, so be aware of such product features. Avoid the physical risks of unnecessary injury by steering clear of dangerous environments and situations. Lastly, be aware of the dangers that everyday stress can inflict on your immune system.

Water

I would say that it is more than ironic that water not only covers over seventy percent of the Earth but is near the same percentage as your body mass. I also think it is safe to say that water is a vital part of life considering you cannot live without it for more than a week, give or take. You should try to drink at least eight glasses of water on a daily basis. Too little water can lead to dehydration, especially during the summer months, and when you are suffering from such illnesses as diarrhea. Believe it or not, too much water can prove to be problem as well. If you consume large volumes of water in a short time, your electrolyte levels will become out of balance and, if not treated, could lead to death.

Not all water is created equal. Actually it was created equally but what happened to it after that is another story. Just because water is bottled, that does not mean it is good for you. The water may only be filtered for particles or may not be filtered at all. One of purest forms of water that you can readily find is filtered by way of reverse osmosis. The reverse osmosis process involves a semi-permeable membrane that allows only specific chemicals to pass through. In the case of purifying water, most harmful impurities such as lead and mercury are blocked by the membrane, leaving near pure water as a product. You can readily find small units that fit in a sink cabinet at your local home improvement store. They can be easily installed in minutes, including to your refrigerator's ice maker/chilled water line, with little annual maintenance required.

If drinking plain water is not something that you know you can stick to, then try incorporating different flavorings. However, be careful what additives you use. Read the product label and see if it has an artificial sweetener such as NutraSweet® or Spenda®. In addition, too much carbonation could lead to weakened bones as well as bloating. The best flavoring is simply a splash of lemon juice. However, be careful when using fresh lemons since the liquid in the lemon's rind is especially corrosive; it can melt polystyrene instantly.

Food

As the saying goes, "you are what you eat" and they are a hundred percent spot on. Every substance that you consume obviously passes through your body, but more important are the chemicals and compounds that are retained. All foods fall into one of three main categories: carbohydrate, fat or protein. A balanced ratio is the key to a healthy lifestyle. Carbohydrates are basically starches and sugars; however, excess sugars are converted into fats and will be stored by your body. Therefore, a diet high in carbohydrates is not much better than eating a large quantity of fats. Fats are stored as energy reserves on your body, and are therefore not easy to shed. You can greatly help your weight, heart, and arteries by not introducing additional fats into your body in the first place. Foods high in protein such as chicken breast and tofu are very good for you since they are lean in fat.

As nature intended, we should avoid processed and synthesized foods. They are typically not the whole food but major components such as fructose and hydrogenated oils. The way that you prepare your food is just as important as the food itself. You can take a healthy chicken breast and ruin it by frying it in oil or drowning it in fatty sauces. Cooked vegetables can lose their vitamins and other beneficial effects if not prepared by steaming. Typically raw fruits and vegetables are better for you compared to their cooked version, but just be sure to wash them with copious amounts of water first. Be sure to cook meats and chicken well enough to avoid bacterial infections, including E. coli and salmonella. Also, keep a clean kitchen and use smart cooking practices to avoid cross contamination by dirty dishes, surfaces and utensils.

Just as important as the quality of the meal is the quantity and caloric value. Having three servings at one time is too much, regardless of how good it is for you. You can be easily amazed when you learn just how many calories are in the smallest of portions and even the healthiest of foods. Stay away from mega and super sizing your meals. One trick is to use a smaller plate, as long as you do not pile the food six inches high. By all means, steer clear of fast foods whenever possible. If you have no choice, try to eat limited quantities of the healthiest food they offer; even a salad can be become unhealthy when the wrong dressings are added.

The frequency and time of day in which you eat are also important factors when it comes to your health. You are better off eating five smaller meals during the course of the day rather than three large meals. Eating at ten o'clock at night is also not the best way to stay fit since the food will sit in your body while you sleep rather than being converted into energy.

Smoking

If I told you to get up every morning, flush five to fifteen dollars down the toilet and then suck on the exhaust pipe of a car for a few minutes every few hours, you would say I am crazy, right? Well what is the difference between that and smoking cigarettes? Actually you are right, you are better off inhaling automobile exhaust since it contains less harmful and addictive chemicals than cigarette smoke.

I do not care how old you are, how cool it may appear, or who else is doing it, there is absolutely no good reason why you should smoke. Furthermore, let me be very clear in saying that smoking anything from cigars to herbs is not acceptable, whether legal or illegal. There are so many toxins in the normal air we breathe every day that we do not need to purposely pollute our sponge-like lungs with additional carcinogens. Just think for a moment how your actions will affect your family when you become stricken with the debilitating affects of tongue cancer, throat cancer, esophageal cancer, lung cancer, or emphysema. In addition, smoking cigarettes greatly accelerates the hardening of your arteries, which can cause a major, irrecoverable heart attack. On top of it all, you are not only trashing your own body, but through secondhand smoke, you are also willingly killing people around you. Lastly, if you think you are getting away with something by hiding your dirty habit from your friends and family, you are only fooling yourself; the Grim Reaper sees your every puff.

Dieting

Unfortunately, there is no magic pill that we can take to lose weight. Dieting is something that needs to be considered very carefully, including the status of your current health. First you should determine if you even need to lose any weight for your specific height and body frame classification. Eating disorders such as anorexia and bulimia hit teens especially hard due to unnecessary peer pressure. Once you are certain that you do need to lose weight, you need to determine how many pounds you can safely lose. If you suffer from any type of medical condition that a diet will aggravate, you need to consult with your doctor first. Assuming you do not have any medical restrictions, be realistic in your goals. If the goal is large, then you may need to have several phases to your diet in order to increase the chances of a successful overall plan.

A successful diet includes three components. The first are the types, quantity, frequency and timing of your meals. The second key factor is an appropriate exercise routine. Without exercise, no diet will be successful short or long term. The last component to a meaningful diet is maintenance. If you think that you can just work hard for a few weeks or months and then go back to your old ways, do not even waste your time starting a diet. You must be fully mentally, emotionally, and physically committed to your new diet if you want long-lasting results. If possible, try to diet with someone else so you can support each other. Also, avoid tempting situations and people who will not be supportive of your new eating regimen. As strange as it may sound, concentrate on the task of eating during meals. You can easily overeat when you become distracted by watching television or reading a newspaper. Lastly, be sure to weigh yourself at the same time of day since your weight can fluctuate by a few pounds from morning to night.

Eating Disorders

Eating disorders such as anorexia and bulimia can be fatal but are controllable. However, they can also be avoided altogether in a number of ways. First, you need to take pride in your appearance no matter how much you weigh. Do not allow peer pressure to dictate the safety of your body. Secondly, be careful of who you select as a role model. People who are constantly under public scrutiny may go to great lengths to look a certain way, which is not always reasonable. Lastly, do not force your body into abnormal conditions for sports or other physically demanding activities.

In addition to the obvious issue of being severely underweight, you could be doing major damage to internal organs and systems. The pH of your stomach contents is not meant to be exposed to upstream surfaces. The acid could do permanent damage to your esophagus as well as your teeth. Unreasonable diets could cause liver or kidney failure, neither of which you may realize until it is too late.

Vitamins and Minerals

Vitamins and minerals should be a regular part of your life. They help your body in the metabolism of various compounds, but by the same token they are no magic bullet. Vitamins fall into one of two categories: water-soluble or fat-soluble. It is important to take the right dosage since you can damage your body by ingesting too many water-insoluble vitamins such as A, D, and E. Excess water-soluble vitamins such as B and C will be flushed out of your system, however, excessive water-insoluble vitamins will build up in your body.

Minerals are classified into two categories, major and trace, which correspond to the body's daily requirements. Examples of trace minerals are copper, iron, and zinc, whereas calcium, sodium, and potassium are considered major minerals. Similar to vitamins, they aid your cells and body. For example, they provide the iron in your blood so it can carry oxygen, the calcium in your bones and fluoride for your teeth. Soft tissue organs such as your thyroid gland require iodine to function properly and prevent goiters.

Best practice would be to start with a typical dose of a multi-vitamin. However, depending on your individual chemical make-up, you may need more of some vitamins and less of others. You will have to pay close attention to your body and observe different trends. Your vitamin and mineral regimen can also change with age. For example, you may need to take additional calcium as you get older. Prenatal vitamins are also very important before, during, and after pregnancy. Just as you would continually re-evaluate your methodology during a challenge, you should monitor your vitamin and mineral needs on a routine basis.

Vaccination

Vaccines are one of the most important discoveries in the medical world. They help protect us from a number of crippling and deadly diseases with little to no side affects. Typical vaccines include: Polio, Measles-Mumps-Rubella (MMR), Diphtheria-Tetanus-Pertussis, influenza, Hepatitis A and B, chicken pox and human papillomavirus (HPV – for girls only). You will receive most of your vaccinations in your childhood years, starting as soon as one month old. It is important that you adhere to the vaccination schedule since many of them require more than one dose. You should also be vaccinated for specific diseases, such as malaria, if you plan on traveling outside of the United States. Since some vaccines, such as those for influenza and rabies, may contain a small amount of egg protein, you should consult with your doctor if you have egg allergies. They can cause a serious adverse reaction if the quantity of egg protein is high enough or your sensitivity is low. If you do have an egg allergy, you can still get the vaccines, but they will be given under supervised conditions in the event you do need to have an antihistamine administered. As a parent, you should request a vaccination schedule from your pediatrician with every child as well as maintain a record of their shots in a safe place. Many schools, ranging from pre-schools to universities, will require proof of immunization before they allow your child to attend classes. Lastly, some people may have religious beliefs that prevent them from getting vaccines. Furthermore, there are some who believe that certain vaccines may cause or be related to mental and physical disorders.

However, the benefits of vaccines greatly outweigh any religious objections or potential side affects.

Sleep

Sleeping is one of the most underrated activities in life. We should spend about one third of our lives sleeping; however, most people do not get enough sleep on a nightly basis. Sleeping allows your body to recharge and heal itself. Cutting into your sleep deprives you physically, which can lead to being mentally sluggish. The quality of your sleep will therefore affect the quality of your waking hours. Eight solid, continuous hours of sleep is the recommended "dosage." Interrupted sleep or fewer hours will put you at a disadvantage the next day. Furthermore, the effects of improper sleep are cumulative over time. Lastly, the quality of your mattress can have a huge impact on the quality of your sleep as well as back aches and pains. Therefore, be sure to rotate and flip your mattress on a routine basis to prevent it from sagging or crowning (highpoint in the middle) and replace it before problems arise.

Exercise

Exercise is one of the most important components of a long, healthy life. As with almost everything in life, exercise should be done in moderation. Try to incorporate thirty minutes every day or every other day into your normal routine; make it as important a part of your life as sleeping or eating. Exercise can take on almost any form, but one of the best is plain old walking. A couple miles of brisk walking every other day will provide you the benefits of elevating your heart rate while placing minimal impact on your muscles, joints, and bones. Exercise can also help in alleviating stress by taking your mind off the challenges of everyday life. If motivation is a problem, try exercising with another person so you can constantly encourage each other. Lastly, exercise is a main component for successful bodyweight maintenance.

The most important component of any physical activity is stretching. This holds true not only for traditional activities such as sports and exercise, but also those which may be an inherent part of your job. Set aside at least ten minutes before you begin the activity to stretch muscles and elevate your heart rate. Pay special attention to the muscles you will be using as well as those in your back which often become the focal point for large stresses. In addition, a simple three-minute brisk walk will gradually raise your heart rate so you are not doubling it in seconds. Just as important as the warm-up phase is the cool-down cycle after you have completed your activity. Gradually lower your heart rate by taking a short, easy stroll, and be sure to hydrate yourself with generous volumes of water for a couple of hours. Stretch out any muscles that might become cramped and apply heat/ice to those which may have been strained. Lastly, avoid liquids such as coffee, tea, and alcohol which act as a diuretic and will dehydrate you quickly.

Sports

Playing a sport is great for many reasons. It has all the benefits of exercise built into it and is a fantastic way to build teamwork skills, assuming it is a group sport. Sports also constantly challenge you mentally and physically while teasing your competitive side. However, always remember to play with integrity and never act or behave unsportsmanlike. This holds true just as much for fans and parents as it does for the players themselves.

Sports can also be dangerous from both a physical point of view as well as mental. Do not allow yourself to get caught up in the competitive aspect to the point where the fun is completely removed. Ensure that you give your body ample time to rest and heal since joints, muscles, and bones can be easily damaged by years of stress and strain. Never take steroids or introduce growth hormones into your body. You will take years off your life by altering your body's chemistry. This also holds true for excessive use of non-FDA or USP approved supplements such as creatine which can wreak havoc on your kidneys. Lastly, if you are lucky enough to have extraordinary talents, just be sure that you have a solid and complete education to fall back on. A single injury can end your career in the blink of an eye, and no matter how much money you have earned, it may not be enough to support you for the rest of your life.

Sexually Transmitted Diseases (STDs)

Sexually transmitted diseases (STDs) are a scary, even fatal, consequence of careless, unprotected sex. You should fully understand what you could be getting yourself into before doing something you will regret for the rest of your life. STDs may not only affect you but also any current or future partners as well. Furthermore, it only takes one experience to ruin, if not end, your life, so do not think you are above STDs or are safe because you know the person. In addition, the disease may not kill you directly, but it may compromise your immune system enough that a relatively mild medical condition will prove fatal. If you ever find yourself in a situation where you have contracted a disease, take responsible action. Contact past partners to inform them of the potential exposure no matter how difficult it may be. Lastly, men and women are equally at risk of the damaging affects of STDs. Below is a summary of common STDs, including their transmission methods and cures, if available.

While pubic lice or "crabs" is curable, it can be very uncomfortable and easily spread. The parasite infests the hair around your genitals but can also

71

infect other body hair, towels, and bedding as well. It can be cured using lotions and shampoos.

Chlamydia and gonorrhea, bacteria diseases, have their own unique characteristics, however, they typically accompany one another. They can both be cured, but if left untreated, they can cause serious damage to reproductive organs in both men and women. Many people may not even realize they have either disease since symptoms do not always surface.

There are five variations of hepatitis (A, B, C, D, and E) with A, B, and C the most common transmitted sexually. All forms have no cure, and some are worse than others. Hepatitis A can be transmitted from all types of unprotected sex as well as through the use of intravenous (IV) drugs. Symptoms are relatively minor, including fever and diarrhea, and you may not even be aware that you are infected. While there is a vaccine for Hepatitis B, it will not do you any good if you already have the disease. You can be infected by Hepatitis B through all types of unprotected sex as well as through skin piercings, including IV drug use, tattoos, and body piercings. Hepatitis B can affect your liver and even cause death. Hepatitis C is much like Hepatitis B, but it becomes chronic much more often than Hepatitis B.

There is no cure for the herpes virus. A common form of herpes (Simplex 1) is a cold sore, however, Simplex 2 results in genital herpes. It can be transmitted through direct contact, including oral sex, and it will remain in your body for life. Prescription medications can only provide some relief from flair ups or outbreaks.

Human Immunodeficiency Virus/Acquired Immunodeficiency Syndrome (HIV/AIDS) are probably the most well known of all STDs, but yet they continue to infect and kill hundreds of people every day. There is no cure for either, and only a cocktail of medications may keep death at bay. You can become infected with HIV/AIDS through all types of unprotected sex as well as through IV drug use.

The Human Papilloma Virus (HPV) virus mainly affects women and may be the cause of several types of reproductive-related cancers, including cervical cancer. It can be transmitted through all types of unprotected sexual activity. A vaccine for HPV is currently available; however, there is no treatment or cure for the disease. Furthermore, symptoms can go completely unnoticed.

Scabies is a skin infection caused by tiny mites that burrow into your skin. The resulting bumps and blisters can be extremely itchy which may also lead to a bacterial infection. The mites are transferred by skin-to-skin contact with an infected person, but medicated creams and lotions can rid you of the pests. Like pubic lice, scabies can be transferred by way of towels and bedding.

Syphilis can be easily cured if treated; however, if left unchecked it can result in brain, eye, ear, heart problems, and death. It is caused by bacteria that can be transmitted through contact with sores and rashes of an infected person. Schubert and Nietzsche both died of syphilis.

Self-Examination

It is imperative to your health that you know every inch of your body inside and out. From head to toe, you need to be able to identify any changes or abnormalities in your body. Having a strong baseline to which you can compare against is vital for early detection. Knowing if you had a spot on your arm, back, or leg a month ago will help you know if you should go to the doctor or not. Either way, you need to approach a potential situation calmly and not jump to conclusions or think the worst. Furthermore, women and men should be very familiar with their breasts and testicles respectively.

You should not feel embarrassed or ashamed in examining yourself on a monthly basis in the shower. Early detection of a lump or other growth can mean the difference between life and death. Women should get an annual checkup from their gynecologist even if they feel fine and everything seems normal. Yearly Pap smear tests, for example, are extremely important in early detection of cervical cancer. Lastly, your knowledge should not be limited to your external body. Knowing what is normal and what is abnormal internally under regular conditions can be a huge indicator of an issue. For example, constant issues with bowel movements can be the result of a poor diet or something more serious such as colon cancer. Just be sure that you track changes over a reasonable amount of time so you do not turn into a hypochondriac.

Illness

No matter how careful we are about our stress levels, eating habits, and exercise, we will all get sick at some point. Hopefully, the frequency and intensity are low for both factors, but when you are sick, especially seriously ill, there are a few things you can do to help yourself. First and foremost is to maintain a positive attitude. While it is not a magic pill, a positive attitude will help your overall outlook, which can reduce stress levels. You should always have hope, if not for yourself, then for the sake of your loved ones. Having a relative or friend to assist you during your illness will greatly help your stress levels as well. Be diligent in taking any medication and following any instructions provided by your doctor. Never let a pain or illness go unchecked since it could develop into a more serious condition. Lastly, give yourself enough time to rest and recover before returning to your normal routine. Jumping back into daily life prematurely can make the illness worse than it was originally.

There is a large selection of physicians out there, so there is no need to settle for less. Any doctor worth their salt should take more than just a surface look at your issue. They should inquire not only about the obvious items such as family history, but they should also factor in your specific lifestyle, environment and emotional conditions. Your issue may be caused by simple reasons or a combination of factors that may not be obvious to you at the time but also may not require costly or unnecessary tests, medications or procedures. Stress and stressful situations alone can mimic symptoms of nearly any real medical condition, so make sure that you are examining and treating the real root cause and not simply masking or misrouting attention. If you find that you are not receiving comprehensive care, I highly recommend that you seek out a physician who does look at the full picture.

If the illness is terminal in nature, you will need to prepare both yourself and loved ones that will be left behind. However, this does not mean that you should ever give up your fight with the disease or condition. Doctors are only human and miracles do happen. This is never easy but may help in your acceptance of the situation. Ensure that you have all your affairs in order, especially your last will and testament, living will, and power of attorney. Make sure that your intentions are clearly defined and try to leave little to chance or open to question. Lastly, try to enjoy the time you have remaining with your family and friends.

Mental Stress

Mental stress is a silent killer. It can easily weaken your immune system quicker than almost any disease or virus. Stress coupled with time is a guaranteed recipe for a shortened life. You should fight off stress with the same intensity that you would a shark attack. Mental stress can attack you physically, which can lead to a simple cold or any number of severe illnesses.

You should always listen to your body. Your body can tell you just as much as any diagnostic test. When you are feeling run down, it is your body's attempt at sending up a red flag in hopes that you will listen. If you do not listen, your body will intensify its message until it changes course and takes over full control. This can include anything from blacking out to a coma.

Drugs/Alcohol

At no time, for any duration, or in any quantity, are drugs acceptable. Illegal drugs are illegal for a reason. Their short-term and long-term effects are worse than you probably realize. Prescription drugs can, but should not, be overused for the same reasons as illegal drugs. Even over-the-counter medications can be abused when taken in large quantities or for the wrong symptoms. The damage that they can do to every organ in your body, especially your brain, heart, and liver, is often irreversible. There are enough toxins in the air we breathe and foods we eat; your body does not need you adding any extra strain to it.

Let me make one thing clear, alcohol is a drug. It can be abused and has the same effects as any narcotic. Moderate drinking by responsible adults is acceptable on occasion. Alcohol itself is not always the problem, but when combined with driving a vehicle, you have a surefire recipe for disaster. You can easily kill yourself, a passenger, another motorist, or a pedestrian if you drive while under the influence of alcohol. There is no excuse for getting behind the wheel, even if you are only "buzzed," so chose not to drink, have a sober person drive, or stay right where you are. Never feel embarrassed or pressured into doing something you know is not right. Lastly, never feel bad about calling someone, including your parents, for a ride regardless of how late it is or far away you are. If you think that phone call is bad, just imagine the one in which a police officer tells us you have killed someone or are dead yourself.

Suicide

Taking your own life, regardless of the situation or circumstance, is never a solution. Before you cause harm to yourself or anyone around you, reach out for help. **The National Suicide Prevention Lifeline is open 24 hours a day at 800-273-TALK (8255) or on the Internet at www.suicidepreventionlifeline.org.** You can get assistance from any number of trusted sources, including a relative, friend, teacher, religious leader, co-worker, medical professional, or free and confidential services. If you are at the point where you have already written a suicide letter, why not share your problem with the people you intend to leave the note with. The important thing to do is to let someone into your world to help you. Try not to let issues build up inside of you to the point of explosion. Chances are that the problem or problems you are facing are temporary and controllable. If they require a long-term solution, there are successful ways of breaking up the issue into smaller, more manageable pieces. You may also need the assistance of prescription medication on either a short-term or long-term basis. If you will not stop your suicide attempt for yourself, then do it for the people that it would deeply affect, especially any children. Also, do not be selfish and consider all the people who are stricken with illnesses such as cancer who would give anything for a second chance at life. Lastly, never harm innocent people if your plan includes hurting others before taking your own life.

Tattoos and Piercings

While the idea of a tattoo may sound really good at the time, you have to be ready for a life-long commitment. Therefore, tattoos are not, by far, for children, and it is illegal to get one if you are under age. Between the design, words, and location, you better be positive of what you are about to do. They can be removed to an extent using lasers, but you may be left with an unsightly scar which might be worse than the original tattoo itself. In general, tattoos have a negative connotation in society. Therefore, if the tattoo is visible when you are wearing typical clothing, you may be judged or stereotyped before you even utter a single word. Lastly, if the instruments have not been properly sterilized, you can be infected with anything from hepatitis C to HIV and AIDS.

While piercings are not permanent like tattoos, they can be just as dangerous. If the needle or jewelry is not sterile, you can be infected by a disease just as you would with a tattoo. However, you have a greater chance of developing a bacterial infection from the open wound. If left untreated, not only will the original site of the piercing become infected, but so too will the surrounding tissue. If this does occur, you should immediately seek medical attention. The doctor will remove the piercing and provide proper medication, including antibiotics. Hiding or ignoring an issue will only cause it to get worse and the damage to become more severe.

Lead

While lead was commonly found in everything from paint to gasoline decades ago, it has since been removed from many products in the United States due to serious effects on our health. If ingested, lead-based paint can cause brain and developmental damage, especially in children who frequently place objects in their mouths. Unfortunately, not all countries have followed us when it comes to lead standards, and imported objects, including toys, may contain lead-based paints. Contaminated toys should be simply discarded immediately. Furthermore, take special care when removing any type of paint that may be lead-based. If you are not sure if the old paint contains lead, you can purchase inexpensive, easy-to-use testers from your local home improvement or paint store. Typically, you simply break a small vial which is within a protective sleeve and rub the cotton swab-like end on the object you want to test. If lead is detected, the swab will change color. If you do need to remove lead-based paint, be sure to protect yourself with a mask or respirator as well as the surroundings from becoming contaminated. Lastly, as part of regular infant health checks, their blood is tested for lead levels, but if you have any doubts, have your child retested.

Asbestos

Asbestos was one of those discoveries that was thought to be the miracle product of the day. It is a naturally occurring material that is fibrous. It was commonly used for its superior insulating properties, however, after many decades of exposure, it was found to be a carcinogen and thousands of people have died as a result of lung cancer. Now you may be asking yourself, why do I need to know about insulation used years ago? Unfortunately, it still can be found in many older homes and buildings, including schools and apartments. In addition, it was a major component of shingles which were used on houses for many years.

On the other hand, if left undisturbed and intact, asbestos insulation and shingles are of no immediate danger. However, once the fibers become frayed and airborne from damage or intentional removal, your health is at risk. If you are not sure if you have any form of asbestos in your location, have a licensed professional evaluate the material. Furthermore, you should never remove asbestos material on your own. Proper removal requires environmental and personal protective equipment to ensure the harmful fibers do not become airborne. In fact, proper procedures include carefully wetting down the material during the removal process. Lastly, asbestos cannot be placed in regular household or commercial garbage and is handled as hazardous waste.

Radon Gas

Radon is an odorless, colorless, tasteless, naturally occurring gas. It does not pose a danger until it is released into the air of enclosed spaces, especially in basements which are below grade and typically have poor air circulation. Radon levels also vary by geographic regions and locations. High or elevated levels over a long time can cause serious health hazards, including lung cancer.

If you wish to retest or have no idea of what your radon expose may be, you can easily test for the gas by purchasing an inexpensive kit from a reliable source such as a home improvement store like Lowes®. Typically you expose a small container or two to an undisturbed, closed environment (such as a basement) for a day and then mail them to a laboratory for analysis. There are both state and federal thresholds for allowable radon gas levels, and a test is usually required in most areas before a house can be resold. Keep in mind that even if you have a finished basement, it will not prevent the radon gas from entering the house.

If an unacceptable radon level is discovered, there is no reason to panic and begin packing. You should retest to confirm the initial results and realize that levels can be significantly affected by the time of year. Remediation consists of a ventilation unit which will pump the contaminated air to the outdoors. It is not an inexpensive system, but living in a contaminated environment is just as dangerous to your lungs as cigarette smoke, so you must take action. Lastly, this is one of those projects that should be left to the professionals.

Mold

Mold can grow in nearly any environmental condition, and it is often found in the hardest to reach or clean places. Maintaining a clean and orderly space will greatly help reduce the chances of mold growth, but the key is not to let it develop in the first place. Mold can cause severe health issues if ingested, inhaled, or introduced to your body in other ways such as by contact with your eyes. However, there are a number of easy steps you can take to prevent the health hazard. One of the major causes of mold growth is damp, humid, or wet conditions. Therefore, you should reduce the potential for mold growth by using a dehumidifier in damp locations such as a basement. You should never leave anything that is damp or wet balled up or in contact with porous surfaces. For example, if you come in from exercising and your shirt is wet with sweat, you should not put it directly in the laundry hamper. Instead, you should allow it air dry. Another common example is wet bath towels. You should always open up and allow wet towels to fully air dry before folding them up. Furthermore, the steam from a shower can create a perfect environment for bacterial growth, especially on porous grout. Therefore, if you do not wipe down the shower walls, you should ensure ample natural or mechanical ventilation by opening a window or turning on a bathroom exhaust fan. Another major, though not required, contributor to mold growth is dark conditions which can range in location from basements to closets.

Mold can visually take on a few different colors. It can be a pale red to brown or black. If you do see any signs of mold growth, be sure to clean the actual spot as well as the immediate area right away. Mold can grow at an exponential rate and, if left untreated, could cost thousands of dollars in remediation/replacement costs, in addition to the health concerns. Therefore, routinely inspect areas in your space that you would commonly expect the environmental conditions to be just right for mold growth; an ounce of prevention is worth a pound of cure.

Insurance

Whether it is auto, home, renters, life, medical, or dental insurance, it is a necessary evil. Even though you may never use it, you still need to have complete coverage. Health insurance can be extremely costly if you have to pay for it yourself, so make sure that you can get as much coverage as possible from your employer. Even if you leave a company for any reason, you can still receive coverage thanks to the Consolidated Omnibus Budget Reconciliation Act (COBRA). In addition, you can help lower your payments by taking a higher deductible (the amount you would need to pay out of your pocket before your coverage begins).

You should never leave your family unprotected without a significant life insurance policy. Term life insurance may be offered through your employer at discounted rates or can be purchased privately from a number of reputable agencies. Just as important as having insurance is reviewing your policy to ensure you have enough coverage. Keep in mind that a life event, such as the birth of a baby, is not the only reason to review insurance coverage. Market conditions, for example, could raise the cost of replacing your home, so be sure that you have adequate coverage at all times. Never go even one day without all types of insurance coverage since we all know the effects of Murphy's Law (what can go wrong, will go wrong).

Safety

"Caution is the parent of safety."
– Traditional Proverb

Safety

No matter what you do in life, big or small, safety should always come first. From using a knife to driving a car, you should always consider your personal safety and the safety of those around you. It may be something as simple as looking both ways before crossing the street, even if it is a one-way street. Think twice about what you are doing, how you are doing it, as well as who and what may also be affected, including your immediate surroundings. For example, if you are working with a combustible material, make sure that there are no sources of ignition in the area.

There are a number of "musts" that you should always observe. For example, you must always wear your seat belt, regardless of the trip's distance or duration. Always wear the appropriate personal protective equipment when working in or near hazardous conditions. This could be as simple as using a pair of safety goggles or not wearing loose clothing. It also holds true for items that are not traditionally seen as hazardous such as blood and other bodily fluids. Take the few extra seconds to perform an activity safely rather than rushing it and causing a potentially dangerous situation. Also, never rush others when they are exercising safe practices such as when waiting to make a turn into traffic.

One small but important detail to pay attention to when purchasing certain types of products, especially those containing electrical or flammable/combustible components, is the Underwriters Laboratory (UL) certification mark. The non-profit, privately owned U.S. company evaluates a host of product types for potential safety hazards such as electrical, mechanical, and fire. If you have a choice between two or more products and one does not carry the UL mark, I highly suggest leaving it on the shelf. Products are not legally required to pass rigorous UL standards, but you should take comfort in their methods and reputation.

Panic

Panic is a normal bodily reaction to a sudden or scary situation. It can be caused by nearly anything, ranging from an unexpected action such as a car stopping short in front of you to something extremely upsetting such as death. While initial panic is acceptable, you need to try to prevent it going too much beyond that point. Relaxing yourself and collecting your thoughts will allow you to better tackle the given situation. Focus on the matter at hand rather than all the implications that may or may not result. Excessive and frequent stress can surface in the form of panic attacks. They can cause all types of physical symptoms, including dizziness, chest pains, vomiting, or loss of consciousness. Therefore, try to learn from past incidences and prepare for future issues to reduce your chances of panicking in any situation.

9-1-1 Emergency Services

Despite what you may have heard, nearly every man, woman, and child in the United States with access to a phone has an insurance policy. While it may not be your traditional type of medical coverage, the 9-1-1 emergency system helps protect us in ways we often take for granted. Whether you are at home, work, in school, or on a cell phone, you can reach out for emergency help by dialing 9-1-1 twenty-four hours a day, 365 days a year. You should never hesitate in dialing 9-1-1 as long as you have a genuine emergency requiring the assistance of the fire department, police, or medical technicians. Never use 9-1-1 for non-emergencies since you will be tying up precious resources which could be otherwise used by people in a real emergency situation. Every call to 9-1-1 will be followed up by someone, even if it was accidentally dialed and you hung up.

Whenever you do call 9-1-1, you should provide the operator with two critical pieces of information as soon as you connect. First, provide them with your location. This is especially important if you are calling from a cell phone since technologies may not be in place to automatically locate you. The second vital piece of information to provide is your name. This will insure that in the event the call is disrupted or you are not able to further communicate, authorities will know where to go and who required the help. In addition, it is important to keep in mind that if you are traveling outside of the United States, 9-1-1 may not be the number to call in case of emergency. Other countries and regions either have a different number to call or may not have a central system in place at all. For example, most European counties use 1-1-2 instead of 9-1-1. Lastly, do not confuse 9-1-1 for 4-1-1, which is the general number for telephone directory assistance in the United States or 3-1-1, which is used for non-emergencies in the United States and Canada.

Emergencies

While you can never be fully prepared for all types of emergencies, you can take some steps before an incident occurs to ensure safety. The most important thing to do is to remain calm and not to panic. Take your time but be deliberate in your actions. This holds true if you are a bystander or a victim. Then, either call for help yourself or have someone do it for you; never be afraid to dial 9-1-1. Next, try to stabilize the victim. You can do this by simply calming the victim down, preventing them from moving too much and further hurting themselves (unless the victim is suffering from a seizure in which case, you should clear the area of objects and not restrain the victim), or applying pressure on an open wound. Take precautions from exposing yourself to biohazards such as blood and other bodily fluids, even if you know the person. If you do contaminate yourself, wash the area thoroughly with soap and water immediately and discard any contaminated items, including clothing. If you have any open wounds, such as a cut on your hand, and become exposed to another person's fluids, you should immediately seek medical attention so the proper precautions can be taken.

If you have been properly trained and the victim requires it, you can start cardiopulmonary resuscitation (CPR). If there is an object penetrating the victim, you should think twice about removing it since they can easily bleed out and die. In cases of burn victims, do not try to remove any clothing or other material that may have been singed into the wound. If you have not been properly trained and you try improper techniques, you can cause additional harm, including death. Always know your limitations and allow the professionals to do the job they have been trained to handle. Sometimes being a hero is not as glamorous as the movies and television would make it seem – less can be more.

Basic First Aid

Unfortunately, life will always have its little bumps and bruises. Therefore, it is important to know how to treat various situations to minimize the damage. Regardless of the scenario, it is important to remain calm and not to panic. If you do not become part of the solution, you might as well be another victim. Therefore, make sure that you become familiar with each of the following techniques and try to overcome any fears, such as the sight of blood, since someone else's life may depend on it.

Shock is a common term used to describe extremely low blood pressure. It can be caused by an open wound, internal bleeding, or a reaction to a terrifying situation. It can also lead to the person losing consciousness. This is something that you want to prevent if at all possible. Do whatever you need to keep the victim awake by talking to them and focusing their attention on anything but their trauma. You can also use "smelling salts" if you happen to have it nearby. It will release ammonia when activated which will hopefully trigger the victim to inhale since it is an irritant to air passage membranes. You can also help reverse the effects of shock by having the person lie down and elevate their legs. This will help in promoting blood flow to the victim's heart and brain. Regardless of the cause of shock, you should have a doctor check you out just in case it is indicative of a more serious issue, especially if it happens with any level of frequency.

Your skin is your largest organ, and it is the first line of defense against infections. If you receive a cut, even if it is just a paper cut, the integrity of the organ becomes compromised. Think of your body as a big water balloon. A pinhole can be just as damaging as a large gash. For shallow cuts and surface wounds that have limited bleeding, you first need to flush them clean with fresh, cold running water and/or hydrogen peroxide. Peroxide is very affective at cleaning wounds, but be careful handling it as it will bleach the color out of porous clothing or fabric. Be sure to get all debris out of the wound before applying an antibacterial ointment such as Neosporin®. The ointment will help prevent bacterial infections and should be applied to all cuts of this nature. Next, cover the wound using the appropriate size and type of bandage. The bleeding should be controlled by the simple bandage, and the wound should be kept dry until it heals.

If you have received a deep or long wound or a small one that has not stopped bleeding, you will need to seek medical attention. Until then, apply steady and constant pressure with a clean paper or cloth towel. You may even need to receive sutures or a butterfly stitch. After you receive professional treatment, you will still need to keep the wound clean and dry. You may be asked to change the dressing daily, and stitches may dissolve on their own in a few days to weeks, or you may need to go back to the doctor to have them removed.

In the case of severed or nearly severed body parts, you will need to act fast. The average adult has ten pints of blood, but that does not mean you can easily spare a few and continue to function. Applying pressure may not be enough to stop the bleeding in some cases, so you will need to apply a tourniquet. Think of a tourniquet as a noose that cuts off the flow of blood. It can be made of nearly any material that can be tightened down and maintains constant constriction on its own. Typically in an emergency, a pants belt can be used as a tourniquet. Once the tourniquet is in place, you should look for the severed body part and place it in a clean plastic bag with an ample amount of fresh ice. Depending on the nature of the cut and damage to nerves and vessels, the part may be able to be reattached. However, if the damage is too extensive or too much time has passed, the part may not be usable any longer but at least the victim is still alive.

Sprains are a common injury not only received as a result of sports but from almost any daily activity in life. The most common types are ankle and wrist sprains. They are most susceptible to injury since they are composed of several small bones and are often a pivot point with heavy loads placed on them. The main cure for sprains is time; however, you can use the Rest, Ice, Compress, Elevate (RICE) method to aid in the recovery of minor injuries. Resting the injury for the first couple of days is critical to the success of the cure. Stay off your feet as much as possible for the first few days for ankle injuries and do not lift anything with a sprained wrist. Next, apply ice to the location of the injury for ten to twenty minutes at a time every three to four hours. Applying too frequent or long of cold will only inhibit the healing process. Using a compression bandage such as an ACE® bandage will also help things along. However, be sure not to restrict blood flow by making the bandage too tight. Lastly, try to elevate the injury above your heart as much as possible. You can do so by using pillows and blankets while lying in bed.

Fractured or broken bones are serious injuries that require immediate and professional medical attention. If they are not set properly or allowed to fester, bigger issues will develop. Fractures and breaks can occur at any age but are most common with active children and adults as well as seniors who may suffer from calcium loss which has led to brittle bones. X-rays can easily determine if a bone is fractured or has a simple or compound break. In the event the bone protrudes through the skin, do not attempt to move or push it back in place. Simply try to control any bleeding by applying pressure, even though it may hurt the victim. Also be careful that the victim does not go into shock since it can be a scary sight. In the best cases, you may be able to get away with a soft cast which is not as rigid as a full cast. Healing time varies with the type of injury and bone, but it is safe to say that you will be out of commission for a number of weeks at a minimum.

Any type of head or neck trauma can be a matter of life or death in minutes. The wrong move can also cause a serious problem no matter how good you feel. Spinal injuries occur far too often and can lead to permanent paralysis. Therefore, treat all types of head and neck trauma as the most serious of matters. Never move a victim of a head or neck injury. Unless they are bleeding profusely, you should not even touch the victim. Instead, talk to them and make sure they remain calm and do not make any movements. Professionals will carefully immobilize and transport the victim to the hospital. Even if you have only had a slight blow to the head or neck, as in the case of a fender-bender, you should seek medical attention. You may feel perfectly fine at the time, but that does not mean that you do not have slow bleeding in your brain that can hemorrhage at any point. Lastly, if you develop any kind of impaired vision, difficulty breathing, or slurred speech, you should get immediate medical assistance.

A stroke can happen to anyone at any age but typically affects older people and those who have just had surgery. It is caused by a small blood clot, air bubble, or fleck of cholesterol that broke free from a clogging artery and has migrated to the brain. The blockage reduces or completely cuts off the flow of oxygen-rich blood to a part of the brain temporarily or permanently. In addition to strokes, there are also trans ischemic attacks (TIAs), which are mini-strokes or warning strokes that are very short-lived (seconds) but could be a red flag of future full-blown strokes.

There are a few physical characteristics that you can use to tell if someone has had a stroke. The victim's face may become partially paralyzed on only one side, they may not be able to raise both arms fully or equally, they may not be able to walk without a problem or have slurred to no speech. When you come across someone who has had a stroke, time is of the essence. If you can get them to a hospital and have medication introduced within the first couple of hours of a stroke, its affects may be reversible. Even if you are not sure, it is better to err on the side of caution since you cannot go back in time to reverse the effects of a stroke.

All types of burns are painful and should be treated appropriately and immediately. Keep in mind that they do not have to be caused by fire either. Burns can also be caused by chemicals such as acids and bases, hot objects such as metal, as well as electricity. In general, burns are classified into three different levels of severity. It is very important that you carefully determine which category a burn falls into since treatments are different for each degree. However, regardless of the severity, you should seek proper medical attention to avoid complications such as infection and nerve damage. Never apply non-sterile substances such as butter or oil on the burn since that can lead to infection. Lastly, chemical burns can be tricky since the substance may react with water if you try to flush the wound.

First-degree burns are the least severe of all burns. They are typically reddish in color and swelling can accompany the damage to the upper layer of skin called the epidermis. The best remedy for this type of burn is rinsing with clean cold water and applying an antibiotic ointment such as Neosporin®. It will take a few days for the wound to heal and minor too little scarring will result.

Second-degree burns are worse than first degree burns. Unlike first-degree burns, second-degree burns affect both the first and second (dermis) layers of skin. Burns are considered second-degree as long as they are less than ten to fifteen percent in total area. You can also suffer from the chills, a fever, and blistering of the site, which should not be disturbed. Any clothing or jewelry that fuses to the wound should only be removed by a medical expert. Scarring will usually accompany this type of burn, and you should seek immediate medical attention.

Third-degree burns are the most severe form you can receive. They can look wet in nature in addition to being brown or black. In this case, bones, muscles, nerves, and other organs may have been damaged in addition to the first two layers of your skin. Pain may or may not accompany this type of burn since the nerve endings may have been destroyed. The victim may suffer from shock, lose consciousness, stop breathing, or go into cardiac arrest. About all you can do to treat this type of injury is to dial 9-1-1 and try to keep the victim calm. Scarring will definitely occur and skin graphs could be used to help in the healing process. Lastly, you may not be able to visit a third-degree burn victim while in the hospital since they are especially venerable to infection. Many weeks of physical and emotional rehabilitation will accompany the healing process.

Risk

Risk, like people, comes in all shapes and sizes. There is good risk and bad risk, which can completely make or break you. There is risk in everything in life. It is not limited to tangible items like money but may be as simple as crossing a busy street. The first step to take is to determine the degree of the risk. You not only need to make this initial assessment, but you also need to continually reassess the severity of the risk during the process or event. Typically the level of risk is proportionate to the reward. The environment that you are in can also play a factor in your decision. For example, if you are young and investing in the stock market, it will be reasonable to invest in more aggressive stocks. However, if you are planning on retiring in the next five years, you are better off placing your hard-earned money into more conservative stocks, money market accounts, or bonds.

Always evaluate the level of risk in everything you do ranging from the types of friends you keep to your line of work. While it may be exciting to be in a risky situation, weigh the potential negative effects against the potential benefits. Regardless of the situation, idea, or action, always keep in the back of your mind the old expression of "A bird in the hand is worth two in the bush." Sometimes going with what you know is not as exciting as the unknown or untested, but at least you are relatively guaranteed a positive result.

Preventative Maintenance

As the saying goes, an ounce of prevention is worth a pound of cure. Actually, in some cases, there may not be a cure, so preventative maintenance may be your sole option. Preventative maintenance applies to almost all aspects of your life. Whether it is exercise and a proper diet to help lower your cholesterol levels or changing the tires on your car before they burst, chances are you will save much more time and money performing a little work upfront rather than having to deal with a situation in the future. Preventative maintenance does not have to cost a ton of money either. Often you can make something last longer just by keeping it clean. Preventing an issue, especially those of the emergency type, can keep your stress levels low since you have mitigated the risk upfront. Keep in mind that you cannot prevent or plan for all incidences. Be sure to think of contingency plans in the event a problem does arise. Simply stated, plan ahead!

Accidents

While it would be great to go through life without having to worry about accidents, this is simply not reality. Hopefully, any accidents you experience will be minor in nature, but there always exists the potential for something major to occur. You should try to be as careful as you can so as not to cause an accident, but when they do happen, large or small, do not panic. With minor accidents, first make sure that you are not hurt, and then clean up any mess that was made. If you caused damage to someone else's property, do not try to hide it or cover it up. You should be open and forthright with the person as soon as possible and apologize sincerely. If you lost, broke, or damaged someone's property, you should replace it with a new copy. If that is not possible, you will need to figure out what you can do to make up for it. On the other hand, if someone comes to you saying that they lost, broke, or otherwise damaged something you own, you should not hold it over their head if it was truly an accident. This may become more difficult the larger the incident; however, we are all human and we should not let an accident cripple us mentally. It is also usually best to "get back on the horse" as soon as possible since the more time that goes by, the less likely it is that you will ever face the challenge or situation again. Even if you do have a major accident where, God forbid, you lose an arm or leg, know that it is not the end of the world, and that it could have been worse. If you feel yourself getting depressed, talk to someone, anyone, before it develops into something much worse. Life is such a precise gift that every moment of it, for better or worse, should be cherished.

Believe it or not, there is such a thing as a good accident. Methods and products, ranging from explosion welding to Teflon®, came about as a result of unintentional events. This is just another good reason to always keep your eyes and ears open for new opportunities.

Allergic Reactions

Allergic reactions can seriously injury or kill people and animals if immediate action is not taken. Allergens can come from diverse sources, including nuts, shellfish, bee or wasp stings, latex, and antibiotics. Even though there are tests available to detect if you are allergic to some substances, most people do not discover that they are allergic until they have already been exposed. Furthermore, the quantity of the substance you are exposed to does not have to be large. In some cases, when two different types of food are processed on the same machinery, it can cause serious harm. In most cases, swelling or outbreaks over your body are a sign of a negative reaction. Allergic reactions can also lead to airways being closed or a reduction in blood flow to vital organs.

The treatment for each type of allergic reaction is specific to the substance. Typically a dose of adrenalin can combat the effect of bee and wasp stings. Anti-inflammatory medications such as Benadryl® can help reduce swelling. Regardless of the type, duration and seriousness of a reaction, you should seek immediate medical help. Allergic reactions can occur in pets too, as in the case of antibiotics such as penicillin. Keep in mind that even if you are not allergic to certain substances or situations, others around you can have serious reactions. Therefore, take precautions before serving foods with allergens such as peanuts or peanut butter and, as always, ask a parent's permission before giving a child any type of food.

Negative Interactions

Whenever you introduce a substance into your body, you not only have to think of the potential consequences or side-affects it may have on its own, but you also have to consider any potential negative interactions with other items either already in your system or that will be taken at the same time. In addition, doses do not have to be large and the impacts may not always be obvious; you could easily be doing harm to internal organs and systems and not realize it until it is too late. Furthermore, many times people think that combining two prescription medications is the only source of potential harm; however, there are a host of other types that could prove just as dangerous. For example, if you are on blood thinner medication, you have to be careful when eating certain types of vegetables. Vegetables that are high in vitamin K, such as broccoli, can interact with the dose of blood thinner, thereby causing problems ranging from bruising easily to cuts not clotting. Mixing two over-the-counter drugs, such as when treating a cold, can have adverse affects. Even combining something as simple as aspirin or acetaminophen with alcohol or other over-the-counter drugs can have damaging effects on your organs. Therefore, always read the product label before taking any substance. If you are not certain if two or more substances will have a negative interaction, contact your doctor or ask a local pharmacist. Lastly, be leery of information from questionable sources such as the Internet.

Your Eyes

Of all your five senses, I think everyone would agree that your sight is the most valued. Imagine never being able to see your family or the natural beauty of a summer sunset ever again. Taking care of your eyes is a lifelong commitment, especially considering you only have one set of eyes. Be sure to get full eye exams annually, including checks for glaucoma. If you wind up needing glasses, be sure your prescription is up-to-date and they fit properly. An old or inaccurate prescription can cause everything from eyestrain to headaches, not to mention safety issues, especially while operating a vehicle or other potentially dangerous equipment.

The most important lesson when it comes to your eyes is physically protecting them. The primary way to offer the best protection is through the use of safety glasses and sunglasses. You should always protect your eyes when using tools or in a hazardous environment, no matter how uncomfortable or unfashionable they may seem. You can easily lose your vision from a large or small foreign object, including solids, liquids, and gases. By the way, have you ever wondered why you cry while cutting unions? Well, they can contain high levels of sulfur, which mixes with the moisture in your eyes to form sulfuric acid. The acid irritates your eyes and therefore they will tear in an attempt to dilute and clear the acid. A way to greatly reduce their weepy affects is to chill them in your refrigerator for an hour before cutting.

No matter if you purchase a five-dollar or five-hundred-dollar pair of sunglasses, you should make sure they come with ultraviolet (UV) protection. The thin layer of protection will block the harmful component of sunlight. Otherwise, without the coating, your eyes can be damaged since sunglasses dilate your pupils (opens them more than usual) and allows more light to pass into them. If you are unsure if your sunglasses have a UV coating or if you suspect it has worn or been scratched off, then throw them out immediately and get a new pair. You can do more damage wearing sunglasses without the coating than no sunglasses at all.

While your eyes may be the windows to your soul, they are also the superhighway to your body for germs and viruses. As much of a habit as it may be, you should never touch your eyes with your hands unless you have just washed them. This holds especially true while out in public since everything from door handles to shopping carts are a breeding ground for all types of bacteria and viruses. If you are unable to wash your hands or do not have any hand sanitizer with you and you do need to wipe your eye, use the back of your hand, which should be less contaminated.

Lastly, as tempting as laser corrective surgery may seem, I highly recommend you do not undergo it. While statistically the chances of a problem occurring are low, you do not want to be one of the people who suffer complications. The complications can be relatively minor but still a nuisance, such as having to constantly rewet your eyes. Furthermore, even with some types of surgeries, you will still need glasses for reading and other up-close activities starting in your forties or fifties. Instead, I recommend extended, disposable contacts which you can wear for a few weeks at a time; you can even sleep without having to take them out. If anything does happen, at least you can take the contacts out and wear glasses. The same cannot be said for the corrective surgery.

Cleanliness

Cleanliness truly is next to godliness. This holds true for everything from personal hygiene to your surroundings. Make sure that you wash your hands often, especially in the winter months, to keep bacteria and viruses from making you and your family ill. Always wash your hands before working with food and keep your kitchen tidy when preparing raw foods such as chicken. Keep your surroundings clean and clear of debris to avoid ants, mice, or worse. Maintain your possessions by wiping them down or washing them to keep them looking and working like new. You should not have to waste hard-earned money by replacing items that should have been taken care of along the way. Take pride in your community by cleaning up the property around you, even if it is not your mess or your property (the street or a hallway for example). One of the automatic benefits of cleanliness is that it helps keep things organized as well.

Fire

Fire of any size or source should be treated with great respect. Fire is much like us in that it is born, lives, and dies; however, it is a force of nature that we cannot always control. Playing with fire is something that is fit for no one since it can easily lead to major destruction, including loss of life. Not even trained and seasoned firefighters are exempt from fire's fury. Never play with matches, lighters, or sparking devices by themselves or in conjunction with other materials. We are constantly surrounded by combustible and flammable solids, liquids, and gases so no matter how careful you think you are, a small flame can lead to an inferno at any time. Burns can be mild to severe in degree but are one of the most painful, slow healing and disfiguring types of wounds you can receive.

When a fire does break out, it should not be the first time that you try to figure out what to do. There are a few important guidelines that can limit damage and help save lives. However, if the incident is or has the potential to get out of control, you should always dial 9-1-1 from a safe location so firefighters can restore order quickly and safely.

You and your family should have a home evacuation plan and perform annual drills at all times of the day and night. An important part of the plan is the designated gathering place where everyone should meet once they have evacuated. However, not all meeting locations are the same. The best place to meet is on the sidewalk of the next-door neighbor's house. You never want to cross a street, especially if you have children. Fire engines and other apparatus will be coming in from all different directions, and they will not be able to stop on a dime if your child runs into the middle of the street. You will also want to be close to your home, so you can report to the fire department either that everyone is out of the house or if someone is unaccounted for and potentially trapped inside the structure. Senior-ranking fire officers wear white helmets on the scene, so look for one of them, but in a pinch any firefighter will be able to communicate your message to the appropriate commander. By the same token, you do not want to be in the way of the fire department, so the fire hydrant a couple of houses away is not a good gathering location.

Fire extinguishers should always be available to you; in fact, it is legally required in both public and private structures. However, not all extinguishers are the same and size can make a huge difference. Depending on the size of the extinguisher, you can have anywhere from ten to thirty seconds worth of fire-extinguishing agent. That is not a very long time; therefore, you need to make sure that your decision to stay and fight a fire is the right one before you pick up the extinguisher.

In general, there are four types of extinguishers. The first type, know as Class A, consists of plain water under pressure. This is useful for small ordinary combustibles such as wood, most plastics, and fabrics. The second type of extinguisher, Class B, consists of carbon dioxide (CO_2) in a gaseous form under high pressure. Class B extinguishers can be used on petroleum-based fires such as gasoline and oil. One of the benefits of using a CO_2 extinguisher is that it will not leave damaging extinguishing agent residue on or near the incident. The next type of extinguisher, Class C, should be used on electrical fires. It is comprised of a dry chemical powder under pressure; you should take precautions in limiting your exposure to the dust, which can be easily inhaled. The last type of extinguisher is Class D and is used in very specialized situations such as burning metals, including sodium, magnesium, and titanium.

You should always use the proper type of fire extinguisher on the appropriate fire, or do not use one at all since you can harm yourself as well as spread the fire. Class A fire extinguishers should never be used on an electrical fire due to the risk of electrocution. Class B extinguishers should not be used on light combustibles, such as a pile of dry leaves, since the force of the CO_2 can spread the very same fire that you are trying to extinguish (use Class A instead). In most cases, you will find combination ABC extinguishers which can be used for the majority of common incidents.

A, B, and C class extinguishers are all operated in the same manner. Most of these fire extinguishers come with a gauge. If they do, the first step is to check and see that the extinguisher is not low or empty. There is no sense wasting precious time with an empty or near empty extinguisher. Depending on the model, some can be refilled but not by consumers on their own. The next step is to remove the safety pin that prevents the trigger from being accidentally activated. If you are using a Class B extinguisher, you should remove the horn from its holder and point it in the general direction of the fire. You should hold the horn by the handle and never point it at yourself or anyone else since rapidly discharging carbon dioxide is extremely cold and can cause damage to eyes and skin. The last step is to activate the extinguisher while pointing it at the base of the fire using a sweeping motion side to side. If the fire is still not under control, leave immediately and dial 9-1-1 for help. However, even if the fire appears to be completely extinguished, you should carefully sift through it and the surrounding area to ensure that it has not spread to other surfaces, locations, or objects and there is no sign of embers, smoke, or flames. You should also remove the debris to a safe, non-combustible, open location such as outdoors on concrete or asphalt. Never put a partially used extinguisher back into service without replacing or having it refilled first.

As silly as it may sound, fires do not just happen in houses. A fire can break out in any building or location, and therefore you should prepare yourself no matter where you are or how long you will be there. For example, for locations that you routinely visit such as a school or an office, you should be very familiar with the layout of the building and know of at least two ways out to safety. In addition, even if you are in a building for just an afternoon, such as to attend a wedding, you should take a quick look around for at least two exits. Furthermore, take notice if the room has strobe lights to warn of a problem, fire extinguishers, sprinklers whose heads may be behind decorative covers or plates as well as pull boxes near the exits that can be used to sound an alarm in case of an emergency. By the way, water will continue to flow out of a sprinkler head even after the fire has been extinguished; only the fire department can/should turn off the sprinkler system. Lastly, even if you are traveling on a bus or airplane, you should take a moment to look around for the exits, keeping in mind that the nearest exit may be behind you.

There are a few miscellaneous pieces of information that can help you in fire-related emergencies. For example, never try to use water on a kitchen grease fire. There is a good chance it will spread the fire as well as cause the hot oil to splash on to you. Instead, use a pot lid or baking soda to blanket the grease and extinguish the flames. Never run a gas or electric clothes dryer or dishwasher while you are sleeping or out of the house. If a fire does develop, you will have less of a chance to extinguish it or escape to safety when you are not home or sleeping respectively. One important, potentially life-saving, sign to look for involves truss floors and roofs. Truss construction is a lightweight, less expensive alternative to traditional "stick" construction. The sign indicating the use of trusses will have an "F," "R," or "F/R" in a triangle which represents the use of truss floors, roofs, and both floors and roofs respectively. The sign will be posted at the entrance of the commercial building or private residence such as townhouses, condominiums, and apartment buildings. However, keep in mind that the absence of a sign does not necessarily mean that the floors and roofs use standard construction techniques. There is a major safety issue when you combine trusses and fire. The structural integrity of an individual truss section can be compromised within a few minutes of direct flame contact. Furthermore, once one member of the truss roof or floor becomes compromised, the entire roof or floor is at risk of collapse. It is no wonder trusses have the distinction of being nicknamed "firemen killers". (The two World Trade Center towers utilized truss floors whereas the Empire State Building, which was hit by a World War II era bomber, remained intact with relatively little structural damage.) What does all this mean for you? It translates into less time to safely escape a roof or floor collapse in the event of a house or building fire. Also, keep in mind that a truss roof was not designed to take into account any extra load such as heavy boxes or furniture. For this reason, you should never store anything in your attic if the roof is constructed with trusses. Imagine what would happen if you or your rescuer became trapped under not only the weight of the collapsed roof but all your college textbooks and unused clothes. You can quickly determine if you are looking at a truss by the triangular sections formed by wooden cross members which are held together by metal fasteners called gusset plates. A gusset plate is basically nothing more than a group of staples whose teeth penetrate the wood less than a half an inch. If that is not enough to catch your attention, take a drive through the next new housing development you see. To say the least, the truss sections may not be delivered or stored in the best of conditions, leading construction workers to hammer mangled gusset plates somewhat back into place.

If you become trapped in a structure during a fire, you should try to get to a window and signal for help. If that is not possible, you should get as close to a doorway or wall as possible. Firefighters place either their right or left hand on a wall and follow it throughout the area to orientate themselves during the search. Therefore, if you are in the middle of a large room in smoky conditions, you may not be seen or found until it is too late. By the way, this search technique could be very useful if you are disorientated due to smoke or darkness in either a familiar or unfamiliar environment such as a hotel. Furthermore, children like to hide when they are scared. Hiding in a toy box, under a bed, or in the back of a closet will greatly hamper rescue efforts. Therefore, children should be taught never to hide from smoke, fire, or firefighters who can look rather scary when they are in their gear and sound like Darth Vader. Lastly, never be lulled into a false sense of security just because a structure has a sprinkler system since they can malfunction at any time.

Water

Over seventy percent of the Earth is covered with water, and that is not even including swimming pools. As refreshing and relaxing as water can be, it can be just as dangerous if not treated with respect. Children and water do not mix. In fact, a child can drown in a fraction of an inch of water. Never leave children unattended in or around any body of water, no matter how shallow or calm. Always have preventative measures in place, such as fences and locked gates, so as not to make it easy for a child to get to the water. Always make sure that an adult who knows how to swim is present when children are in the water.

Rivers and streams can cause additional hazards due to fast-moving currents. Even though the water appears to be flowing at a slow pace, it does not take long for a child or adult to be swept away from the shoreline. Rivers and streams can also swell or flashflood with downpours and melting ice. Lakes can contain many biological and animal hazards due to their stagnant nature, so always wash off after swimming and never swallow lake water. Do not be lulled into a false sense of security by the calm water of a lake either. They can contain soft, silt floors which your hand or foot can easily get stuck in. Furthermore, the fine particles can make visibility almost nonexistent, which could hamper rescue efforts if something does happen.

When it comes to the ocean, you have to treat it with extra special care. Always swim within the protection of a lifeguard. Never go swimming in the ocean before, during, or after a storm, no matter how good/big the waves may be. Be especially aware of any rip currents, which can quickly exhaust and drag you out to sea. If you do get caught in a rip current, do not swim directly into shore. Instead, swim parallel to the coast until you clear the dangerous section of water and then swim back to the shore.

Boating, no matter how big the vessel, does not make you invincible to the dangers of the ocean. In fact, you could be at risk of even more hazards in a boat. First and foremost, never set foot on a boat unless the captain is licensed and experienced. Secondly, ensure that the captain has and is not drinking alcohol; an intoxicated captain can be worse than an inexperienced one. Next, make sure that you have easy access to a lifejacket that fits you and that there are enough for all onboard. Never act recklessly while on a boat; accidents can easily occur due to slippery surfaces, sharp objects, and rough seas. Be fully prepared for your journey, including food, drinkable water, and sunscreen. Lastly, make sure that someone knows where you are going and when you are expected back. Cell phones will not always be in range of a tower while on the water, so a boat's radio may be your only means of communication.

Regardless of the body of water, never swim alone and always be aware of current and future weather conditions. No matter how desperate you may get, never drink salt water. In extreme cases, and as unpleasant as it may be, you can drink your own urine. It is comprised mostly of water and is sterile. No matter what, always respect the water just as you would any of nature's other elements like fire.

Choking

Choking is one of the scariest medical incidences that can happen to you or someone right in front of you. It can appear to happen so quickly yet seem like an eternity until the object is dislodged. It can occur to anyone, at any age and, in the case of children, it does not always have to involve food. Therefore, you should be prepared to quiet any panic and treat all cases swiftly and quickly.

First, you should know and recognize the universal sign for choking. If you are choking, you should put both hands around the front of your neck in a clutching motion. Next, determine which form of the Heimlich maneuver (also known as the "Hug of Life") you should use to treat the victim. There are methods for babies (under one year of age), adults, pets, and even yourself in the event there is no one else around to help. Follow the steps below for each type of victim.

Adults and Children (above One Year Old)

1. Stand behind the victim. If they are sitting, have them stand up.
2. Wrap your arms around the victim's waist.
3. Make a fist with one hand (with your thumb pressing into the victim) and place your free hand in front of your fist. Place both hands just above the victim's belly button. Stay clear of any ribs or other bones.
4. Pull your hands towards you in an upward motion. Do so forcefully enough and as many times as necessary to dislodge the foreign object.

Babies (under one year old)

1. Rest the baby on your forearm face down. Lower your forearm ensuring the baby's head is lower than their feet.
2. Carefully but firmly hit the baby's back with the palm of your free hand five times between their shoulder blades.
3. Move the baby so he or she is face up on your arm. With your third and fourth fingers of your free hand, give five chest thrusts.
4. Repeat the above steps until the foreign object is dislodged.

Animals

1. Place the animal on its side on the floor. For larger animals, such as dogs, straddle them from behind while they are standing.
2. Place both your hands behind the last rib and press down, quickly, firmly, and slightly forward.
3. Open the animal's mouth and remove the foreign object (easier if you have someone help you while you are administrating the compressions).

Self

1. Make a fist with one hand and place your thumb between your belly button and your rib cage.
2. Grab your fist with your other hand and press it into yourself with a quick upward thrust.
3. If that fails or is not an option for some reason, you can thrust your upper abdomen into the edge of a chair, table, or railing.

After any incident, you should see a medical professional or veterinarian to confirm that no damage was caused by the foreign object or when the Heimlich maneuver was administered.

Cardiopulmonary Resuscitation (CPR)

While I hope you never to have to use cardiopulmonary resuscitation (CPR), you should be able to execute the procedure since someone's life could depend on it. Furthermore, you should be equally familiar with both one and two person resuscitation methods as well as the differences between adult, child, and infant CPR. CPR is as easy as ABC: Airway, Breathing and Circulation. The basic idea is to get air into the victim's lungs and their blood pumping by compressing their chest. Below are the basic steps as a refresher; however, you should not rely solely on these instructions for saving someone's life. There are many local hospitals and first-aid squads that run courses so you can become not only certified but comfortable when an emergency does occur. In addition, you should also be familiar with the purpose and usage of a defibrillator. Automated external defibrillators (AEDs) are becoming more readily available in public locations and should be used in the event of an emergency. However, you should not wait until something happens to start learning how and when to operate an AED. You can always visit the Red Cross web site at www.redcross.org for further information on local courses.

If you have another person assisting you, one person should perform the breathing while the other performs the chest compressions. In a perfect world, you would have a breathing mask to help protect you from any of the victim's bodily fluids. However, life and emergencies are not usually that convenient, but try to take as many precautions as possible. The number of breaths and compressions remains the same regardless of one or two person CPR. Be aware that CPR will not always revive a victim. In actuality, the odds are against you, but then again, you have nothing to lose. Cracked ribs are a common complication of CPR but better to have a few broken ribs and be alive than no broken ribs and be dead. If you hear or feel any cracking, use less pressure with the compressions. This holds especially true when working on infants and children. Lastly, you may accidentally deliver some breaths into the victim's stomach which may cause them to vomit. If they do, tilt their head to one side and clear their mouth of any debris.

Adult CPR (victims older than eight years old)

1. Confirm that the victim is unconscious by calling out to them and/or carefully tapping them.
2. Lay the victim on their back on a firm surface. Tilt their head back if they do not have any apparent head or neck injuries. Do not tilt their head too far back.
3. Listen and feel for any breathing.
4. Check for any foreign objects or debris that might be blocking their airway if they are not breathing.
5. If you clear their airway and they start breathing on their own, do not continue with CPR. Otherwise start rescue breathing.
6. Pinch the victim's nose closed so the air you deliver will not escape. Administer two full breaths and see if they start breathing on their own.
7. Assuming they are not breathing, continue with CPR by checking for a carotid pulse (on their neck).
8. If the victim does not have a pulse, place the heel of your hands on top of one another approximately half to three-quarters of an inch above the end of the breastbone in the middle of the chest.

You can use two fingers at the end of the breastbone to "landmark" your hand position.

9. Locking your elbows and using your bodyweight, compress the victim's chest approximately two inches and hold for half a second.
10. Relax the compression for half a second and repeat the compressions another fourteen times.
11. Administer two more rescue breaths and check for a pulse.
12. Repeat steps 8-11 three more times until you establish a pulse or professional help arrives.
13. If you do get a pulse but the victim is still not breathing, continue with rescue breathing by administering one breath every five seconds.

Child CPR (victims between one and eight years old)

1. Confirm that the victim is unconscious by calling out to them and/or carefully tapping them.
2. Lay the victim on a firm surface on their back. Tilt their head back if they do not have any apparent head or neck injuries. Do not tilt their head too far back.
3. Listen and feel for any breathing.
4. Check for any foreign objects or debris that might be blocking their airway if they are not breathing.
5. If you clear their airway and they start breathing on their own, do not continue with CPR. Otherwise start rescue breathing.
6. Pinch the victim's nose closed or place your mouth over both their mouth and nose so the air you deliver will not escape. Administer two breaths and see if they start breathing on their own. Children's lungs are smaller so adjust the delivery pressure and volume appropriately relative to an adult.
7. Assuming they are not breathing, continue with CPR by checking for a carotid pulse (on their neck). If the breaths did enter the victim, administer two more breaths.
8. If the victim does not have a pulse, place the heel of one hand on their breastplate in the middle of the chest. Place the heel of your other hand directly on top of your first hand.
9. Compress the victim's chest approximately one inch and hold for half a second.
10. Relax the compression for half a second and repeat the compressions another twenty-nine times.

11. Administer two more rescue breaths.
12. Repeat steps 8-11 until you establish a pulse or professional help arrives.
13. If you do get a pulse but the victim is still not breathing, continue with rescue breathing by administering one breath every three seconds.

Infant CPR (victims less than one year old)

1. Confirm that the victim is unconscious by carefully tapping them on the shoulder or chest.
2. Lay them down on a firm surface and tilt their head back carefully and slightly so as not to pinch off the windpipe. Do not tilt their head too far back.
3. Listen and feel for any breathing.
4. Check for any foreign objects or debris that might be blocking their airway if they are not breathing.
5. If you clear their airway and they start breathing on their own, do not continue with CPR. Otherwise start rescue breathing.
6. Place your mouth over both their mouth and nose so the air you deliver will not escape. Administer two small puffs and see if they start breathing on their own. Infant's lungs are very small so use mostly the air in your mouth.
7. Assuming they are not breathing, continue with CPR by checking for a brachial pulse (inside of the upper arm, between the shoulder and the elbow).
8. Place two fingers in the middle of their chest just below their nipples. Deliver three quarters of an inch deep compressions using the other two fingers.
9. Relax the compression for half a second and repeat the compressions another twenty-nine times.
10. Administer two more rescue breaths.
11. Repeat steps 8-10 until you establish a pulse or professional help arrives.
12. If you do get a pulse but the victim is still not breathing, continue with rescue breathing by administering one puff every three seconds.

Poisons

While nearly any substance, including water, can be poisonous, there are a number of common items to be aware of. Furthermore, the toxicity of a substance is determined by the type, quantity, method, and duration of exposure. Exposure routes can be inhalation, injection, ingestion as well as contact with your skin or eyes. The manner in which you treat a poisoning can vary and depends mainly on the specific substance. Depending on the toxin, inducing someone to vomit may make the situation worse. The American Association of Poison Control Centers can be reached nationally by calling 1-800-222-1222 or online at www.1-800-222-1222.info. It is comprised of local centers organized at a state level. Never be scared or wait until the situation worsens before calling. Be sure to follow their instructions and never begin administrating any type of aid unless directed. The only immediate safe action you can take is to get the victim to fresh air if the case warrants it. However, only do so if it can be done safely by not turning yourself into a victim as well, as in the case of high carbon monoxide levels.

You can never prepare for or prevent every type of poisoning, but you can take a few simple steps to ensure that help is available right away. Post and label the phone number for the Poison Control Center on telephones and in several conspicuous locations such as the kitchen, bathrooms, and the garage where most household toxins are located. Always keep poisonous substances in a locked cabinet or far out of reach to prevent children from poisoning themselves. Keep in mind that an accidental poisoning can also happen in the workplace. Typical toxins include household and industrial cleaning products, alcohol, over-the-counter, illegal, animal, natural and prescription medications, and carbon monoxide, carbon dioxide, propane, or natural gases which poison or displace breathing oxygen. In addition, it is important to remember that just because a substance is a gas, that does not mean it will rise. For example, you may have a leaking propane cylinder connected to your barbeque grill in the backyard. Since propane gas is heavier than air, it could easily enter and collect in your basement through a nearby opening such as a basement window. On the other hand, carbon monoxide is lighter than air and will therefore rise. So for example, say your clothes dryer is located on the second floor of a two-story home and the vent line was accidentally disconnected or blocked. Someone who was sleeping on the second floor may never wake up since the deadly carbon monoxide gas will pool on the upper level before making its way down to the first floor. Furthermore, know the signs and be able to recognize various types of poisonings. For example, one sign of carbon monoxide poisoning is cherry red lips. Ensure that everyone living and working in the space is aware of the location of potential toxins as well as the national hotline. Lastly, you can have ipecac syrup and activated carbon/charcoal at the ready. If directed to, use the syrup to help induce vomiting and the activated carbon to aid in absorbing toxins.

Security

Security is a broad topic but one that is very important on many levels. Like safety, security is something that typically only takes seconds out of your day and should become an integral part of your routine. Even if you have the most expensive security system in place, unless you actively and religiously use it, it is worthless.

Your personal security, and that of your children or others in your care, should be your primary concern at all times. Ensure that you do not put yourself in harm's way by entering a dangerous environment. This can take the form of a bad neighborhood or simply the time of day (late at night). Always be aware of who is in your environment and be observant of any patterns in case you are being watched or followed. Also, only carry what you need in terms of money, credit cards, and identification and place it in your front pocket so it is harder for a thief to get at. For example, if you are going out for the evening to a club, only take a small amount of cash and your identification such as a driver's license. Leave everything else safely at home in your wallet or purse. Never leave your purse or wallet in your vehicle since a thief will get an extra bonus if your vehicle is stolen. Lastly, never carry your Social Security card with you; it should be at home in a safe or in a bank safety deposit box.

Your normal actions can lead to an insecure situation as well. When walking to your car or entering your apartment/house, be sure that no one is behind you. Always lock your doors and windows and never leave valuables out in the open. Also, avoid parking your car out of plain sight or between two large vehicles. It is not only traditional items such as money and jewelry that you should be concerned about protecting either. You should secure all unused checkbooks, credit cards, and cell phones since they are small but pack a ton of value. You should secure documents, including postal mail, which may have your identity on them. Be sure to shred all junk mail and old documents before tossing them into the trash. You should also help ensure the personal safety of others when possible. For example, if you are dropping someone off, wait until they are safely in the house or building before driving away. Another common scenario is when guests are leaving your house late at night. Ask them to give you a ring or call when they arrive home safely.

Just because your valuables are in your house or apartment, that does not mean they are completely safe either. If you can afford a home security system, it will help deter, but not completely prevent, a break-in. Remember to activate it when you are not home and at night. Furthermore, leaving house or car doors and windows unlocked will defeat the purpose of your security plan. Keep spare keys out of plain sight as not to tempt a thief or make his or her job any easier. Next, secure all important documents in a heavy-duty, fire-resistant safe that is bolted to the floor or within the wall. Keeping the safe in your possession is a vital component to its effectiveness. Secure all data sensitive electronic files with a password, even if just used at home. Back-up your files frequently and secure them in the safe. Close and lock your vehicle's doors and windows even if it is sitting in your driveway or garage. Someone can easily gain access to your house if you have a garage door opener hanging from the visor of your car in the driveway (they can also get your home address from your insurance card, registration, or GPS unit if it is in the vehicle as well). If someone does gain access to your house and garage, do not make it easy for them to drive off in your unlocked vehicle. Lastly, reinforce any basement doors and windows and consider frosting clear glass to prevent a potential thief from getting a good view of your possessions.

AMBER Alerts

AMBER (America's Missing: Broadcasting Emergency Response) Alerts are very important to know about both as a parent and as a fellow citizen. Amber alerts are notifications to the public of a child's abduction and are available throughout the nation. They are named after Amber Hagerman, who was sadly abducted, raped, and murdered in Texas in 1996. Messages of a problem are typically broadcast on television, radio, e-mail, wireless devices, and dynamic highway signs and can contain a license plate number or other descriptive information related to the incident. In order to have AMBER Alerts sent to you by way of e-mail, register at www.amberalers.com, and for wireless devices such as cell phones, go to www.wirelessamberalerts.org. As a motorist, you should be vigilant when an alert has been issued; call upon your observation skills to help a parent or guardian in need. Hopefully, the system will not be invoked very often, but it is comforting to know that it is available.

Self-Defense

You have every right to defend yourself, regardless of the attacker or nature of the situation. Young or old, you may need to defend yourself from either a verbal or physical attack. Use any techniques or objects at your disposal to ward off the aggression. Keep in mind that the best defense is not provoking someone or something in the first place. You should always be aware of your environment and avoid those that may bring you harm. Take the time to complete self-defense classes so you can be prepared for an attack and know that you are capable of holding your own before something happens.

Your reputation or character may also come under fire at some point in your life. You should take swift, yet accurate, action in repairing the non-tangible asset using facts and not emotions to clear your name. You should never let people walk all over you; however, there may be a time where the best thing to do is not to fight back. This may be the case when you are heavily outnumbered or overpowered; however, you should never stop resisting or preparing yourself for a next move.

Weapons

Weapons, no matter their size or potential to cause harm, should be respected all the same. A weapon, not only the traditional types such as guns and knives, can be nearly anything if used improperly. Unless you are a law enforcement professional, there is no need to carry or own a weapon. You should, however, know how to handle weapons in case you do come across them. You should always consider a gun loaded if you do not know its status. Never go near the trigger of a gun, but if you do need to move it out of harm's way, pick it up by the handle only. Never point a weapon at yourself or anyone else, and always keep them pointed down towards the ground. If you do need to carry a weapon for your job, always be sure to keep it locked and out of the hands and sight of children while it is in your home.

Trust

Trust is gained only through experience and observations. You cannot buy trust; it must be earned. No matter how much someone may tell you to trust them, you need to listen to your gut and go with how you feel. There are a ton of bad people in the world that may try to gain your trust to take advantage of you mentally, emotionally, physically, or financially. Evaluate people by their actions towards you as well as others. Furthermore, just because someone may appear to be a traditional authority figure, that does not mean they are incapable of taking advantage of you. For example, if you are pulled over by an unmarked vehicle or undercover officer, you have the right to request a uniformed officer be sent to the scene. This may anger and annoy the first officer, but better to be safe than sorry, especially if it is late at night or on a quiet road.

Strangers

While it is acceptable to be cordial to strangers, their trust is something that needs to be earned. This is especially true for children who should never interact with a stranger since their intentions may be harmful. As the number one job of parents is to protect their children, you should never let a stranger come in contact with your children. You should always count on a nightly question from a parent: Did you meet anyone new today? This holds true not only for meeting someone in person but also on the phone or online. Parents should never let their children on the Internet, post content, or access e-mail and instant messaging without supervision. Parents can also use the power of the Internet through various free web sites to learn the whereabouts and background of registered sex offenders in the area.

If a stranger does try to do something to you, you should do everything in your power to be noticed by screaming for help. Strangers may try and use many different tactics to lure you in. They could say that they are a family friend, use food or animals as lures, dress as a traditional authority figure in a uniform, or say they were sent by your parents. You should never trust or go with someone that you do not know. In the unfortunate event that you are either approached or successfully taken by a stranger, you should try to remember as much detail about the person, surroundings, and timing as possible. This could help in your rescue as well as the prosecution of the perpetrator. Details such as tattoos, scents, sounds, foods consumed, and traveling durations can greatly assist the police.

As adults, we are not safe or off limits to strangers either. Women can be especially vulnerable to unwanted aggression ranging from harassment to rape. As with everything you do, be aware of your surroundings and keep a watch out for any suspicious or unusual activity. Never be scared or intimidated to speak up or ask for help if you suspect someone does not have your best interests in mind. The potential harm that could be inflicted on you always outweighs any repercussions.

Gangs

There are two main influential sources in life, nature and nurture. Exposing yourself to a gang or any other type of negative organization is a one-way ticket to disaster-ville. In fact, you should do just the opposite and surround yourself with people of high caliber. Whether they are direct or indirect influences, never let yourself feel pressured into joining a gang. Your association with a gang will inevitably lead to a failed future, including criminal involvement which can prove fatal in the end.

If you cannot overcome the need to belong to something bigger than yourself, at least find a positive and meaningful organization. It can be religious in nature or secular such as the 4-H Club, Boy Scouts, or Girl Scouts. You could also take up a new sport and be part of a team. The possibilities are endless, and you should not shortchange yourself by limiting your potential.

Survival

There can be various degrees of survival situations, but hopefully you never find yourself in any of them. However, life can take some crazy turns and unfortunate luck may come your way one day. Therefore, you should have a basic understanding of what to do in various situations so you can maintain your mental and physical composure until help arrives or you find it on your own. Keeping calm and not panicking is your greatest weapon for survival. If you are planning an adventure, think ahead and plan accordingly, including a basic survival kit just in case. It should include items such as a knife, device to produce a flame or sparks, water purification tablets and plastic bags to help keep items dry or for collecting water. There are even rescue devices that you can purchase as an insurance policy which are based on global positioning system (GPS) technology.

If you find yourself in a survival situation, one of the biggest decisions you may need to make is whether to stay at the location or leave towards civilization. There are three main factors that should influence your decision. The first depends on whether or not anyone knows where you were going to be. If the answer is no, then you should consider heading out. Another factor is not only current weather conditions but what may develop in the coming days. Coupled with the weather are the other factors of available water, food, shelter, and clothing. Weighing all these conditions at once, you should determine if it makes more sense to stay and build a fire and shelter or head out towards a populated area. If you do choose to head out, be sure to leave behind a note or indication of who you are, when you left and in which direction you are headed.

Depending on how you found yourself in the situation, you may be able to use some of the otherwise nonworking objects. You may be able to use batteries and wire as an ignition source or flammable liquids to support combustion. Synthetic or natural cloth, cushioning, or other material such as insulation can be used to keep you warm or as kindling when starting a fire. Be creative in using what limited resources you have available to you. However, do not try to take everything with you; they can quickly weigh and slow you down, thereby wasting precious energy.

Use nature's resources to make equipment if manmade objects are not readily available. For example, you can braid vines together to make a rope. If stranded in a rainforest or jungle-like conditions, you can lash bamboo and balsa woods together to form a crude raft.

If an artificial source of fire is not available, you can always use the old-fashioned method of rubbing two pieces of wood together, whose friction will eventually produce embers. It may take some time and energy, but it will work if the wood is dry enough. A fire will not only provide warmth, but it can be used for cooking small animals, drying out wet clothing, and it can act as a signaling mechanism when combined with leaves to produce smoke. You should always be aware of your environment, especially for dangerous wild animals. Never leave food or food waste (cooked or uncooked) lying around. The scent can be picked up by hungry animals miles away.

If you do decide to start on a trek for civilization, you need to be aware of basic navigational principles. For example, the sun always rises in the east and sets in the west. On clear nights, you will be able to use the North Star as a guide and reference point. When walking in a wooded area, never pass trees on the same side. You can easily wind up walking in a large circle if you do. To determine south from north, use the path of the sun and know that if facing north, west and east always spells "WE."

Having a good general knowledge of trees and plants can help save your life. Some plants can have berries or fruits that may be poisonous or cause diarrhea, which can lead to dehydration. However, other plants, fruits, leaves, and roots can provide fresh water and valuable energy; knowing the difference can be a matter of life or death. Other plants and trees may produce fluids that can be used for medicinal purposes, such as to prevent infection. If drinkable water is not available, you may be able to pull it out of thin air using socks or other strips of clothing to gather moisture from morning dew.

If you find yourself lost or stuck in a mountainous area, you should try to find your way downhill and look for flowing water like a stream or river. Chances are it will lead to a larger body of water and/or a populated area. If you are faced with a freezing environment, you may need to prepare a shelter on a nightly basis. No matter what you do or situation you find yourself in, keep yourself mentally stable by never giving up hope. Use whatever motivational techniques you need to keep your spirits up.

Driving

Driving an automobile is a privilege and not a right. It is a large responsibility to have and should not be taken lightly. Just as fun and exciting as a ride or trip could be, the potential for fatal consequences is always looming. Tens of thousands of people die every year in automobile accidents; try not to become one of them. Just stop and think about that fact for a minute. It is the equivalent of a medium-sized town disappearing each and every year. Before you even get in the car, take notice of the vehicle's condition while walking towards it. Are the tires low or flat or is there anything hanging or leaking from the car or truck? As you walk away from your vehicle, use your sense of smell to detect any odors emanating from melting or burning objects. Make sure that you can see out of all the windows. If any of the windows or mirrors are dirty and obscure your vision, then clean them before shifting out of park. If there is snow or frost covering any of the windows, either scrape it off or allow enough time for the defrosters to do their job. Next, make sure that you use your lights if it is getting dark or still not daybreak yet.

Always wear your seat belt and ensure that all your passengers are as well. You would not ride a roller coaster, which is on a set of tracks and moves slower than a car, without using a restraint system, so why would you not wear a seat belt while driving a vehicle that can reach high speeds, collide with other vehicles and flip over? In addition, make sure that children are in the proper size car or booster seat, facing the correct direction and seated in the proper location (front versus back seat) based on their age, height, and weight. Furthermore, air bags can kill children instantly while some will not deploy if your seat belt is not fastened. While driving, take your time and allow a safe distance between vehicles, including those behind you. If someone is following you too closely, then safely change lanes as soon as you can. Never antagonize another driver by making sudden moves or obscene gestures. Always be aware of your surroundings for a way out in the event you have to suddenly swerve or change lanes. It also helps to try and anticipate another driver's next move, especially for those who may be distracting themselves by talking on a cell phone. The brake light patterns of vehicles in front of you speak volumes of what is about to come. You never know when an animal, person, or debris may cross your path, so always give the road your full and undivided attention.

Simply put, speeding equals death. While I will not lie to you and say that drifting five miles per hour over the speed limit is uncommon and unacceptable, excessive speeding can have deadly consequences. When you travel above the speed limit, you are reducing your reaction time and exponentially increasing the amount of energy for a crash. Couple speeding with reduced visibility, poor road conditions, or alcohol, and your chances of a fatal accident skyrocket. If you do not believe me, look at a simple formula. Kinetic Energy = 0.5 x mass x velocity squared. If you do the math, a two-ton vehicle traveling at seventy-five miles per hour has the same amount of energy as more than two sticks of dynamite. If that little fact does not hit home, pay a visit to the local junk yard and get a firsthand view of the unrecognizable, twisted plastic and metal that was once a car or truck. In addition, if you think you are safer in a sports utility vehicle because it is heavier, take a look again at the formula. The more mass the vehicle has, the more energy available in the crash, not to mention the higher center of gravity. Lastly, while you may not be the driver of a speeding vehicle, being a passenger can be just as unsafe. Never get into a vehicle with an unsafe driver, whether they are intoxicated, tired, speeding, or acting recklessly.

It is almost impossible to go a whole driving career without being pulled over at least once. No matter if it is for a good reason or no good reason at all, there are certain actions and attitudes to take when an officer strolls up to your vehicle. Moving violations can be quite costly in terms of time and money, not to mention your personal safety if you literally make the wrong move. The first action you should take is to pull over to the side of the road at the first safe opportunity. However, do not let too much time or distance pass before you do so since it may appear that you are trying to evade the officer. By the way, active emergency vehicles (police, fire, and ambulances) always have the right of way so you should safely pull to the right and allow them to pass without difficulty. Next, you need to check your attitude. You should give the officer nothing less than full respect, including "Yes, sir or ma'am." This is not the time to be hostile or confrontational, by any means; this includes your passengers as well, who should remain silent unless spoken directly to by the officer. After you have safely pulled over, you should fully roll down your window, shut off your engine, take the keys out of the ignition and place them on the top of the dashboard above the steering wheel so they are in plain view. Be sure to leave your seatbelt on. Activate your hazard lights for additional safety and turn on your exterior and interior lights if it is nighttime. Then, slowly gather your paperwork, including license, registration, and insurance card. Adding a Police Benevolent Association (PBA) card to the stack does not hurt either if you have one. Answer and comply with all instructions given to you by the officer. Lying will not help the situation since your stories will be as transparent as your windshield. If you do need to retrieve something from inside the vehicle, do it slowly and inform the officer of your intended actions before you act on them. Make sure that your actions are deliberate otherwise, you may find yourself in an unfavorable position; inappropriate actions can easily get you shot or killed.

Hopefully, you will never find yourself involved in a car accident; however, if you do, there are a number of steps you need to take for everyone's benefit. First of all, regardless of if it was your fault or not, you need to act responsibly. Never leave the scene of an accident, no matter how insignificant or catastrophic. It is for this reason you should always have full and up-to-date automobile insurance, with the most coverage available to you. You should always have a police officer summoned to the scene so they can generate an accident report – be sure to obtain a copy and review the report as soon as it is available and be honest with your testimony. Lastly, never simply accept money or someone's information in exchange for pretending the incident did not occur. If you do not heed any of these recommendations, I guarantee that the past will come back to haunt you.

Driving a vehicle also places the responsibility for its maintenance onto you. Pay attention to any unusual sounds or degradation of the ride quality. Never let the fuel go below the three quarters empty level. Make sure that you have enough wiper fluid, especially in the winter months. Keep track of the last time items were replaced or inspected. Each vehicle has its own schedule for maintenance, so be sure you know the specifics for your car or truck.

You should have an emergency kit in the trunk of your vehicle at all times that contains the following versatile items. They should be neatly stored in a plastic tote for convenience and protection. Furthermore, you should immediately replace any items that have been used or expired.

Vehicle Emergency Kit

Item	Purpose or Function
Adjustable Wrench	Tightening or loosening bolts, nuts, and more. Can be used in conjunction with Vise-Grip® pliers.
Band-Aid® Bandages	Small box of various-sized bandages for keeping wounds clean and protected.
Bottled Water	Use for anything from drinking to cleaning wounds. Carry at least two bottles (be careful of freezing in winter months).
Duct Tape	When electrical tape is not strong enough (such as a leaking hose).
Electrical Tape	Repair and bind objects together, including wires.
Flares or Reflective Signs	Warn others of your location (safety or rescue).
Flashlight	Aids in viewing objects as well as personal safety at night. Also include an extra set of batteries.
Gloves	For warmth and hand protection while working on the vehicle.
Sanitizing Lotion	Clean and disinfect hands or wounds.
Jumper Cables	Heavy duty cables to jumpstart dead batteries.
Plastic Bags	Sealable and garbage bags useful for gathering water, keeping items dry, and cleaning up messes.
Rope/Cord	Useful for binding or tying down objects or creating a tourniquet.
Screwdrivers	Flat head and Phillips to tighten or loosen screws.
Small Blanket	Multipurpose from keeping you warm to providing a clean surface.
Snacks	Dried fruits and nuts provide long-lasting and convenient calories.
Towels	Paper or cotton towels for absorbing all types of liquids.
Vise-Grip® Pliers	Strong locking pliers to hold two items together.
Utility Knife	Multipurpose knife. Also known as a box cutter.
Waterproof Matches or Lighter	To start a fire for warmth or signaling.
Whistle	To signal for help.

The Armed Forces

The men and women who make up our armed forces (including the National Guard and the Coast Guard) are dedicated people who unselfishly give of themselves for our country on a daily basis. Hundreds of thousands of them, past, present, and future, sacrifice their own lives in order to protect not only our lives but our freedoms. They do this not for the money or the glory but for the honor of serving our great nation. Active military personnel as well as reservists serve with the same level of dedication and can find themselves in harm's way just the same.

Whether at war or peacetime, you should always respect and honor the patriots who comprise our military. You may not agree with a war, but you should always support the individuals who are on the front lines carrying out their duties. Keep in mind that soldiers do not get to pick and chose which wars they wish to fight in, so do not hold them accountable for decisions made by others, including politicians who return to their warm, safe homes on a daily basis. You should have respect not only for the men and women in the military but their families as well. Children, wives and husbands, boyfriends and girlfriends often go without seeing their loved ones for months or years at a time; some never get to hold them ever again.

September 11, 2001 (9/11)

The morning of September 11, 2001 was absolutely perfect until the calm, sunny sky over New York City was forever shattered at 8:46 a.m. America had never before seen such horror inflicted on innocent souls, even when compared to the attack on Pearl Harbor in 1941. Being a rookie volunteer firefighter at the time, I headed straight to the firehouse after leaving work. It was not until then that I saw on television 343 of my brothers and thousands of others perish as the towers fell, the Pentagon burned and the results of the brave men and women in a Pennsylvania field. Years later, the shock is just as strong as it was that sacred day. Thousands of mothers and fathers did not get to come home and hug their children that evening, as I am blessed to do every day. The victims were not soldiers, just everyday folks trying to put food on their table and make it through the day or another shift. That is the real tragedy.

The biggest lesson to learn from the tragic events of 9/11 is to live life to the fullest since you never know when it may be your last day. Be extra kind to your fellow Americans and hug your family and friends a little tighter that day every year. No matter where you are or what you are doing, be sure to pause for a moment every year at 8:46 a.m. to honor those who lost their lives and to reflect upon your own life. Learn of and be inspired by all the resulting brave actions of both ordinary people as well as those who put their lives on the line daily to keep us safe. It is a grim but important reminder that we always need to keep our eyes and ears open for not only our own safety but for all our fellow citizens.

Education

"A man who has never gone to school may steal from a freight car; but if he has a university education, he may steal the whole railroad."
– Theodore Roosevelt

Education

There is no replacement for education; everyone needs a strong base upon which experience can be built. This holds true even more so in today's day and age since, simply put, there is just much more to know. Technology has catapulted our society hundreds of years in just the last ten years. Every stage of education is more important than the last, and continuing your education past high school is paramount. While experience is vital to your overall knowledge, it may only take you so far in life, especially in the high-tech and corporate work environments. Though to be perfectly honest with you, on more than one occasion, it will be more a case of who you know than what you know. Even in your later years, learning helps keep your mind sharp. There is always something new to learn, and it is impossible to know everything. Having a diverse educational background is just as important as being an expert in a specific subject.

Reading

Reading is a base requirement for life, no ifs, ands, or buts about it. It is important to both master and enjoy reading at an early age. Frankly, if you do not learn how to read, you will not be successful in school or be able to hold a meaningful job. You would find yourself constantly looking for ways to avoid reading and fighting off the embarrassment that comes along with it. Illiteracy can also endanger your life and the lives of others, especially when it comes to such things as warning labels, signs, and medication. Lastly, if you cannot read, you cannot write.

You may not always enjoy the material you are reading, especially while in school. However, do not let what you have to do spoil it for everything. Read books, magazines, and articles on subjects that you do enjoy. Reading opens up whole new worlds and can allow your imagination to run wild.

Writing

Having refined writing skills is essential in life. Whether you are writing a report for school or a formal document for work, you will need to develop a strong understanding and use of the English language. A key building block to your writing abilities is your vocabulary. Creating and maintaining a diverse vocabulary will ensure successful writing skills. Furthermore, knowing how to write in another language can help your career exponentially. Always keep in mind the simple principle of "tell them what you are going to tell them, tell them and then tell them what you told them." From essays to presentations, this basic method of constructing an introduction, body and conclusion will help you be successful in ninety-nine percent of writing projects.

Writing does not only need to be for formal communication either. You can expressive yourself creatively by writing poetry, songs, or fictional works. You may even want to keep a journal or diary for yourself. Just do yourself a favor and keep your private thoughts off the Internet; it will save you a ton of problems later on. This includes any type of blogs, social networking, or other freeform, publicly accessible web sites.

Spelling

Despite the abundance of electronic spell check functionality in computer-based applications, there are many times when it is not available in everyday life. Having a strong vocabulary and ability to spell words will save you from a lifelong series of embarrassing situations. Avoid slang at all costs and eliminate the use of words such as "yeah," "nah," and "like" from your vocabulary. Unfortunately, people tend to remember you for your worst quality or an unfavorable incident, so do not provide them with a memory. It is never too late to start building or polishing your spelling skills, especially in a world where a new word or phrase is coined each and every day. From handwritten notes to official documents, always re-read and spell check your work before sending it out. Moreover, with critical documents, ask someone with strong language skills to double-check your work.

History

Would it not be great if you could learn all of the things that have worked or failed since the beginning of humankind? What if you could learn about them all in one place and for little to no money? Well, guess what, you can. It is called history. Ignoring history is one of the biggest mistakes you could ever make. Having a strong knowledge and understanding of history will also help you gain a broader appreciation for all races, creeds, and cultures. Take advantage of thousands of years of history from scores of cultures to make you a well-rounded, informed person. Studying history is also the best way to learn from other people's mistakes, while at the same time, be inspired by great success stories. Pay your local library a visit and I guarantee that you will find hours passing you by as you become enthralled by any number of books.

No matter what interests you, there is probably a rich history behind it. History can also help you in other ways such as innovation. Perhaps someone in the past had a brilliant idea but the technology did not exist in their time to bring it to reality. Understand how we, as a global society, are where we are by learning how we got here. Then, armed with all your skills and knowledge, make your own positive mark on history.

Practice

Practice really does make perfect, or reasonably close to perfection. If you think you will be successful at something without putting in the time and effort or by just "winging it", you are sadly mistaken. While you may have a shot at beginner's luck, there is no way that you can perform consistently without practicing over and over. Whether it is playing an instrument or giving an important presentation, you will need to work out all the bugs and kinks beforehand. One of the keys to successful practice is to train like you work and work like you have trained. This concept is especially vital when it comes to emergency situations; trust me when the going gets tough, your mind will automatically revert back to your training. Even those who appear to have a natural talent need to hone and maintain it through practice. Do not be afraid to get creative (as long as it is safe) in your methods either. Until you are comfortable or able to perform without assistance, use external aids to help gain confidence or accelerate your skills. Often, practicing in front of a small audience can help you gain confidence while providing you with valuable feedback from vantage points you may never have had exposure to before. No matter how lofty, never give up on your goals and know that the road to success is paved with bricks of practice.

Learning

From the minute we are born we start learning and, hopefully, you will never stop. Much how no two snowflakes are the same, we all have unique brains, and therefore different learning and comprehension styles. Learning how to learn is a skill in itself that takes some time to master. Many things may come to us very easily while others can take a considerable time to fully understand. This is perfectly normal and you should not shy away from subjects that you find difficult or challenging. In fact, you should spend more time trying to conquer them. Furthermore, you should always try to apply successful learning methods to the difficult cases. You should also transplant methods that work for other people and apply them to your own situation.

While you may become frustrated with new or difficult subjects, do not become discouraged for long or give up altogether. Sometimes you just need to put down what you are doing and temporarily walk away to clear your head before you become completely discouraged. Never be afraid to ask for help from a fellow student, teacher, parent, or other experienced person. If you are embarrassed to ask a question in front of a group of people, simply approach the teacher or a colleague in private. The only stupid question is the one never asked.

Tests

During your lifetime, you will be required to take hundreds of tests. In fact, the first test given to you occurred sixty seconds after you were born. The Apgar score (0-10) is the standard rating system used to evaluate newborn's health based on the five categories of breathing, color, heart rate, muscle tone, and response to stimulation. Most of the formal testing that you will experience occurs before you are twenty-five years old, but it does not stop as soon as you are finished with school. Therefore, learning successful studying and test-taking methods at an early age will pay dividends for years to come. Much like learning itself, no two people study for or take tests in the same manner. Techniques that might work for some people may not work for others. Therefore, you need to figure out what methods work best for you. Furthermore, as the material gets more complex, you may need to modify your techniques to fit the degree of difficultly. Try as many different traditional and unconventional methods as it takes to best suit your learning style. Try using flash or index cards, mnemonics (using words that represent the first letter of items in a list), or word associations. Create your own study aids using combinations of traditional techniques. Thinking "outside the box" can help you in ways never imagined. Regardless of the method(s), stick with what produces consistent results and works best for you. Just as with learning and comprehension, your environment can play a huge role in your success or failure. Find yourself a comfortable and quiet location to limit distractions. Make sure that you have everything you need in one place before you start so you do not have to stop every five minutes to get something else.

When it comes time to take the test, try to be relaxed and not let your nerves get the better of you. Make sure that you do not have any personal distractions like hunger, and that you are physically comfortable. In addition, be sure to get a good night's sleep; avoid procrastinating and the inevitable late night of cramming. Here are a few good techniques that can help you on every test. When you first get the test, take five minutes to scan it from beginning to end. This will allow you to quickly get a sense for the types of questions as well as perform a quick calculation of how much time you can spend on each question or section. If faced with a multiple-choice question, try to eliminate at least one of the wrong choices right away. Continue your process of elimination for the remaining three or four options. It can be frustrating with the answer is staring right at you, so try not to get upset and remain focused. If you run across a difficult question, skip it and return to it at the end if you have time. Compared to multiple-choice questions, you have better odds with true/false questions so spending more time on them can be valuable. Try to become familiar with the style of the person or organization giving the test. This can help you determine if there will be many trick questions or even simple answers to otherwise complex-looking questions. Lastly, be sure to reread your responses to freeform questions and essays to ensure that you have both full answered the question being asked as well as provided the right response to the right question.

Presentations

Throughout the course of your life, you will give hundreds of presentations. Now you are probably thinking that I am crazy, but presentations do not have to be formal or given to dozens of people at a time. For example, you may find yourself presenting a case to your manager about why you should be given an increase in salary. Regardless of the nature of the presentation, there are a number of common and important elements for success.

The first significant element for a quality presentation is preparation. If you think you can just walk in and "wing it", you are setting yourself up for failure. Be sure that you know the material inside and out. Next, think of some potential questions that may arise, and be sure that you have their answers handy. It also helps to provide relevant examples and samples to support concepts and arguments. If you do not have the answer to a question, you can always tell the person that you will get back to them shortly, or that you can take the issue "offline" if presenting to a group. Furthermore, ensure that you have reviewed any presentation aids such as slides or handouts for accuracy as well as the often-overlooked basics, including spell check, readability, and print layout. Confirm all facts and make sure you can state the source of all your information. Lastly, put your presentation through its paces using "dry runs" or by practicing in front of a mirror. Iron out as many of the kinks beforehand to help calm your nerves.

The next most important factor for a successful presentation is knowing your audience. Whether you are presenting to a group of fellow students or a board of investors, you should target and focus in on their specific characteristics and needs. For example, if you are giving a presentation to a business-oriented group of people, avoid technical details that would not interest them. You can quickly cause your audience's eyes to glaze over and lose their interest if you focus on facets that are not appropriate. Depending on the size or type of venue, you may need to tailor your presentation material to fit. For example, when presenting to a small group, you can provide hardcopies or additional information with ease. However, if you have a larger audience, you may wish to send out the presentation electronically before the meeting or conference call (generally a good idea for any size audience).

One of the most critical elements of a presentation is your delivery. You should always speak loud enough so that everyone can hear you, especially if you are giving a presentation in a room with a speakerphone. Never obstruct your voice by mumbling or chewing gum or candy. Do not speak fast or rush through a presentation. Make sure that you have allotted enough time for the material or tailor it to fit the available timeframe. Do not say "um" or leave large gaps or pauses in your speech. Speak deliberately and without hesitation; a strong delivery can sell ice to an Eskimo. In addition, if you are presenting in person, ensure that you are dressed appropriately for the occasion. A sloppy appearance can discredit you before you even utter your first word. Furthermore, watch your body language. Stand or sit up strong but not too rigid. Avoid extraneous movement such as fidgeting or pacing. Lastly, try to make eye contact with your audience, or for large crowds, focus on a particular point in the distance. You should know your material well enough that you do not need to look down at or read off of notes.

Teaching

Everyone, not just professional educators, needs to possess strong teaching skills. One of the key elements to becoming a successful leader is the ability to effectively motivate and instruct others. Being a good teacher is much like being a good presenter. To begin, you must have an excellent working knowledge of the subject yourself. How could you ever expect to show someone else how to do something if you do not know the "ins and outs" yourself? Next, you must know and target your audience. Depending on your student's background, you may also have to tailor your lesson plan. Are they at a beginner, intermediate, or advanced level? Furthermore, ensure that you have prepared adequately for the amount of time you are given to work within. You should always come fully prepared with any teaching aids, presentations, supporting materials as well as any handouts that students can take with them. Do not be afraid to be relatively creative with your teaching methods, especially when it comes to a more difficult or abstract subject. However, make sure that they are not inappropriate in any manner. Many times lasting impressions are made when you take students out of the traditional classroom and show them real-life applications. Lastly, speak slowly and clearly while making eye contact with your students to help them feel like you are working directly with them even though they are in a group.

Teaching styles are only outnumbered by learning styles. However, based on all the factors previously mentioned, you should be able to arrive at a style that fits the student(s) with the topic. You should have a cache of teaching styles and be flexible in switching between them as well as pulling various techniques from one to another. Regardless of the style you apply, you should always incorporate a few key items. First, always leave time for questions, whether during the session or at the end. Furthermore, make yourself available, directly or indirectly, for follow-up questions after the session. Never intimidate or make your students feel afraid to ask a basic question that they might consider dumb. If you treat the students with respect, you will be given respect in return. Next, use examples, samples, or analogies that the students can relate to. Lastly, think back to your favorite or most impressive teachers and incorporate their techniques into your own style.

Being Observant

Being observant can help you in countless ways; some may even turn out to be life saving. It can help you excel in school, financially and with your own health. Keep your feet on the ground and head out of the clouds since a lack of understanding of your surroundings can lead to missed opportunities or worse. Your observations can make connections that would have otherwise gone unnoticed to the untrained eye. Recognizing patterns based on your observations can prove invaluable in all aspects of your life.

Pattern Recognition

Pattern recognition is not much more than putting two and two together. While it sounds like a simple concept, it is not always as obvious as you would think. Patterns can consist of more than just shapes and numbers; they can be of events, people, places, and thoughts. The most important component of pattern recognition is observation. You should use all five of your senses to help you make connections. Do not be afraid to use your sixth sense or gut feeling during the process either. Become a detective to root out clues to a challenge or help you with problem solving. Use the process of elimination to help clear extraneous information; thereby leaving a concise subset of data that can be managed easier. Turn the object or concept physically or metaphorically on its side or inside out to aid you in your discovery process. Do not become frustrated if a pattern is elusive; give it time and it just may come to you at the most unexpected time.

Adaptation

Being able to adapt to any given situation, short or long-term, is invaluable. Many animals adapt to their surroundings for survival, and even the mightiest of oak trees needs to be flexible in the face of strong winds. Unfortunately, the only thing constant in life is change. The quicker you are able to adapt to changes at home, school, work, and everywhere in between, the more successful you will be. Adapting will also help lower your stress levels since you will not be swimming upstream all the time. Try to build into your personality, skills, and methodology the flexibility to easily accommodate change. This does not mean that you need to be on the bleeding edge of everything either since that realm is usually untested, flawed, and costly. Again, moderation is the secret.

Learn From Everything/Everyone

In life there are a couple of things that could help you without having to do much of anything. For example, learn from other people's mistakes. Rather than just poking fun at them, take what they should have learned and apply it to your own life. This holds true for actions involving any topic so keep your eyes and ears open at all times. Use your observation and pattern recognition skills to help aid you in the discovery process.

Another effortless advantage you may gain from others is when they do something negative. You can inorganically grow while others are sinking themselves. This concept is not something that you should ever rely on as a primary means to success though. Never intentionally sabotage others either since that will surely backfire and put you on the receiving end of trouble.

Work Smarter Not Harder

As the saying states, there is more than one way to skin a cat. Before you tackle any task, you should quickly ask yourself if your approach is the best in terms of time, cost, and energy. There may be several methods or approaches you can take, including manual and automated. Automated efforts usually require a longer set-up or start-up time, whereas manual efforts can start quicker but may take longer overall. There is no one formula to determine which way is the best way. Weigh all the options against each other and see which comes out on top overall. You should also try to determine if you will need to repeat the effort in the future, in which case, an automated solution may work out better for the long run. You should consult with other people whose opinion you trust and value too. Lastly, you may also find yourself applying various smaller aspects of people's ideas to produce a highly synergized methodology.

The other key part of working smarter and not harder is to continuously re-evaluate your approach. Pause for a moment and quickly judge your actual progress compared to the theoretical place where you should be in the task. You may find yourself adapting previously discarded ideas as the situation progresses. Never be afraid or ashamed to completely stop what you are doing to start over. While it is great to get something done on the first attempt, it is by no means required, as long as lives are not in the balance.

Teamwork

Learning how to work together as part of a team is a basic building block in life. Whether you are in school, work, or any place in between (such as marriage), teamwork skills will be used in the smallest of efforts to the largest. Being patient with others, respecting new ideas and maintaining a positive attitude are all elements to successful teamwork. While strong self-reliance is a great quality to possess, you must curb those instincts when working with others. Lastly, do not think you can always "go it alone;" ask for help when you need it as there is no shame or weakness in asking for it.

Mentors, Idols, and Role Models

Working with a mentor can greatly help with both your formal and informal education as well as expand your network of contacts. A mentor can help guide you and provide perspectives that you may not normally think of or be exposed to. If you have an interest in a specific field or profession, try to find someone that is willing to take you under their wing. However, nearly anyone in any field or with a significant level of experience can help mentor you. Lastly, keep in mind that mentoring is not just for "young" people. You should never stop learning, at any age.

Be careful of who you choose to be your role model. While anyone has the potential to be a good role model, not everyone is meant to be one. The responsibility of being a role model has to be consciously accepted by the person as well. The worse thing that can happen is that your role model acts less than favorable and you copy their negative behavior. Some sports figures have come flat out to say that they should not be seen as a role model. The best advice is to select a role model that you know and can trust.

Unfortunately, some folks have poor idol selection skills. Instead of focusing on those who are celebrities for dubious reasons, we as a society should concentrate our precious time on the everyday heroes who make a real difference in our lives and in our world. I do not recall specifically, but I highly doubt the masses were as devastated and upset with the passing of Jonas Salk, developer of the polio vaccine, in the mid 1990s as they have been with the deaths of most pop culture icons. There are literally thousands of people across the country and around the world that selfishly give all of themselves to worthwhile and necessary causes on a daily basis. We need to turn the popular media and paparazzi limelight away from the mundane and shine it onto the people who, for example, develop medical cures and enrich the lives of the less fortunate. I may be going out on a limb here, but I think most people would find more inspiration in learning about those who work with disabled or terminally ill children, for example, than which celebrity shaved off all their hair or checked into rehab for the fourth time.

On the other side of the coin, if you are asked to mentor someone or a group of people, you should take the opportunity to enrich someone else's life by sharing your knowledge and experiences. The mentoring experience does not have to be on a formal basis either. It can be through a program or just a simple get together over a meal on a monthly or quarterly basis.

Higher Education

College, or some form of technical school, is not optional for several reasons. First, you will need more than a high school diploma to gain better employment and open more doors in the future. Yes, while it is possible to be very successful without higher education, it can be a much more difficult road. Secondly, exposure to a college or technical school environment helps you further develop your self-reliance skills and allows you to mature as an individual without as much oversight from your parents. Lastly, a positive environment, with exposure to people of the same or higher caliber, will promote your learning experiences. A college education will never go bad and is more than just a piece of paper.

When it comes time to selecting a university or other institution, name is only worth so much. The real value is the type and quality of education you receive as well as how much you make of it. Often state schools have just as good, if not better, programs, especially when weighing in the cost of tuition. Hopefully, your hard work in high school pays off in the form of scholarships or grants, so you can avoid starting off your professional career with large student loans. In addition, with any luck your 529 savings plans will help defray the large expenses that come with tuition, fees, books, and housing. In a nutshell, a 529 plan works much like a 401(k) plan in that you can take advantage of tax savings, just as long as the money is used towards qualified higher education. However, as with any investment, there is a risk that gains will be little to none; the plan could even lose money if the economic health of the market is poor at the time you need to start making withdrawals. Worse case, even if you do need to take out student loans, the interest is relatively low, payments can be postponed until you complete your degree, and you may have a number of years to repay them.

Foreign Languages

Knowing a foreign language is a powerful tool to have in your educational arsenal. This point has become more and more significant as the world has become smaller and smaller through globalization. Do not put your head in the sand like others have and refuse to learn a language other than English. Lastly, do not stop at learning just one language either; the better equipped you are for the world, the more opportunities will open up for you.

Science/Technology

Science and technology dominate our lives, sometimes more than we would like, on a minute-by-minute basis. Just think how a power outage cripples nearly everyone, even if for just a short period of time. From the foods we eat to the jobs that we build our entire careers on, we are all influenced by science and technology. It is vital to be well versed in the traditional math and science subjects while in school. It is even more important to stay on pace with ever-evolving technologies. Whether it is related to your career or health, being in the dark can hurt you. You should always be asking questions and finding out the "why" behind things. You can get the answers to just about anything from the Internet (just be careful of the source), or for a deeper understanding you can always take a course or training class. Some hobbies can turn into careers just by developing an interest and learning more about them.

Culture and the Arts

It is true that we live in a very high-tech, fast-paced world, peppered with all types of electronic gadgets, but sometimes you need to exercise the right side of your brain as well. Stop and take the time to balance your life with some culture and the arts. There is a fascinating world out there just waiting to be discovered and appreciated. You can read a book, visit a museum or art gallery and attend a play or opera for starts. While these activities are good, they are passive in nature. Do not be afraid to try your hand at any of them. You may not think you are the best artist, singer, or dancer in the world, but at least you are applying your creative side.

Vocations

When I use the term "vocations," I am referring in particular to electrical, plumbing, gas, carpentry, heating, and cooling skills. Why would I raise this topic? In a word, money. It can be very costly to have almost any work done in these areas. It does not matter if you are a man or a woman, it is a great advantage to have a good working knowledge of these fields. Actually, it is more important for women to at least have an understanding of these topics since they may be targeted for inflated costs by unscrupulous contractors. If you do not have a relative or friend that can safely teach you these trades, then pick up a reputable do-it-yourself book or take a course at the local community college or vocational school. You can easily save yourself thousands of dollars with these basic skills.

Continuing Your Education

You never have to stop learning and you never should. There is also no such thing as knowing everything. Just because you are no longer in school, that does not mean that your education should stop. Think of your brain as a muscle. If you do not exercise it, it will atrophy. There are countless ways to exercise your mind. Read books and magazines, take continuing education classes at the local community college or adult school, stop by a local library, or watch television programs on history, science, and documentaries.

However, taking in knowledge is only half of the equation. Now you should do something with it. For example, if you take a cooking class, practice your newly developed skills by creating dishes of your own. If you learn a new foreign language, find someone else that also speaks the language and build on it that way.

The Intellect Triangle

A triangle is one of the strongest geometric shapes found in nature and used by mankind. It can be used by itself or combined with other triangles to form sturdy towers and supports. When it comes to intellect, look to the triangle. The three main components for a strong and balanced intellect are technology, business, and culture. All three areas fundamentally oppose each other, but when combined, they produce a strong stable force. Furthermore, without one of these components or too much focus on one, the balance is shifted and the overall strength of the intellect triangle will be weakened. Be sure to develop each one of these areas individually and learn how they work to compliment each other. Having a strong intellect triangle as your base will allow you to succeed in all aspects of life.

Current Events

You should always stay on top of current events for a host of reasons. First and foremost, you never know when an event or series of events could affect you directly; it could range from a product recall to dangerous weather approaching. Furthermore, how can you be a productive part of society if you have no idea what is going on in the world? You do not have to know every little detail, but you should have a general yet comprehensive understanding of current events. It could be very embarrassing to be engaged in a conversation with someone and have no clue what they are talking about. Do not limit your awareness of the world around you to just the popular news stories on television either. Lastly, you should be aware of local information just as much as what is occurring on a global level. Take an active role in society; do not keep yourself in the dark or let life pass you by.

Career

"Aim high in your career but stay humble in your heart."
– Korean Proverb

Career Selection

Education can be both expensive and time consuming to say the least. Therefore, the sooner you are able to determine a career path, the greater the advantages you will have compared to your compatriots. There are several factors that you need to consider when deciding on a career path; this is the time when parental guidance and an experienced mentor will really pay off. One of the best ways to organize all the facts and consolidate your thoughts is to create a matrix or grid. You can then easily plot the various types of careers versus important factors. Lastly, while money plays a significant role in life, it should never be the primary criteria for entering into a career. Always be honest with yourself regarding your interests and career goals.

Below is a list of components that you should take into consideration while evaluating career paths. Also keep in mind that some of the items may vary greatly from company to company as well as region to region.

- Initial, base or starting salary
- Salary growth potential
- Maximum salary
- Bonus existence and potential
- Individual or team-based position
- Travel requirements
- Demand for type of job/career (current and future)
- Level of education required
- Continual education required
- Skill-set transferability (company to company as well as career to career)

- Hours per week required, including overtime (paid or unpaid)
- Mental, emotional and/or physical demands
- Health risks and/or environmental conditions

Employer Selection

Just as important as the career path you select is the organization you work for. Chances are you will work for a number of companies during your career so as important as the interview is to the employer, it should be just as important to you. Below is a list of factors that should be considered when evaluating a potential employer.

- Company size: small, medium, large, or self-employed
- Company type: public, private, government, or non-profit
- Company nature: conservative, trendy, middle of the road, bleeding edge, or risk taking
- Company history (years in business, mergers, acquisitions) and reputation
- Financial stability
- Health benefits/coverage, including disability and life insurance
- Other compensation (company vehicle, fuel, insurance, telephone, etc.)
- Extra benefits (discounts, pre-tax spending accounts)
- Time off (vacation, sick, personal, compensation time)
- Any special restrictions or limitations
- Performance review criteria and frequency
- Management and supervisor structure
- Workspace conditions (office, cubical, warehouse)
- Commuting time and distance
- General feeling you get about the work environment
- Parking facilities (costs, security)
- Building security
- Dining facilities

Career

As early as thirty years ago, the career that you set out on was the one that you retired with. In this day and age, the complete opposite is true. You may find yourself changing careers as often as you change your shirt; this is typically driven by extremely fluid market conditions and environments. It is for this reason that your educational background should be as diverse as possible. In addition, a strong mentor can provide invaluable guidance in steering you towards the best areas of study, including those that can weather the harshest of economic storms.

As far as career paths, you should always try to be involved in areas that interest you. If you do not enjoy interacting with others, then a career in sales is probably not the best for you. You may not always enjoy the job you have (hence the term "work" and not "fun"), but you should not go through life hating what you are doing on a daily basis either. Unfortunately, the more fun career paths are not always paved with gold. You will need to make a decision as to how you will balance your income versus your career type and path. If you have a family to support, you may need to take a more stable, less favorable position for the time being. However, this is not to say that you cannot enjoy your true passion as a hobby, volunteer work, or side job.

As previously mentioned, you are not forced into any career situation. If you do not have the educational background to qualify for a position, go back to school and get it. The effort can be either part time or full time, at a local community college or Internet-based training. The main point is to never settle for less if you do not have to. Feel no shame in filling a less desirable role while taking the time to improve yourself. Take charge and make changes in the few areas in life that you can, no matter how long it may take you.

When it comes to your job, never fly too close to the sun like Icarus and think that you are irreplaceable; no one is immune. However, there are a few steps you can take to help insulate yourself from potential replacement or elimination. First, the more tangible and specific your education, skills and talents the better. Having too general of an education or skill leads to easier replacement. Secondly, have and continually gain experience in as broad a range of areas as possible. Think of it as skill diversification which has the same benefits as investment diversification. Having all your career eggs in one basket places potentially damaging limits on yourself, especially if you are pitted against others or if the main aspect of your job runs into its own form of a recession. Thirdly, the strength of all your positive traits will greatly work in your favor just as much as the power of your negative traits will work against you. Their daily impacts may be small, but over time they will accumulate and define your ever-important reputation. Lastly, keep in mind that sometimes employment decisions are made that appear to completely defy logic. That may truly be the case in some instances, but in others you may just not be aware of all the factual details. In either case, act mature and do not take any actions you might regret later.

Being Your Own Boss

Just because you are working, it does not mean it has to be for someone else. Being your own boss and having your own business can be both exciting and terrifying at the same time. With the highs of the good times naturally come periods of worry and panic, for not only your own income, but perhaps that of any employees you may have. However, when you combine all your positive qualities with old-fashioned hard work and dedication, there is little that will stand in the way of success. There are many factors to consider when thinking about starting your own business, especially if it means leaving your current, often more stable, employer. No matter what you sell or what service you provide, you will need to size up your competitors and perform market research. Ensure that your potential new business is not flooded with competitors or completely barren of opportunity. Next, be realistic about any start-up costs in addition to reoccurring daily and monthly expenses. You may also need to purchase supplies or equipment, rent office, manufacturing, and/or warehouse space which can become costly. In addition, will your business rely on resources whose cost can greatly fluctuate such as gasoline or electricity? Furthermore, you will have to consider if you need new insurance to help protect and isolate your personal finances from potential legal action. Be sure to investigate all forms of funding and/or low-interest loans, especially from state and federal sources. They are typically more readily available to certain groups of folks, including women, veterans, and minority-owned businesses. Lastly, always keep in mind fundamental business principles. For example, it was not the '49ers who went out West during the Gold Rush that got rich, it was the people who outfitted and supplied them that made the real fortunes. Before you make any serious commitments I would highly recommend that you speak with a professional accountant or financial planner who may suggest that you set up a specific type of organization such as a limited liability company (LLC).

Depending on your personal financial situation as well as your family's needs, you may or may not be able to get the business off the ground and sustain it. Chances are if you have a mortgage to pay and several mouths to feed, you will find a difficult road ahead of you. Furthermore, consider the potential of long hours and strain that the fledgling business may have on your relationships and any children. You may opt not go it alone by joining forces with a business partner or two. While this may seem like a viable solution on the surface, you need to be extremely careful when it comes to business relationships and money, especially if friends or family are involved. No matter what choices you make, ensure that you do all your homework before committing significant money to the effort, and that it does not adversely affect your family.

Summer Vacations

Capitalizing on the summer months between grades is one of the smartest things you can do with your time. Help yourself gain numerous advantages by working in your field of interest during the summer months instead of wasting them away at the beach, at a petty job, or hanging out with friends morning, noon, and night. You can find such opportunities by contacting your guidance counselor, college advisor, mentor, parents and their friends/colleagues. Whether you are paid or work for free, you will not only gain valuable experience, but you will be exposed to working with potential future employers and making contacts in your area of interest. If not for anything else, working during your high school and college summers can help validate that your area of interest is truly what you want to get into before committing all your time, money, and energy to it.

Professionalism

Professionalism is not a quality limited to the work environment. You should extend a professional attitude and work ethic in everything you do, including school, home, and on the playing field. Much of professionalism is tied to respect, and therefore should be in place at all times. It can help in all aspects of your career, especially in the form of promotions and monetary compensation.

Unemployment

Unemployment can happen to anyone at any time and at any age. These days, companies downsize, go out of business or relocate on a daily basis. Throughout your life, it would not be uncommon to find yourself unemployed more than once. The key is not to be in that position for very long. While you can sometimes rely on severance and public assistance for unemployment benefits, it is only a short-term and partial solution to the problem. Furthermore, whether you leave a job on good terms or bad, you should never "burn your bridges." As much as you may like to tell someone off, you should refrain from the bad habit. You may need a reference from them one day, and you never know who is friends with whom; just play it safe and do not turn yourself into a victim of bad karma.

Hopefully, before you became unemployed, you had been making business connections and relationships which would help aid in future job searches. This is the time when your reputation and all your other positive traits should pay off. Hit the ground running from the time you learn of your job separation. Do not wait until the last week of your supplemental income to start a resume and look for a job. Use all forms of media, including the Internet, newspapers and career fairs to assist you in your job search. While being between jobs may seem like good timing for a career change or for starting your own business, consider all the implications of your decision. Lastly, your pride should keep you from becoming a burden. It should motivate you not only in finding a new job but perhaps in improving your career status.

Finances

"Money often costs too much."
– Ralph Waldo Emerson

Finances

When it comes to your personal finances, you need to be proactive and vigilant. Whether we like to admit it or not, money makes the world go round. Without money, you will not get very far in life, but keep in mind that it will not solve all your problems or make you happy either. You should always have a plan that takes into consideration your current status, where you would like to be, and where you would like to end up (retirement). A solid, expansive education should provide you with the necessary foundation to build your wealth upon. Never rely on other people or public assistance as a primary means of living.

Armed with the tools for a career, you should secure a job that compensates you appropriately, whether in the form of cash, commissions, bonuses, or other resources such as a company vehicle. Early in your career, you may need to take jobs that are lower paying due to your lack of hands-on experience. However, this should be a relatively temporary situation, and you may need to leave the organization after some time if you cannot grow within the company.

Your spending habits, especially early on in life, should be frugal. The last thing you want to do is put yourself in debt from the start. This, however, may be the case when it comes to educational bills in the event you were not able to secure funding in the form of grants and scholarships.

When you do make money, you should separate the total into several parts. Obviously, you will need to pay any outstanding bills; however, one part should be for savings. If you are having problems with the whole saving concept, think of it as another bill that must be paid. Another important component of your finances is saving for retirement. Since we cannot be sure what the future will hold for programs such as Social Security or Medicare/Medicaid, we need to invest ourselves. You can open a Roth IRA, money market account or purchase stocks and bonds. When you start working, you should contribute as much as you can to a 401(k) program. Hopefully, your company matches a percentage as well, for which you should contribute at least the maximum that they match.

Before you purchase something, you should think to yourself (1) do I really need it? (2) can I afford it? (3) I am getting the best price? and (4) is the quality of the product or service worth the expense? Credit cards are not a license to buy anything you like. They should be used only on a month-to-month basis where you pay off the balance in full at the end of every month. Interest rates on credit cards are extremely high, and if you get yourself into deep enough debt, it could take $30 or more to pay off that $10 sale item. One way to gain "financial feeling" back is to use cash instead of credit cards whenever possible. You can easily become numb or indifferent when swiping a credit card, but handing over cold hard cash will most likely have a physiological effect on your spending habits.

Being an educated consumer automatically saves you money and may open up a few new doors. For example, when it comes to girl's and women's shoe sizes, there is an overlap. A girl's size six is the same as a woman's size eight. Not only does this little conversion fact work in your favor by giving you another option, especially with the popular size, it can also save you money since girl's footwear may be less expensive when compared to the woman's counterpart. Being an educated consumer can also help save your life. For example, do you know that automobile tires have a shelf life? Even if a tire has never touched the road, it begins to degrade after six years (think of an old rubber band that starts cracking over time). Therefore, the next time you need to replace a tire, be sure to check the manufacture date before it is mounted on the rim. Simply look on the sidewall of the tire for the last set of digits of the serial number. They will tell you the week and the year the tire was made. For example, a serial number ending in 2301 translates into the tire's birthday of the 23rd week of 2001. If you were to come across a tire with this serial number, you should leave it on the shelf and insist on a newer tire.

Lastly, unless it is an emergency, try to avoid loaning people money, including, and sometimes especially, family. It could lead to permanent relationship problems in the future. Even worse than loaning money to a friend or family member is cosigning on a document. Whether it is for a loan or an official document, you are exposing yourself to potential financial and legal risk at the hands of someone other than yourself. About the only person you should cosign with is a spouse, but even that may be a dicey situation unless the marriage is completely stable and trustworthy.

Credit and Credit Scores

Your credit status is one of the most important financial factors throughout your life. Poor credit can cause you to be declined for car loans, credit cards, mortgages, and home equity loans/lines of credit. Perhaps worse yet, if you are approved for the credit, a "less than perfect credit" status can have you paying higher interest rates. Your credit status boils down to a three digit number between 300 and 850 known as your FICO® (Fair Isaac and Co) score. Typically your credit score is a blend of individual scores from the three main credit bureaus: Experian, Equifax, and Trans Union. The average credit score in the United States is 700.

There are several factors that can affect your credit score. Believe it or not, you can actually have a low score if you have little to no credit history. Therefore, it is important that you establish your own credit history early in life so when you do need to make a large purchase or apply for a major credit card, there will be no issues or delays. To first break into the credit game, you can apply for department store or gas station cards, which are usually willing to give you a low credit limit initially. Once you have a few of the smaller cards in hand, you can expand your profile by applying for the major cards such as Visa and MasterCard. Credit card companies also rely heavily upon marketing campaigns at colleges and universities to target the typical money-starved student.

Another interesting credit phenomenon is that you can lower your credit score if you have no debt or pay off your debt promptly. Credit card companies allegedly call people who pay their monthly bills in full "deadbeats" since they make little to no money from them. However, you should be a deadbeat as much as possible to avoid paying interest. Credit card interest rates can easily exceed twenty percent, which makes that nice sweater you bought on sale triple the price if you do not pay it off right away. Furthermore, credit card companies can raise your interest rate without any warning.

By federal law, you are entitled to a copy of your credit report once a year from each of the credit bureaus at no cost. You can instantly and securely receive a copy of your credit reports online from https://www.annualcreditreport.com; however, it will not contain your credit score. While there are several web sites that claim you can have a free credit report, many require that you enroll in one of their programs for a fee. You should examine your credit reports very carefully on an annual basis, at the minimum. Identity theft can cost you time, money, and a ton of aggravation if not kept in check. There are also many credit monitoring services that can alert you to suspicious activity or make you aware of potential problems before they snowball out of control. Lastly, throughout the United States, you can place a freeze on your credit information with the three bureaus for little to no money such that inquires cannot be made without your knowledge. However, companies that you have existing relationships with may have unfettered access to your information. Freezes usually can be temporarily lifted when necessary, as in the case of doing business with a new cell phone or utility company.

Identity Theft

Protecting your identity in the highly digital world we live in is extremely important. Your credit and reputation can be ruined with the click of a mouse. Always shred or destroy any physical media that have any personal identifiable information on them. This holds true for old postal mail, outdated documents, credit cards, bills as well as floppy disks, compact discs, hard drives, DVDs, and other portable media such as flash drives. No matter how many times you may have deleted or formatted a storage device, a trace of the old data could remain.

Be especially careful when you are giving out information over the Internet. Make sure forms are secure and you are truly on the site you think you are (a scam known as phishing). Never give out information as a result of an e-mail or transfer private information over e-mail unless encrypted. Lastly, use only one specific credit card when purchasing items on the Internet to help limit your exposure.

Review you credit report on an annual basis at a minimum. Keep an eye on your bank account and credit card transactions on a daily or every other day basis to mitigate potential damage. Never share your passwords with anyone and make each user name and password different so as not to allow cross contamination if one if breached. Guard your private information more closely than you would cold hard cash.

Bankruptcy

Bankruptcy should never be seen as a quick and easy way out of debt. Whether you file for Chapter 7 or Chapter 13 protection, your credit will be ruined for the next seven years at a minimum. If you file Chapter 7 bankruptcy, you must surrender your assets, which will then be sold off to pay creditors. Chapter 13 bankruptcy protection allows you to keep all your possessions, but part of your future income must be given to creditors for a period of time, usually three to five years. The easiest way to avoid bankruptcy, like any addiction, is not to get in over your head in debt in the first place. Emergencies do occur, and sometimes you have to do whatever it takes, but bankruptcy should only be a last resort.

Gambling

Gambling with real money is something that should be done on rare occasion. There is no problem with playing the lottery for a dollar or two every so often, but once you start "investing" more than twenty dollars at a time, you are headed for potential disaster. Whether it is betting at the racetrack or taking a trip to a casino, your habits can quickly become an addiction. Therefore, the best way to avoid any gambling issues is to steer clear of it altogether. Gambling debts can easily pile up, especially when you are using non-cash sources such as credit cards or playing over the Internet.

If left unchecked, your gambling problem can start to affect your relationships and family. Do not gamble with your marriage, family, and/or house because it is a sure bet that you will lose everything. If you do feel the need to gamble, take only a small amount of cash with you (leave all credit and debit cards at home) and use that money until it is gone. If you do win, I would recommend placing your profits aside and walking away when you have depleted your initial funds. There is nothing wrong with just playing for fun with a group of people either.

Charity

Unfortunately, medical, natural, and manmade events have the potential to impact all types of people in bad ways. Donating to a charity is noble and should be a regular part of your life. While you should always donate unused clothing, furniture, vehicles, and other objects, giving money to a charity should be equally part of your character. The amount of the donation does not need to be sizable, but it should be at least one percent of your income. If you are able to give more, you should not hesitate in doing so. One easy way to help you remember to donate is to pick the same day every year. For example, you may wish to donate on your birthday or on a noteworthy holiday like Memorial Day or Thanksgiving.

The only word of caution is that you donate to a well-respected and fair organization. Unfortunately, there are people in the world that try to take advantage of good people's generosity since the definition of a charity is a relatively broad one. If you choose not to donate to a well-known or respected organization such as the Red Cross, be sure to check into the financial background of the group before making a donation. Charities often post their 990 federal tax form on their web site, so they can be reviewed at any time. You can also research charities using various web sites such as

Charity Navigator (www.charitynavigator.org). Also, keep an eye out for the 501(c)(3) tax status, which means the organization is truly non-profit. Furthermore, investigate how the money is distributed, ensuring that it does not fund questionable causes. Keep in mind that the charity or organization that you donate to can help animal shelters and other non-traditional causes as well.

Shopping

Careless shopping is one of the major contributors to a failing financial situation. If you really need the item or service, you should first ask yourself if you are getting the best price or rate. Granted that price and quality are often directly proportional, but there are thresholds that you should be willing to accept. Be sure to research the product or service before purchasing and always save the receipt in case you change your mind later or if a problem develops. Using the Internet is a quick and easy way to comparison shop and view customer feedback (though I am always a little suspicious of the feedback source). It also helps to keep an eye out for sales and coupons, especially if you do not need the item right away. Avoid buying items sight unseen; be sure to inspect products with an eye for potential points of failure and premature wear. Lastly, ask friends, family, neighbors, classmates, or coworkers for their opinions and experiences.

Stock Market

The stock market is a very complex yet vital part of our economy. "Stock market" is actually a general term; there is no single stock market. The market is comprised of several stock exchanges throughout the world. The large exchanges in the United States are the New York Stock Exchange (NYSE), National Association of Securities Dealers Automated Quotations

(NASDAQ), and American Stock Exchange (Amex). There are also several regional exchanges in the United States.

When you invest, you are providing money to an entity in hopes that they grow and succeed. Your reward for being a part of their success is an increase in the value of the investment. In the case of stocks, you are investing in a company. Similarly, you can invest in other types of organizations such as cities or countries which are the case with municipal bonds and treasuries respectively. Some investments, such as bonds and treasuries, may provide a guaranteed or fixed return on your investment. However, the return is typically lower compared to the potential of stocks; a trade off for lower risk.

Just because the market is "bad" or in a "correction" phase, that does not mean it cannot be good to you. Much like you should wait to purchase a name brand item when it is on sale, you should always bargain shop for the right investments at the right time. The key is to recognize patterns and trends that the cyclical market typically experiences. Just as Newton provided us with his third law of motion (for every action, there is an equal and opposite reaction), the world runs on cause and effect. Though there is no guarantee and there is always an element of risk, you could profit relatively easily while others are sinking. For example, when the proverbial you know what starts hitting the fan, investors like to seek shelter in commodities such as gold and other precious metals. Now the time to buy gold is not when it is at a high but rather when the market is experiencing favorable conditions and the price of gold is relatively low. Furthermore, take advantage of stock when it is at a lower price, as long as it is with a "staple" company that cannot only weather the economic storm but come back strong in the relatively near future. The second key to the puzzle is recognizing when the economic climate is changing so you can cash in on your smart investment. In order to perform that action successfully, you need to keep your eyes and ears open to the world, especially for current events. Kick your observation and pattern recognition skills as well as knowledge of history into high gear to maximize your profits. Lastly, do not feel bad if you miss an opportunity, make less than you planned or lose money in the process. The important lesson is to walk away from the experience wiser so when and if it starts happening again, you do not make the same errors.

I would consider investing in the market a necessary evil. Not that there is anything innately bad about the market, just that you can lose as much money as you can gain. The market can be as sensitive as a box of hundred-year-old dynamite. At times, it seems like a strong breeze could lead to disaster. Actually, that is not too much of an exaggeration. For example, if a hurricane has the potential to hit oil-drilling platforms on the Gulf Coast, you may see crude oil prices increase significantly. Therefore, given the daily, weekly, monthly volatility of the market, it is definitely not ideal for short-term investing. Rather, investing in the market should be seen as a long-term goal.

The following are a list of factors that can drastically affect the performance of any investment, ranging from commodities to 401(k) plans. Furthermore, depending on the factor, it could have short or long-term implications.

- **Economic** – stock market, recessions, supply/demand, federal funds rate, inflation, unemployment, consumer confidence
- **Environmental** – climate and weather patterns, "green" movements
- **Global** – international relations, population trends, diversity patterns
- **Government/Political** – regulations, party in power, treaties
- **Man-made Events** – terrorism, war
- **Natural Events** – floods, hurricanes, drought
- **People** – latest trends, age, health, priorities, basic necessities
- **Technology** – bleeding edge, obsolete, upgrade/maintenance costs
- **Transportation/Natural Resources** – gasoline and oil prices

The most important key to investing is portfolio diversification. The basic concept is that as long as you spread out your investments and do not put all your eggs in one financial basket, you will be able to weather any economic storm. While you are younger, you can afford to take greater risks by investing more heavily in stocks that may have greater potential. There may be newer players to the market such as initial public offerings (IPOs) or those that base most of their success on specific results such as Federal Drug Administration approval. As you get older, you should become more conservative in your strategy by focusing on more stable investments such as bonds.

You should start investing as early on in your adult life as possible. Doing so will give you the greatest chance of accumulating wealth that can be used throughout your life and perhaps allow you to retire earlier. However, simply investing a few thousand dollars will not do it alone. Much like any living creature, you will need to continually feed it in order for it to grow strong. Therefore, set aside funds on a monthly or quarterly basis to bolster your investment potential. Unfortunately, the market can be a financial roller coaster. When the time comes for you to start liquidating your investments for such things as purchasing a new home or retiring, the market may be at a low point. In general there is not much you can do in the short term other than sticking it out until the market recovers and your investments become more valuable again.

Real Estate Investments

Investing in real estate has similar risks as the stock market and then some. Returns on your investment can be slow or quick, large or small as well as positive or negative. There are several factors that will influence the success of your endeavor, including the type of real estate, health of the housing market, interest rates, duration of investment, property location and condition. Unless you are well versed in all aspects of investing in real estate, you should not jump in and expect a huge windfall. In fact, you can easily lose hundreds of thousands of dollars and ruin your credit through bankruptcy or foreclosure.

There are a number of different types of real estate that you can invest in, including residential and commercial, which can be further divided into renting, leasing, or flipping. Flipping is the practice of reselling a property after holding on to it for a short period of time, typically after making improvements or in hopes of a large return. Laws vary greatly, so be sure to be fully versed in all the details before you commit any money to a project. For example, renting out Section 8 housing guarantees a large portion of the monthly income from the federal government. In any case, do not hesitate in consulting with a financial planner, accountant, or real estate attorney if you have any questions or feel uncomfortable with a situation.

The current as well as the future health of the real estate market will have a significant impact on your profits or losses. If you are planning on purchasing a house with the hopes of fixing it up and reselling it in a few weeks or months, you will not need to worry about real estate market conditions too far in the future. However, if you plan on purchasing new construction and flipping the home, it could be months to years before you close. During that timeframe, the housing market can change drastically, and you could easily lose hundreds of thousands of dollars. Conversely, you can probably find many bargains in a bad housing market, either from people desperate to unload a house or through foreclosures.

Unless you have cash on hand to invest in real estate, chances are you will need to borrow money in order to fund your project. Depending on your existing financial situation, you may be able to use the home equity available in your primary home, or you may need to take out a relatively short-term loan. The danger in either case is if your funding is variable and dependent on the prime interest rate. The prime rate can easily double, triple, quadruple, or more in a relatively short period of time. Therefore, you should be very careful and think not only about current monthly payments but future increases that can either cut into your profits or put you in debt.

When it comes to real estate, there are actually only three factors: location, location, and location. Where your investment is located will greatly affect your ability to rent, lease, or sell it. For example, is it located in a busy traffic area? This could be good for a commercial business but is not favorable for a residential investment. Your venture can also be influenced by natural disaster factors such as fires, mudslides, hurricanes, floods, and tornadoes. In addition, your property may be subjected to seasonal influences. For example, if you are investing in southern Florida, the population varies with the seasons (known as snow birds) such that the winter months are the only time people tend to be in the area or thinking of purchasing a retirement/vacation home.

Lastly, the physical condition of your real estate investment can make or break you. If you plan on renovating an older home or apartment building, it may take longer than expected to complete the work, which can result in additional monthly payments before you are able to sell or rent it out. Furthermore, if you plan on doing the work yourself or with the help of others, you better make sure that you can handle the job and that your crews are reliable as well. In addition, if you are a landlord, you are responsible for maintaining the structure for which repairs can be costly, especially if they are major like a new roof.

If you do get in over your head, either on your primary residence or investment property, there may be four potential options available before having to foreclose. Keep in mind that every case is unique and laws/rules vary greatly from state to state and lender to lender. The first potential option is a short sale. You will have to sell the house for less than you would normally make, but it is the cleanest solution to a difficult situation. Another potential alternative to foreclosing is a deed in lieu. In this case, you will be handing over the deed to the house to the lender in return for the forgiveness of the outstanding loan balance. Your credit will suffer for a relatively short period of time, but not quite as much as it would in the case of foreclosure. You can also ask that the transaction be recorded as "paid as agreed" to help limit the hit to your credit. In cases of hardship, you may qualify for a repayment plan or a loan modification. The repayment option may be available to you if you had a temporary negative financial situation but are now back on your feet. Loan modifications are for more drastic cases where there is now a major difference from when you first had your mortgage. You may be able to work with the lender to alter the terms of your obligation such that monthly payments are reduced, for example. In either case, you will need to substantiate your hardship with official records such as medical bills and pay statements.

Purchasing a Vehicle

During the course of your life, you may find yourself leasing or owning anywhere from five to twenty vehicles. They are not inexpensive, so you definitely want to make sure that you consider several factors. The first consideration that you need to think about is whether you should buy a new or used car. Do not be fooled by the term "certified pre-owned" or similar phrase that just means used car. In general, new cars do not have as many problems, and if they do, they may be covered by a warranty. Most new cars come with warranties that cover major problems or defects and can be extended if you plan on keeping the car for a long period of time. If the vehicle turns out to be a "lemon" (typically the case if you have an issue with the same item three or more times), you have legal rights that can help protect you. On the other hand, used cars have a greater potential for having problems. Those problems can be due to simple wear and tear on parts as well as how the vehicle was treated earlier in its life. If someone knows that they will be trading in a car, they are less likely to drive or take care of it well. Since you do not know how well a used car was treated, you may wish to spend the extra money on a new car for peace of mind. If you do purchase a used car, you may wind up, sooner than later, needing to replace costly items such as tires and brakes. However, before you commit to a used vehicle, be sure to investigate it as much as possible by purchasing a vehicle history report from a reputable source such as CARFAX.

Vehicles come in all shapes and sizes, so often the problem is having too many choices. However, there are some questions you can ask yourself to help narrow down the selection. First and foremost, you need to consider safety. If the car or truck is not well built or is only an inch off the ground, you should pass on it. The next obvious factor is cost. You can either finance or lease a vehicle if you cannot afford to purchase it outright. If you do not plan on putting excessive miles on the vehicle, or if you know that you will want another car in the near future, leasing may be your best option. Furthermore, you may be able to use the monthly lease payment as a business-related tax write-off. While constantly leasing cars may appear to be like renting an apartment (spending thousands of dollars and having nothing to show for it), it could very well be the best option given the fact that automobiles lose their value or depreciate so quickly. Leases typically require a down payment and other fees which may add up to a significant amount, so be sure to read and understand all the fine print before you sign any contracts. No matter what the circumstances, ask as many questions necessary to make you feel comfortable. On the other hand, you may wish to purchase a vehicle if you do not plan on putting many miles on it, which in theory should enable it to last longer.

If you are having a difficult time making up your mind between vehicles or you want to confirm your expectations, try renting the vehicle(s) for a few days. This way you can get a better sense of all their positive and negative features before spending thousands of dollars and committing years of your time. Never feel pressured into purchasing a vehicle. Remember, you are the one in the driver's seat, not the salesperson; no pun intended. Lastly, you may wish to use timing to your advantage. In order to meet sales numbers, dealers become much more eager to put you in a vehicle at the end of the month and the end of the quarter.

One other major factor to consider is the purpose or usefulness of the vehicle, not only in the short term but the long term as well. For example, if you live in Vermont or Seattle, purchasing a convertible may not be the wisest move. Furthermore, if you plan on starting a family soon, a small two-seater is not going to be practical for very long.

The final consideration, which really should be your first, is the environmental friendliness of the vehicle. Hybrid vehicles are a great start to reducing our dependency on fossil fuels, regardless of source. If you are unable to purchase a hybrid or similar vehicle, then look for one that gets the most miles per gallon of gasoline.

I highly recommend that you do not purchase a used vehicle from a private party. Even if you know the person and have had someone with a good working knowledge of cars inspect the vehicle, the purchase can lead to disaster. That is not to say that purchasing from a commercial business may be much better, but if something bad does happen, you may have a better chance at being awarded some compensation.

Selling a Vehicle

Since no vehicle lasts forever, there will be many times when you will have to part with your current car or truck. If you are sure that you have received the most out of your vehicle, or it is no longer safe/reliable to drive, there are a few good options available to you. If you are purchasing a new vehicle, you can trade in your old one to help defray the cost of the new car or truck. You can also try selling it to a company whose sole business is buying old vehicles. Lastly, if the value of the vehicle is so low, or it is in such bad condition, you can donate it to a reputable charity for a tax deduction. While you may be able to get a higher price for the old car or truck by selling it privately, you run the risk of a number of headaches. With the cost of advertising, dealing with people not showing up or trying to haggle on the selling price, it is not worth your time and the additional stress. Furthermore, even after you sell it, there always exists the chance that the buyer will come back to you months later if something happens to the car. Regardless of how you sell your car or truck, never try to tamper or alter documents and records such as the odometer reading. You should also make it a point to turn in your old plates and get a receipt at the motor vehicle department. This will help protect you in the event your old plate numbers/letters are used fraudulently in the future. Lastly, before you turn over your old vehicle be sure to clear out any codes used in the built-in garage door opening system (such as HomeLink®), and do not forget any personal items such as sunglasses, CDs, and DVDs.

Renting

It is likely that you will, at least once in your life, need to find a place to live but not be able to afford a mortgage for a house, condo, or townhouse. In general, renting should be seen as a short-term housing solution since you are not gaining any value in return for your monthly payment. There are several important factors that you should consider when renting an apartment or other living space. As usual, security should be your primary concern. If the building is not located in a safe neighborhood, the parking situation does not feel safe, or the laundry room is an incident just waiting to happen, you should look elsewhere. Ask questions of the landlord/building manager regarding security systems and access, including maintenance workers. Always be aware of your surroundings and those around you since attackers often strike when you are entering the building.

Next, if you do need to take on a roommate, be sure you find out as much about them as possible before locking in to any agreement. Only live with people you can trust, such as someone recommended by an honest source. Remember that all your possessions, including items that make up your personal identity, can be exposed to your roommate or mates. Lastly, protect yourself by purchasing renters insurance. It is relatively inexpensive and can cover you for fire, water, and smoke damage as well as theft and liability. Keep in mind that the owner's policy, whether on a personal or commercial property, will not cover your personal property.

Buying a Home

Purchasing a single-family house, townhouse, condo, or other living space is most likely going to be your biggest financial investment in life. Just as there are many factors to consider when renting, there are even more when owning a house. The most important thing to remember is to be honest with yourself since you can easily get in over your head. The first question to ask yourself is if owning a house given your current personal, family, career, and financial situation makes sense now. Hopefully, if you were renting an apartment, you were able to save money to cover such things as the down payment. If you do think that a house is right for you, consider what type of person you are compared to the level of responsibility each type of home comes with. For example, if you do not have the time or skills to maintain a single-family home, you should strongly consider purchasing a condo or townhouse where you can pay to have those items taken care of through fees. Furthermore, if your career has a significant travel component to it, or you are just beginning a demanding job, perhaps the additional burden of a house is not the best challenge to tackle at this time.

If you are ready to fully commit to a house, I would recommend taking the following steps. First, make sure that you can comfortably afford the monthly payment. Keep in mind that that does not simply consist of the mortgage payment. You will also need to factor in the cost of utilities (water, gas, electric), garbage removal, property taxes, maintenance fees, homeowner's insurance, and potentially private mortgage insurance (PMI) if you put less than twenty percent down on the house. As a rule of thumb, these costs should not exceed more than two thirds of your total monthly salary.

Just like vehicles, houses come in two basic flavors, new and used. While a new construction house may seem favorable at first, it too has several points to be aware of. Regardless of size, make sure that the builder is reputable. Big companies can fall on hard times just as quickly as the little guy who spot builds. Next, take the delivery date that the builder gives you and add at least a few months to it. Rarely are homes finished on time. Be sure to have a qualified attorney review the contract before you sign on anything more than a binder. A binder is a small, usually refundable deposit that is used to reserve the home/lot while you are reviewing the contract. Do not be afraid or pressured into any terms that you are not comfortable with. While you will never have all the points of the contract go your way, you should be reasonability comfortable with the conditions of the items in question.

The next item for consideration is determining what house factors are important to you. They can include the style or age of the house, number of bedrooms and bathrooms, if it has a basement, and the size of the property. Think not only for the short term but also long term; you may plan on only being there for a few years, but life has a funny way of changing on you, whether it is due to a new baby or the health of the housing market. Chances are you will not be able to find a house that has everything that you are looking for, so you may need to compromise on some of your requirements.

You can probably guess what the next most important factor is by now, safety. Make sure you do your research on the location and surroundings of the house. While it may be in a safe neighborhood, if you have to travel through undesirable areas or are next to questionable towns, you should keep looking. Visit the house during the day, at night, on the weekends, and during the week to get a better sense of everything from traffic to background noise. While you may not have kids yet (or any of school age), you should do additional research to ensure that the public school system in town is good. If not, you may have to spend additional money on a Catholic or private school. If you need daycare services in the area, make sure that you research them as well.

When you are ready to look at a house, use a checklist to track all the points of consideration. If there are obvious issues with the house, do not hesitate in walking away from it. The evaluation process is a little harder when looking at new construction, but you can get a general idea of the workmanship quality and materials used when you view a finished model home or similar houses under construction. If everything is looking good with your selection, you should have a licensed home inspector review the [existing] house. Depending on the results, you may be able to work with the current owner on reducing the sale price to offset repair costs. However, if the damage is significant and/or structural in nature, I would recommend that you continue your search. On the flipside, with new construction you can compile a punch list of items that require repair and submit it to the builder after you close. However, in reality, unless it is a major issue, chances are you will wind up needing to fix the problems yourself.

Selling a Home

There are countless reasons why you may need to sell your house. It may be due to an expanding family or relocating for a job, but whatever the reason the process is the same. There are two main ways you can go about selling your house. The first, and more common, is with a real estate agent. They will take care of most of the running around and paperwork, but more importantly, they will be able to get your house the exposure it needs by way of the Multiple Listing Service (MLS). Unfortunately, all these benefits come at a price. The typical sales commission is six percent though it can be negotiated to a lower value such as five percent. This adds up to thousands of dollars that will take away from your potential profits. However, realistically, it is the only sensible option if you wish to sell your house in a reasonable timeframe.

The second and more difficult method of selling a home is privately. While you will save the thousands of dollars on the real estate commission, you may waste more time and energy trying to sell it. Furthermore, if you sell your house privately, you will not be automatically listed on the MLS and a subscription will run to a few hundred dollars. If time is not an issue, than putting your house on the market yourself may be a reasonable option.

Regardless of the selling method, you need to set a reasonable selling price. There are a number of free web sites available to estimate your home value as well as see the price that other houses in your area have sold for. You will need to adjust your price based on the features that your house may or may not have. Furthermore, if you are in a rush to sell your house, you may need to price it lower so it will sell quicker. The important thing to remember is not to fool yourself into thinking your house is worth more than it is. Be reasonable and realistic and it will sell within a normal timeframe. Unfortunately, the situation may get more complex when you need to sell your house in conjunction with purchasing a new one. This can be an extremely stressful time for you and your family, but try to remain calm and everything will work out in the end.

There are some things you can do for relatively little money that can add thousands of dollars to the selling price, or at least make your house stand out from the rest. Typically kitchens and bathrooms are what sell a house. However, there are a number of less expensive and quicker things you can do to make the house more attractive. The first step is to de-clutter the space. Hopefully, you do not have a lot of knickknacks lying around, but if you do, get rid of them before you have to move them anyway. The next step is make sure that everything is clean and orderly, including closets, cabinets, and entire rooms such as the garage or basement. Next, a fresh coat of paint can work wonders. You do not have to paint the whole house, but hit the rooms that need it the most. Furthermore, make sure that you tone down any wild colors which may make a bad impression on a buyer. That does not mean that the entire house should be beige, but hot pink and lime green will definitely hurt your chances of selling.

You can also update your house quickly and easily with small touches. They can include light fixtures or ceiling fans, flooring, and window treatments. Also, try to give the space a light and airy feeling, especially if the rooms are small. Another smart tactic is to stage your house. You can do the staging with items you already have, or you can rent all types of furniture and accessories for open houses. If worse comes to worst, renting your current house may be a viable option until you are able to sell it.

Mortgages

There are dozens of different mortgage products, but they generally fit into one of two main categories. There are fixed rate mortgages which are typically for ten, twenty, thirty (even forty) years where your monthly payment remains constant for the life of the loan. The thirty-year fixed rate mortgage is the most common; stay away from forty-year mortgages since you will wind up spending much more money in interest compared to a thirty-year mortgage. The other major type of mortgage loan is an adjustable rate mortgage (ARM). They come in several different variations, including 1/1, 3/1, 5/1, and 7/1. Most of them are based on the prime interest rate which can change several times a year. For example, with a 5/1 ARM, you will pay the same interest rate for five years, but then it is adjusted, up or down, on an annual basis for the life of the loan. The initial interest rate is usually lower than a fixed mortgage, but the rate, which directly affects your monthly payment, can double when the fixed period ends. It is not uncommon for mortgages to be several hundreds of thousands of dollars, so a small mistake can add up to big payments, or foreclosure, quickly. The last product variation that applies to both fixed and ARMs is known as "interest only." This means that for a set period of time, you will only be making interest payments and none of your monthly payment will go towards the original principal. An interest-only product has benefits to only a few situations such as lower initial payments and should be avoided by most people. The only other built-in benefit is the tax write-off for all the interest paid.

Whenever you talk about borrowing money from a bank or other financial institution, the discussion becomes dominated by the prime rate. It is a major driving force when it comes to how much interest you will be paying on the money you borrow. The prime rate is based on another factor known as the federal funds rate. The federal funds rate is the interest rate that lenders use to charge each other to borrow money overnight. It sounds complicated, but it is relatively straightforward. Basically the United States Federal Government requires by law that banks and other lenders maintain a certain level of reserves (money) with them. If a lender's reserves fall below the minimum, the lender will borrow the difference from another lender who is above the minimum level. The interest rate that the one lender charges the other is based on the federal funds rate. The members of the Federal Reserve currently convene eight times a year at Federal Open Market Committee meetings, and depending on the economic climate, they may increase, decrease, or allow the federal fund rate to remain the same. The other option a lender has is to borrow money from the government itself. The interest rate that the lender would be charged in that case is known as the discount rate. The discount rate is higher than the federal funds rate, and therefore the latter method is not often employed. The government can set the discount range exactly, however, the federal funds rate is actually a range in which they set the nominal rate.

With all that said, the prime rate is approximately three percent (or 300 basis points) more than the federal funds rate. Often, banks and lenders use the prime rate as a basis for the interest rate they will charge you for a mortgage, auto loan, education loan, or line of credit. Depending on many factors, including market conditions, the quality of your credit, loan amount, and product type, the bank or lender may add to, subtract from or use the prime rate itself as your specific interest rate.

Another important topic when it comes to borrowing money and interest rates is amortization. An amortization schedule will detail out the portion of your payment that will be applied towards the principal and the interest. In the early years of your loan's life, almost all of your payment will go towards the interest portion of the loan. As you make more and more payments, the interest portion and principal portion will begin to equal. After that point, more of the payment will be applied towards the principal until the loan is finally paid in full. The sad reality is that for a thirty-year mortgage, you will be paying approximately three times the original value of the loan if it takes you all thirty years to repay. For example, the loan that you took for $300,000 can cost you $900,000 when all is said and done. Therefore, in general, the quicker you can pay off a mortgage, the better.

Another key financial value to pay attention to is the annual percentage rate (APR). The APR is a simple value resulting from a complex equation that you can use to compare loan offers on a level playing field. In addition to the interest rate itself, the APR will take into consideration fees specific to that lender. In theory you can then compare offers from all the lenders on an equal footing. Lastly, paying points on a loan is nothing more than pre-paid interest. Essentially, you can pay more points (money) upfront for a lower interest rate on your loan.

Once you have a mortgage, it does not mean that you should stop paying attention to it. Keep an eye on rates since they may fall significantly enough compared to your current mortgage. If the current rates are approximately 1.5% or lower than your fixed rate mortgage, it would be a good time to start thinking about refinancing. Refinancing is nothing more than a short stack of paperwork that needs to be completed with either your current lender or another lender. There could be a few thousand dollars worth of fees involved with the refinance, but you are usually able to roll them into the new mortgage itself. In addition to lowering your rate, you may even be able to reduce the duration or terms of the mortgage. For example, you may be able to go from a thirty-year mortgage to a fifteen-year mortgage. For adjustable rate mortgages, you will need to refinance before the balloon payment is due at the end of the initial term of one, three, five, seven, ten etc. years. The balloon payment is nothing more than the balance of the loan.

Since buying a house is probably going to be your largest purchase in life, you actually have a chance to change your mind. It is one of the few times in life when you get a legal "do over." The three-day right of rescission gives you the opportunity by law to cancel your mortgage or home equity application without major penalty. You may lose your application fee, but it is a small price compared to getting in way over your head.

One of the best and easiest actions you can take to help pay off your mortgage or home equity early is by making extra payments (assuming there are no prepayment penalties). Making just one extra principal payment a year or making payments biweekly instead of monthly can shave years off of your obligation. Even if you can only add a hundred extra dollars a payment, it will have a significant impact on the loan timeframes. Just be sure that you specify that the additional funds are to be applied towards the principal and not escrow or some other area.

Home Equity Loans and Lines of Credit

Another financing option that you can tap into if you own a house is a home equity (HE) loan or line of credit (LOC). The amount of available equity is the current market value of your house minus any outstanding liens, such as your mortgage, that you have against it. They are not something that you should use freely since monthly payments can become very costly. The main difference between a loan and line of credit is that the interest rate for a loan is fixed and usually higher than a line of credit. The interest rate on a line of credit can go up or down almost on a monthly basis; your monthly payment can easily double if the federal funds rate consistently rises. Use a HE loan or HELOC only in a case of emergency and never like a credit card. However, you can use a home equity line or loan to consolidate high interest debts such as credit cards. While you can use a home equity for home improvements and other types of financing, you should try to save up a significant percent of the total first. Always read and understand all documents before signing and do not hesitate to contact a financial planner or professional before committing to such a large responsibility. Lastly, the interest portion of your payments is also tax deducible.

Taxes

It would be very interesting to see the reaction of the Founding Fathers to all the taxes we have today. It seems like every other month there is a new tax or an increase to an existing one. Furthermore, taxes are rarely lowered and almost never disappear altogether. However, taxes have become a tolerated part of everyday life and most do go towards worthwhile or necessary programs.

There are far too many different types of taxes to cover in one book, not to mention just part of a book. However, let us review the most common and hardest hitting taxes. Unless you are working "off the books" or "under the table," you will be contributing a significant portion of your paycheck to federal and state governments. The percentage of each varies on the amount of money you make (though there are minimums and maximums), the state you work and live in as well as the number of dependents you claim. The more dependents you claim, up to five, the less federal and state taxes that will be withheld from your check.

Working in conjunction with your paycheck withholdings is income tax. Income tax must be filed with the Internal Revenue Service by April 15th of every year. Depending on the state you live in, you may also need to file with the state by tax day. Depending on your specific financial situation, you may either receive money back or need to pay additionally. There are many factors that influence the calculations; however, you should always file your taxes every year. Furthermore, paying a knowledgeable certified accountant to handle your tax return is money well spent since they are familiar with all types of ways to help save you money. To prove just how serious the tax laws are, after all the notorious actions the infamous mob leader Al Capone took, it was the failure to pay federal taxes that imprisoned and brought him down. While it is tempting to cheat on your taxes, do yourself a favor and pay your fair share. The penalties are not worth the risk. Besides, there are numerous ways to be creative and still fall well within the tax laws.

Now you may ask yourself, why should I surrender thousands of my hard-earned dollars to the local or federal government? Well, if you enjoy and would like to keep the armed forces, state police and programs like the Federal Drug Administration (FDA) or Environmental Protection Agency (EPA), then paying your taxes is your way of contributing to the country. In addition to offering protective and emergency services, your federal and state taxes help support social programs that assist and aid people in need. While you hear many people complain about having to pay taxes, we often and easily take for granted just how much we get in return for a relatively small price.

The next major type of tax to be concerned with is property tax. This tax applies to all people who own a home, including single-family houses, condominiums, co-ops, townhouses, businesses, and investment properties. People who rent apartments do not have to pay separate property tax, but the building owners factor the expense into the monthly rental fee. Property taxes are typically due on a quarterly or annual basis and nearly no two people pay exactly the same amount, even if they live on the same street. Your property taxes are mainly based on the value of your home and not necessarily how much land you have. People who purchase new construction homes often pay much more in property taxes, as much as double or triple, compared to a person who has lived in the area for a few years. Furthermore, each town has there own tax rate, which can vary greatly from city to city. Before you purchase a new or previously owned home, be sure to find out the cost of the property taxes. This additional expense on top of a mortgage may force you to look at different houses or in a different city altogether. Surprisingly enough, the majority of your property taxes are used to fund local public schools. The municipal portion of your property taxes can be as low as five percent or less. Volunteer services, such as fire companies and first-aid squads, help to keep your tax rate low, which is another good reason to support your local volunteer organizations.

Sadly, even when someone dies, taxes can be a part of the occasion; as they say, nothing in life is guaranteed except death and taxes. Depending on the state, inheritance tax may be levied on assets willed to you by a relative or friend. There are some different techniques such as trust funds to help insulate you from getting hit with large tax fees. However, one of the best ways around inheritance tax when it comes to money is if the person gives you a significant portion of your inheritance before they pass away. As long as they keep cash amounts significantly less than the Internal Revenue Service (IRS) reportable threshold of $10,000 at a time and not withdraw the money every day, you can collect most of the money intended for you without it being taxed yet again.

Sales tax is one of the most interesting of all taxes. Sales tax is a typical three to eight percent of the total cost but is not charged in every state. It is applicable on a wide range of products and services, yet it is not inclusive of all the items you purchase. In general, you pay sales tax on all commercial and business services. For the most part, you will pay sales tax on clothing, food, and prescription drugs but not over-the-counter medications. You should always review your receipt before you leave a store or before signing for services to ensure you will or have been charged the proper amount. Do not be afraid to ask for an explanation or confront a business on an overcharge; the sooner you resolve the issue the better.

Believe it or not, you pay a whole host of taxes on a daily basis without even realizing it. For example, every time you fuel up at a gas station, you are paying taxes used for road construction and maintenance. Take a careful look at your receipts the next time you go on vacation. Hotels and other tourist-related organizations such as airlines and car rental companies often levy a number of small taxes that can add up quickly. Furthermore, there is such a thing as a luxury tax which must be paid on items that cross a certain threshold amount. While not taxes in the strict sense of the term, over the course of your life, you will be paying thousands in fees and/or surcharges for items such as medical or hazardous waste disposal costs which you may think are already part of the overall product or service. The point of this entire section is that you need to look deeper than the surface or advertised price since there are often many hidden costs by the time all is said and done.

Gifts

Between birthdays, engagements, weddings, baby showers, housewarmings, so on and so forth, there are many occasions when you will need to bring or send a gift. In general, the closer you are with the person, the larger the value of the gift. However, there is a minimum amount that you should spend on even the most distant of friend or relative. Fifteen to twenty dollars is a reasonable minimum gift value. If you are not sure what the person may like or want, a gift card to a local or national store is a cordial gesture. Giving cash or a check is only appropriate for large gifts such as for a wedding. If you do purchase clothes or other specific items for a person, be sure to include a gift receipt in the event they wish to return or exchange it for any reason. If you are in a bind, you can always "chip in" with another person or a group of people for a shared gift.

Although there seems to be some type of gift-giving occasion nearly every other week, sometimes the best gifts are those given when there is no special occasion. In other words, do not wait for a commercialized holiday to give a little something to a person. The best gifts are often given for no specific reason at all since you care about them all year long.

When someone gives you a gift, no matter the value or occasion, you should be appreciative. You will undoubtedly receive some gifts that are, let us just say, less than what you were expecting. Even in those instances you should be polite and gracious. The fact that they took the time to think of you is worth more than any present. In return for their generosity, you should always say thank you at the time you receive the gift, but you should also follow up with a handwritten card. Even though in this day and age it is quick and easy to send an e-mail, text message, or leave a voicemail, there is nothing classier than a personalized message written in your own hand. This shows that, just as they took the time to be considerate of you, you took the time to be considerate of them.

Daily Life

"Every day of your life is a page of your history."
– Arabian Proverb

Home

Your home will and always should be the safest place on Earth. You should always feel comfortable and relaxed in your home. Know that you can always count on your home being there for you, no matter what may be going on in your life or the world around you.

Right and Wrong

I would like to believe that knowing right from wrong is what separates us from animals, but unfortunately, that is not always the case. Furthermore, it is not only knowing what is right but making sure that your actions reflect it. A good litmus test for right and wrong is a simple question: Would I want this published on the front page a national newspaper? If that is not a good barometer, be honest with yourself and go with your gut instinct. While some people catch on to this concept quicker than others, some never do at all and continually make the wrong choices in life. Hopefully, your upbringing is solid and reliable for most situations, but always make sure that you learn from your mistakes. Always be able to look at yourself in the mirror and know that you are leading an honest life and are a productive member of society.

Fun

No matter what you are doing in life, try to have some fun. How you enjoy your time on the journey from point A to point B is just as important as getting to point B. Most of the great times of your life will not come with fireworks and large fanfare, so learn to appreciate the little things that make you pause and smile. Take the time to stop and smell the roses every once in a while; it will greatly help get you through the day. Granted, there are times when it is not appropriate to be jovial but seeing the glass half full does wonders for your attitude, reputation, and health. While "work" is not called "fun," it does not mean that you cannot make the most of it. The last thing that you want to do when you are old and gray is look back and realize that you went through life without enjoying it.

Whenever possible, dispel the saying that "youth is wasted on the young." Being a kid is not always easy in this day and age, but be sure to make the most of it; trust me, it seems to pass in the blink of an eye. Do not let petty items and actions stand in your way of enjoying your youth. It is the time in your life with the least amount of difficult, real-world responsibilities, including but not limited to paying bills, providing for your family and raising children. Your high school years will probably be one of the most fun times of your life, second perhaps only to college, so make the most of them. However, this does not mean that you can act irresponsible or have no one or nothing to answer to. Just be a kid and have some good, old-fashioned clean fun.

Saying "I am Sorry"

Saying "I am sorry" is not only a sign of maturity but also the three most powerful words you can utter. Regardless of the magnitude of the situation, saying you are sorry will cost you nothing and can instantly defuse the most volatile of situations. Being stubborn for the sake of trying to win an argument or hiding from the truth is foolish. Learn to be bigger than yourself and only good will come of it, I promise. As always, learn from the situation to prevent future occurrences.

Affection

Think of affection as an emotional vitamin. Yes, you can live without it, but a healthy daily dose will help enhance all aspects of your relationship, especially given the hectic lives we all lead. A daily gesture does not have to be anything grand or large-scale either. In fact, a simple hug or small bunch of fresh flowers converts your thoughts about a person into actions that they can acknowledge and appreciate. These little nuggets of love will help get both of you through no-fault emotional dry spells until you can properly show your love for one another. Furthermore, affection should be a two-way street with both people giving and receiving. However, never keep score or "nickel-and-dime" someone when it comes to affection.

Communicating

We take many things for granted in our daily lives, but the most overlooked power we have is the ability to communicate. Even though we are the self-proclaimed most intelligent species, I sometimes think that the plant and animal worlds have better communication amongst themselves. Lack of communication, or poor quality thereof, results in everything from small inconveniences to war, death, and destruction. Good communication is composed of three very important components. The first part is the quality of the communication. This applies to all forms of communication, including verbal, written, and body language. Since you are not always able to clarify matters, as in the case of written communications, you need to make sure that your message is clear and leaves no room for misinterpretation. The second key element to good communication is its frequency. While some people could talk a dog off a meat wagon, there is no such thing as over communicating. Too often, people do a good job at communicating when they do, but the problem is that it is just far too infrequent. This can lead to everything from missed opportunities to people's minds wandering off to places that it should not, whereby perception becomes a false reality. The last, and maybe most important, factor in good communication is initiation. Never be shy or feel like you are "giving in" by initiating a dialog. If you are not comfortable with talking to someone in person, you can at least pick up the phone or send them a letter or e-mail, though there is no substitute for in-person interaction.

Now this may sound like a complete contradiction to what I have just told you, but sometimes saying less is the best thing to do. You can easily dig your own grave by talking too much. Usually the best thing to do when you find yourself in this type of position is to remain silent and listen to what the other person has to say, whether you agree with them or not, and let the situation pass on its own. This is especially helpful when dealing with superiors, such as a boss or parent, but can be just as effective with colleagues and friends alike. Hopefully, you will develop this skill before you put your foot in your mouth too many times or jeopardize valuable opportunities and relationships.

Believe it or not, good communication starts between yourself. You need to be personally open and honest by routinely having a talk with yourself. Next, you need to ensure that you are communicating properly with your immediate family, especially your spouse. This will not only promote healthy relationships but will make your life much easier. Finally, make certain that your communication skills are up to par with friends, coworkers and yes, even strangers. There is no reason why you cannot smile or say hello to someone you see every morning or on an elevator. Continuously hone your communication skills and I guarantee it will pay off rich dividends throughout your life.

Challenges

Whether it is a small or a large challenge, all you need to do is remain calm, tap into your previous training, knowledge, and experiences and apply them to the new situation. It also greatly helps to reduce large efforts or tasks into smaller, more manageable tasks. Never accept from anyone, including yourself, that a challenge is too difficult or impossible to overcome until you have given the effort your all and than some. Use your organizational skills and knowledge of history, technology, and pattern recognition to aid in your efforts. Allow yourself to wander outside of your comfort zone every once in a while and I guarantee that you will thank yourself later. New challenges help your mind and body grow. They also help in keeping your mind and skills sharp, especially later in life when people typically slow down and fall into monotonous routines. Lastly, conquering many challenges also helps you become a strong leader.

Friends

Throughout the course of your life, you will have many friends. Some you will keep for a lifetime, some will be "fair-weather friends" and others may come and go based on your stage in life. Furthermore, you will have even more acquaintances that may or may not transform into friends. The key point to remember is that it is not the quantity of friends that you have, it is the quality. Sure, everyone would like to be Mr. or Ms. Mayor, but life is more than just a popularity contest. Make sure that you select your friends for the qualities they possess and actions they take. Avoid associating with people you cannot trust, are not responsible or that may cause you mental, emotional, or physical harm. True friends will be understanding of temporary or transitional situations which may last days, weeks, months, or years. Lastly, do not be afraid to either start new friendships or eliminate those that may adversely affect you and your character.

Traditions

Traditions, big and small, are special moments that you always remember and hopefully look forward to. Whether it is having Sunday dinner together as a family or going around the Thanksgiving table to tell what you are thankful for, traditions help build fond memories and give us something to always count on. Traditions can be of any size, and you should look to start a few new ones of your own. While you may not fully understand some traditions as a child and others may embarrass you, carry them forward through the years and pass them on to your own children one day. Keep in mind that it is not the size or number of traditions that matters, it is the quality.

Dreams and Goals

Dreams and goals, while related, are distinctively different and equally important to have in your life. Dreams help us in many ways. They provide us with an escape from the tangible world and can give us hope and pleasure. They do not cost anything and can be whipped up at any time. Dreams can also help form and provide the motivation to achieve our goals in life. Lastly, hopes and dreams can help us think of alternative ways and paths to take in achieving our goals.

You should have three different types of goals in life: achievable, stretch, and ultimate goals. You should further classify your goals as short-term and long-term. A short-term goal can be something as simple as completing a list of tasks by the end of the day. Long-term goals would consist of how far you want to take your career or the size family you want to have one day. You should start off slow with smaller achievable goals and continuously chip away at larger goals. Always set the bar higher and higher for yourself and never become complacent. Never let anyone step on your dreams or say you cannot do something, but by the same token, be realistic with yourself and not let your dreams overtake reality. Lastly, avoid setting monetary goals. Instead, set financial goals for yourself at every age. Between get-rich-quick schemes and not focusing on the small, yet achievable goals, you will waste more time, energy, and money trying to be the next millionaire.

Think Ahead

While thinking ahead and being prepared may sound the same, they are in fact different. You will be prepared by thinking ahead, but you do not have to be nor can be prepared for everything in life. The point is simple: take the time to think one, two, or three steps ahead so that you can be better prepared. Furthermore, you may need to adjust your initial action or thinking throughout the process. Realize too that the more complex or important the action, the further ahead you may need to think or evaluate your actions. Keep in mind that the world and life is made up of a series of connections, some of which you can influence but some are out of your immediate control.

Timing

Timing is an interesting characteristic. It can be influenced by a number of factors, ranging from luck to precision research, and could impact everything from the mundane to your very life. For example, the year you graduate college may be one in which companies are not hiring many with your type of degree. As with so many other areas of your life, the important concept to always keep in mind is to control the forces that you can as best you can. Being at the right place at the right time will only get you so far and is not a method that you should ever rely upon. On the other hand, you may simply be at the wrong place at the wrong time; hopefully, any effects are minor. However, you should always use all your observation and pattern recognition skills to ensure that you are making well-informed decisions to maximize benefits and minimize negative consequences. This is especially important when it comes to vital aspects of your life such as safety, career, and partner selection.

Reading between the Lines

While the world may appear to have good intentions, that is not always the case. Therefore, you should develop and hone your skills for reading between the lines. Now the goal is not to turn you into a skeptic or a conspiracy theory junky but rather to wipe away any naivety. A big motivator in life is money. For example, when you see businesses tout how they are "going green" and have a strong commitment to the environment, it usually means that they are trying to find ways to save money but cutting back/altering services or aspects of their products. This concept can also hold true for all types of people, including friends, family, and perfect strangers. Learn to discern when someone is genuinely sincere versus when they are just buttering you up for other short or long-term reasons. Be careful not to take everything at surface value since there may be hidden ulterior motives.

Problem Solving and Issue Resolution

It is nearly impossible to be successful in life without sound problem-solving skills. You may need to solve a problem for yourself, as in the case of a test, or you may need to help someone else with a problem as part of your job. The severity of the problem may be nearly insignificant to a medical emergency. In any case, there are a number of common themes and techniques that apply to all situations. First and foremost, you need to remain calm and not panic. You will never be able to arrive at the solution to a problem if your head is clouded and unfocused. Next, you should take a moment to clearly define and understand the problem. Now this may sound silly, but if you are not careful, you could easily come up with a solution to the wrong problem. That will not only waste precious time, but it will take away from your focus. Often related to understanding the problem is being able to reproduce it. While one person may be experiencing the problem, others may or may not. It is extremely difficult to arrive at an answer or fix if someone else is not experiencing the same problem. Always look for general or specific patterns and trends when investigating any issue.

Once you have positively identified the problem, you need to draw on all your skills, observations, and experiences to solve the problem. One technique that works well in many cases is to try and isolate the problem to a specific area or segment of an overall process or condition. You can easily do this by identifying the absolute start and end points and work your way inward until you isolate the specific problem area. This will greatly help you conserve time, energy, money, and resources by not wasting them on areas that are in perfect working order. A great example of this technique in action is with a garden hose. If you press the nozzle and no water comes out, you should first confirm the water is turned on (the starting point) and then make sure the nozzle (the end point) is working by removing it from the hose to see if water is flowing or if the nozzle is clogged with debris. Assuming there is no water flowing out of the open end of the line, you should work your way back to the beginning of the water supply to see if there is a kink in the hose. If you are not able to solve a problem on your own, and assuming it is not a test, you should then take stock of the resources and talents around and available to you. You may be able to easily find the answer by looking on the Internet or by tapping into the expertise of a trusted friend, relative, or colleague. Moreover, when you find yourself in a situation where you cannot provide someone with an answer to their question or problem, you should not just say that you do not know and continue on your merry way. Instead, you should either propose alternative methods or solutions to their issue or attempt to place them in touch with someone who may be able to assist them. Never simply shrug your shoulders or "pass the buck."

While problem solving and issue resolution are mutual exclusive, they often accompany one another. However, problem solving is only one part of issue resolution. To successfully tackle a larger problem or issue, there are a number of steps you should take. First is to execute all the aforementioned problem-solving steps. You should then notify all of the people you may need to resolve the issue and ensure that they have all necessary information and resources at their disposal. The next wise step is to alert the appropriate people who may be affected by the problem along with any impacts it had, is having or will have as well as an estimated issue start and end time. Next, frequent and accurate updates should be provided until the issue is resolved, including a revised resolution time estimate. Once the issue has been resolved, you should close the loop by investigating the root cause of the issue to ensure it does not occur again in the future. Lastly, it is a great idea to document the issue and associated details. This information will not only be useful in the event the problem occurs again, but it can be extremely helpful in protecting yourself, your team, and organization from blame, losses, and legal action. However, the most important factor in any issue is be as open and honest as you can with everything, even if you are at fault, since any type of lying or covering up can cause a problem that may become bigger than the original issue.

Priorities

Prioritization is the organization of your tasks, actions and goals. For example, you may have to prioritize a simple list of daily chores to complete. On the other hand, you may need to secure a job, rent an apartment, and then buy a new car. Regardless of the complexity of the tasks, you should always try to apply common sense. Do not force yourself into a difficult situation by doing things out of order. Lastly, you should constantly re-evaluate your priorities at both the micro and macro levels. Having your priorities in order will hopefully lead to less stressful situations and reduced overhead on your immune system.

Having set priorities not only helps organize yourself but may also determine the timing that you need other people to act. If you have a list of items for someone to complete, you should include as part of the instructions or request the priority of each task. This will clearly define and set expectations for everyone. Keep in mind that not everyone has the same set of priorities. Lastly rather than trying to enforce your style or set of beliefs on someone else, respect the manner in which they get the job done.

Self-Assessment and Size Up

No matter who you are, where you are, who you work for, or what school you are in, you should always have a finger on the pulse of your colleagues and competitors. Just as you would not tackle an emergency situation without first sizing it up, you should avoid going through life like a piece of driftwood. This is not meant to be viewed as a negative trait or make you paranoid, but you should have an awareness of how you rank and fit into the bigger picture. You can use this method to highlight areas that you may need to improve upon or enter into for the first time. It can also help you evaluate if you are in an environment that has intellectual potential, or if it is a mental dead end. You should perform this self-evaluation on a regular basis to ensure that you do not get stuck in a scholastic or career rut.

Holidays

Holidays are special occasions that often bring people together for the day. However, holidays are more than just a day off from school or work and a reason to have a barbeque. Whether it is a religious or federal holiday, take the time to learn the history and reason for the occasion. Understand the reason why you eat turkey on Thanksgiving or fast on religious holidays. Lastly, be sure to pause for a moment to remember those for whom the holiday honors, as in the case of Memorial Day.

Representation

The moment you set foot out of your home, you become part of something bigger. You automatically become a representative or reflection of someone or something else. While you may be remembered for a positive action, you will definitely be remembered when something negative occurs. First and foremost, children are a reflection on their parents. This is true for everything from attitude to wardrobe. Behave as you would when you are not with us as if you were. However, there are many more associations to be concerned about other than the obvious. For example, when you don a uniform of any type, you become a representative of that school, business, or organization. Your actions have a direct impact on the reputation and image of the larger institution.

Other examples of representation can be very subtle. For example, if you are driving badly, you can quickly enhance a negative stereotype for your state when someone looks at your license plate. Furthermore, if you have an organizational license plate such as a firefighter or police, you are tarnishing the reputation of groups held to higher standards. Even if you have no clear physical ties to a group by what you are wearing or your surroundings, you will always represent the United States when abroad. America does not need any additional bad press, so please do not add to it. Always think twice about how you not only portray yourself but also the reputation of a greater organization, including your family.

Personal Involvement

Unfortunately, the world is not a perfect place. Most likely, on more than one occasion, you will find yourself in a situation that you wish you were not. Knowing when to get involved or stay out of a situation takes some experience. Furthermore, there are no hard and fast rules; however, there are some general guidelines that can help you make the best decision. When two or more people are having an argument, you should try to steer clear of it. Do not involve yourself in other people's business unless it is going to lead to someone becoming physically hurt. Whether you know the people or not, you should try and prevent abuse or violence from occurring, especially to those who may be at a physical disadvantage. You should never allow a child to be mentally or physically harmed. This can be an especially difficult situation which may require anything from extra finesse, as in the case of having an existing relationship with the people, to contacting the appropriate authorities. Another time in which you may find yourself getting involved is when the problem has become chronic. There are times when the victim may be afraid or accepting of an abnormal situation. In those instances, let them lean on you for support until they build up the courage to get additional, preferably professional, help.

On some occasions, you may find that instead of getting personally involved, the best position to take is to just give the other person, group, or organization enough rope to hang themselves. More often than not, people are their own worst enemy, so rather than getting your hands dirty, let them take care of the matter themselves. In the end, the situation will play itself out, leaving you unscathed and with the results you desire. Last but not least, there is the golden rule of things to avoid discussing in public: religion, politics, sex, and finances.

Cooking

Knowing how to cook and/or bake is one of the healthiest skills you could possess. It can be relaxing, challenging, and exciting all at the same time. Knowing what ingredients go into foods will help you eat better; you may be very surprised at some of the things that are in your food, including the quantity. In addition, if you cook at home, you will save money compared to eating out. Furthermore, since you are controlling what goes into your food, you can cook healthier and lighter. For example, you can easily and undetectably replace vegetable oil with applesauce when baking your next cake, brownies, or muffins. Once you are comfortable in the kitchen, you can start experimenting with different combinations and substitutions. Lastly, sharing the kitchen with someone else can also help strengthen bonds between family and friends.

When it comes to microwaves and plastics, there has been some controversy. Some argue that harmful chemicals leach out of the plastic and into your food while others say there is no evidence to support the claim. Therefore, the safest route to take is to err on the side of caution by only using microwave safe glass containers to heat food. As always, never place metal objects of any kind in the microwave; sparks and fire will instantly result if you do. By the way, the same controversy also surrounds plastics when containers, such as water bottles, are placed in the freezer.

Weather

While there is nothing you can do to influence or stop the weather, there are a number of actions you can take to be prepared for what Mother Nature doles out. Every season has potential for adding risk to your daily life. Even though you may not live in an area where severe weather occurs, you should be aware and understand all types of conditions. Anything can happen just about anywhere, and you never know when you may find yourself traveling to an area about to be affected by bad weather.

In the wintertime, ice and snow can cause serious injury, and even death if you are not careful. The best way to avoid any issues is to not place yourself in harm's way in the first place. Unless it is an emergency, there is no reason why you should be out on the road during a snow or ice storm. Instead, make sure that you have enough basic supplies in your home to get through any situation that may arise, such as a power outage. Snow and ice can build up on power lines, making them very heavy and causing them to snap like twigs. You should never go near a downed line even if you think it is not live. If you are stuck in your car with a line touching it, you have to jump clear of the car by not allowing yourself to come in contact with both the car and ground at the same time else you can be electrocuted. Lastly, never grab directly onto a person who is electrified since you will experience the same powerful results as they are. Instead, use a non-conductive object like a wooden/fiberglass broom handle or piece of lumber to move them away from the hazard.

At home, you should always have on hand a reasonable supply of bottled water, flashlights, batteries, and food that can be eaten with little to no preparation/cooking. Never use candles since they can easily start a fire. Sources of combustion can cause carbon monoxide poisoning, which can quickly and easily kill you. Carbon monoxide is a by-product of incomplete combustion and is a colorless and odorless gas. It will not be detected by electrically operated devices if the power is out or by battery-operated monitors that have dead batteries. Therefore, you should never use your stove or oven as a source of heat. Remember to open a window or door if you use a kerosene or propane heater and never run a fossil fuel powered generator indoors.

The springtime in many areas is one filled with heavy rains as well as melting snow. Therefore, you should always keep an eye out on deteriorating weather conditions since you may need to leave your house to escape rising waters. Flashfloods and fast-moving water can happen instantaneously, thereby leaving you little time to gather even the most basic of supplies, not to mention valuables and irreplaceable objects. Be aware of both your natural surroundings as well as any manmade objects that may cause water to trap you in your house. Melting snow can cause earth to be undermined and potentially lead to dangerous mudslides.

Never try to drive through standing water, no matter how shallow or easy it may look to ford. Your vehicle can easily stall, become stuck, or get washed away if waters are moving even lightly since your tires will act as ineffective floatation devices. If the water is deep enough, you can even become trapped in or stranded on the vehicle. It is not worth totaling your vehicle or tempting fate when you should just stay put or find an alternate route. On the other hand, even a small amount of water can be dangerous. Hydroplaning is caused by a combination of speed and a thin layer of water between your tires and the road surface. You can easily lose control of your vehicle if you drive too fast when the road is wet (even if it is not raining). Most vehicles are equipped with an Anti-lock Braking System (ABS) which will help you when hydroplaning, but it will not prevent it from happening altogether. The proper action to take in a hydroplaning event is maintaining steady pressure on the brakes until the car is once again under your control; do not "pump" the brakes as you would do in an older vehicle without an anti-lock braking system. Let the vehicle's computer do its job and never try to power through the situation by accelerating. While a dashboard light will most likely illuminate when the system is activated, you will hear and feel the affects of the system when it is invoked.

Hurricane season, officially June 1st - November 30th, can be instantly fatal. Never ignore local warnings and keep a close eye on weather predictions for the path of the storm. Even if you are not directly in the path of the storm, high winds and rising waters can prove just as deadly. Do not wait until the last minute to evacuate and be sure to prepare a list of items to take far in advance of any danger. Remember to pack medications and other irreplaceable items as well as ample supplies of food and water. Do not forget about special considerations for pets and babies such as formula and diapers. Your house is replaceable, but your life is not. It is also a good idea to double-check your homeowner's insurance policy for full coverage, including flood, wind, and hurricane, which may not be covered under your standard policy.

Tornadoes are even more difficult to predict than hurricanes, and therefore should be taken extremely seriously. While tornadoes are the most prevalent in the Midwest, they can occur nearly anywhere with the same deadly consequences. Where tornadoes occur with some frequency, local warning systems can help you prepare for such an emergency. Seek immediate and secure shelter if a tornado comes through your location. You may need to get a little creative in finding shelter while outside of your normal surroundings. For example, if you are stuck outdoors, you should tuck yourself in a ditch until the tornado clears the area.

To say the least, lightning storms can pose a great threat to your health. If you see lightning in the area or it is traveling in your direction, you should get indoors immediately. Just because it looks far away, that does not mean you are safe. If you are not able to get into a structure, seek shelter in a vehicle. If you are stranded outdoors with no means of seeking shelter, you should stay away from trees which can attract lightning strikes. You can improve your chances of survival by getting down on all fours. In this position, you will not act as a lightning rod and, if worse comes to worst, the electricity can pass through you in a relatively safer manner. Lastly, while indoors, it is a good idea to unplug electronics such as computers and televisions to avoid damaging the sensitive components and costly units.

Even when the sun is shining brightly above, you can be in danger. As the mercury starts rising, so does the potential for dehydration and heatstroke. Your body's natural cooling mechanism, sweating, can only work successfully to an extent, especially if it is very humid. Once you stop sweating, you are in definite trouble. You need to drink plenty of fluids, preferably plain water, to keep yourself hydrated. Interestingly enough, your body absorbs room temperature water quicker than cold water. Do not drink alcohol in any form since it will only further the effects of dehydration. If you need to work outdoors, take frequent breaks to reduce the stress on your body. Lastly, make sure that you apply sunscreen to protect your skin from the harmful rays of the sun and wear a hat whenever possible.

Losing Things

Misplacing or losing something can range from no big deal to devastating. In any case, it can be a frustrating experience which may lead to panic. However, as in the case of any emergency, you should remain calm and focused so you can tackle the challenge. You should begin your search by thinking back to the last time you saw or had possession of the object and work your way forward. Do not be embarrassed or afraid to stop and ask others if they have seen the item or to request their assistance in your search.

The importance of the item is directly proportional to how quickly you will need to act in finding it. For example, you may lose a pen or pencil which presents little to no problem even if it was your favorite. However, if you have lost a credit card or your wallet, then you need to act quickly. If you are not able to locate it within a reasonable amount of time, say two hours, you will need to begin protecting yourself. Hopefully, you have previously written down the customer service phone number for the credit card company so you know who to contact. If not, you will have to try and find the number online, which can waste valuable time. You should cancel the credit card and have a new one issued immediately. It may seem like an inconvenience but better to be safe than sorry. You should also confirm that no charges have been made on the card while it was out of your possession. Most credit card companies will only hold you accountable for a small amount before they forgive the remaining balance. If you lose your driver's license or social security card, you will need to contact the appropriate agency and have a new card issued as well. It may take more than just one phone call or visit to get a new card issued, but it is well worth the trouble compared to the problems that may be caused by future discrepancies. Lastly, you should consider signing up for a credit watch program, if you have not already, or manually keep tabs on your credit on a daily basis.

The worst-case scenario of losing something is a child. Unfortunately, this occurs far too often than it should, and it can prove to have horrible consequences. You should not let more than thirty seconds pass by before you alert an authority to your missing child. If you are in a store, you should notify someone who can have a manager lock down the building, hopefully preventing anyone from leaving with your child. Be sure to teach your children never to hide while in a store, especially in the maze of clothing racks. If you are in a public area, you should dial 9-1-1 immediately and provide the police with an accurate description of your child, including what they are wearing. Never be afraid to alert others since the slightest delay or hesitation can have fatal results; with any luck, your child will be located or surface on their own, and you can continue on with your life.

While there are dozens of inexpensive global positioning system devices on the market to provide you with directions, more than likely, you will find that you yourself are the lost item. You should not feel embarrassed having to stop and ask for directions, as long as you do it safely. Whether you are alone or with others, it is daytime or nighttime, you should stop in a relatively safe location such as a gas station to ask for directions. If the area you are in looks a bit shady, be sure to close your windows and lock your doors while searching for a safe place to stop. Use your observation skills to help you out of the jam. For example, utilize the little-known fact that odd-numbered United States routes usually run north/south whereas even numbered routes generally run east/west. Furthermore, to avoid running out of gas at an inopportune time, be sure never to let your fuel level go below three quarters empty. The fuel level rule is also important since you never know when an emergency will occur. The last thing you want to have to do is stop at a gas station to fill up on your way to the emergency room or animal hospital.

Keep It Simple

To be honest, the full phrase is "keep it simple stupid" (K.I.S.S.) but that is not very nice to say to someone. In any event, there is much merit to the old adage of "less is more." Regardless if you are hosting a party or designing a widget, you should try and keep things as simple as possible. While it is nice to "go all out" once in a while, for the most part keeping things small and intimate proves to be just as nice, if not better. In addition, the less complex something is, the less chance it will break or completely fail. Furthermore, usually the more simple the action, object, or event, the less expensive it will cost, initially and for future maintenance. Lastly, always keep your audience's style in mind since you can easily over do it and ruin your own efforts.

Appearance versus Reality

There is an old saying that "all that glitters is not gold." You need to make yourself aware of the various techniques used to make things appear one way when they are in fact made or based on something completely different. Hopefully, you will learn about them before experiencing them firsthand since they can be found in almost every aspect of life. This is not to say that you should turn into a complete Doubting Thomas, but you should know enough to ask the right questions and put it through the appropriate tests for authenticity and accuracy. For example, almost anything physical and non-tangible in the world can be counterfeited. Before you spend a large amount of money on an object or even a little on something that should cost a lot, you should do your research to ensure you are not being cheated or scammed. Chances are that if it is too good to be true, it is.

People also try to sell themselves under false pretenses. They may pretend either to have experience or knowledge on a subject, as in the case of many a resume, or put on heirs that do not fit them. People often forget where they come from and lose sight of what is really important in life. Do not be fooled or falsely impressed by the clothes people wear, the cars they drive, or the houses they live in; chances are, they are up to their eyeballs in debt. Try to avoid anyone who practices these forms of illusion since you usually cannot trust them as far as you can throw them.

Conflict

Conflict, while usually never good, is inevitable. How you react and handle conflict is paramount, whether on the offense or defense. Similar to anger, the obvious solution is to avoid conflict. However, that is not always possible, and in fact, it may be more beneficial to tackle an issue rather than letting it fester or pretending that there is no problem at all. If you do find yourself on the offensive, first try to resolve the issue calmly. It may require that you allow some time to pass so you can cool off, gather your thoughts, and formulate a sensible plan.

If you are in a defensive situation, first try to defuse the aggressor by talking through the issue. Try to work through the problem amongst yourselves, but in some cases you may need to bring in a neutral third party. They can be someone whose decision process and skills you trust and value, or if the situation warrants it, a legal arbitrator. Just as with anger, violence is never the solution.

Incompetence

Unfortunately, the world is not a perfect place, and part of the reason is because of incompetence. Incompetence is rooted in people and can be on an individual basis or within a group of people. Furthermore, incompetence can infect an entire company, organization, or institution. Public, private, for profit and not-for-profit companies as well as local, state, and federal governments can all have pockets of crippling incompetence that make forward progress come to a screeching halt. However, you can take one of two approaches when you come across incompetence. The first is to just complain about it and let it get in your way. Clearly this is the less desirable approach, but often it is the typical path taken by most people. The second, more preferred, method of dealing with incompetence is first recognizing that its existence is just about everywhere and then figuring out how to work around it to accomplish your task. It sounds like a simple concept, but you would be surprised at just how many people let incompetence stand in their way. Using the latter method will not only help you in your personal life, but it is an effective tool in the workplace as well. In fact, the success of your entire career may be based on your ability to deal with incompetence, as in the case of project managers. Think of incompetence as a speed bump that may slow you down, but never let it prevent you from reaching your goals.

Favors

Requesting and performing favors is as much a part of daily life as getting up in the morning. The intensity and duration of a favor can range from trivial and mere seconds to complex and very time consuming. Unless it is a trivial matter, before you ask someone for a favor, you should first make sure that you have exhausted all other possible means. By the same token though, you should never become lazy and rely on others to constantly do little favors for you either. Even before you approach someone for a favor, you should be prepared to return their goodwill in kind or better. There are any number of ways to repay a favor, including a similar level effort at a later time, an appropriate gift or token of your appreciation or an open-ended favor that can be "cashed in" at any time in the future. On the other hand, when someone asks you for a favor, you should be amenable when and if possible. Keep in mind that you should never request or perform a favor that is illegal, unethical, or inappropriate, including the abuse of relationships of those who may have access or influence over a given situation. Lastly, while you should always repay a favor performed for you, you should not automatically expect something in return for your efforts.

Secrets

Secrets can range from good to bad, but they all have one thing in common. Once it is known by more than one person in total, it is no longer a secret. An example of a good secret is a surprise birthday party, whereas a bad secret would be the fact that someone is embezzling from their company. In any case, you may be put in a position where you find yourself having to lie. Telling a little white lie is acceptable when the secret is in regards to something positive. However, you may find yourself telling bigger and more significant lies if the secret is negative in nature. Be very careful with your involvement in bad secrets since they could lead to direct guilt, especially with illegal matters. Be sure to distance yourself from such cases, but in some instances, you may find yourself having to decide whether or not to contact the authorities. Use your best judgment and be sure to associate with positive people to avoid getting yourself into awkward situations in the first place.

Advice

Whether you are on the giving or receiving end, advice can be a double-edged sword. Advice is not much more than an opinion, so you should treat it as such. Always factor in the source of the advice and weigh it against their character. It is always good to hear and consider advice, but do not listen to it necessarily; think of it as a suggestion and you should be fine.

On the other hand, you may find yourself in the position of giving advice to someone at several points in your life. It may be to a friend, colleague, relative, or your own child. In any case, be sincere and never be malicious or steer someone in the wrong direction. Base your advice on your own knowledge and experience and not on the opinions or beliefs of others.

Gratuities

A gratuity, better know as a tip, is a very important part of our culture and economy. Those few extra dollars are more than just a "thank you" for most service providers since it represents a significant portion of their income. The base pay for wait staff, taxi drivers, and delivery people, for example, is typically very low, so your generosity, or lack thereof, has a huge impact on more than just their feelings. For example, the standard minimum tip is 15% of your dining check. You can easily calculate the amount in your head by simply adding 10% of the total (just move the decimal place over to the left by one digit) to one half of that same amount. For example, if the bill came to $82.00, the tip would be $12.30 ($8.20 + $4.10). In some cases, a flat rate is a more appropriate method of tipping. For example, you may give a furniture delivery person $20. Whenever you are on the giving end of a tip, always round up or be extra generous; just put yourself in their shoes and think how you would like to be rewarded. On the other hand, if you are on the receiving end of a bad tip, do not become discouraged, but do review the situation to see if you in fact could have performed better.

Opinions

Opinions are like heads, everyone has one. However, the value of all opinions is not equal. You should view opinions as suggestions or recommendations but never as an absolute. Like advice, you need to first trust the source of the opinion. Next, evaluate the opinion in the context or experience that it was developed. The same situation may or may not apply to you, so look before you leap. Lastly, I would never turn down an opinion; just politely hear the person out. At worse, you may be able to apply the new information to a related or unrelated topic or take the inverse of it and put it to good use.

Statistics

Statistics are like opinions, there are thousands of them out there, and you have to question each and every one of them. Statistics can be made to fit almost any desired outcome. Whether it is the numeric value itself or the way it is presented, you should never take a statistic at its face value. In addition, you should always check the source of the data as well as who may have sponsored the study. This information, as well as the methods used to arrive at the final conclusions, is not always provided upfront. For example, if a pharmaceutical or tobacco company funded a study that becomes public, chances are the outcome will be in their favor. View unconfirmed statistics as propaganda until you have a chance to confirm their source, method of calculation, and assumptions/basis.

Success

Success is a relative term; it comes in all sizes and degrees. You may experience a small success by completing a task, or a large success such as graduating from college. Regardless of its magnitude, you should take pride in your accomplishment and set aside some time to appreciate and reflect upon it. Success is not determined by how much money you have, type of car you drive, or the size of house you own. You can be successful at any level and at any time. Also, be sure to take time to congratulate others in their accomplishments and encourage future success.

Tools

Having the right tools to successfully and safely complete a job is paramount. Granted you may be able to complete a task or job without the proper tools, but quality and the overall time it takes to complete the task may suffer. The term "tool" can refer to a literal item such as a wrench or screwdriver, or it could be non-tangible like training or a skill. Regardless of the challenge at hand, you should first evaluate the tools that you need compared to what you have at your disposal. If the task requires a physical tool that you do not have, you can purchase, borrow, or rent it. If the task requires a skill or training, determine if you can get yourself up to speed in time, or seek assistance from a trusted resource that can help you. If you are not able to acquire the proper tools, then consider delaying the project until you do. Furthermore, if you are not capable of completing the task due to lack of skill or experience, you should let people know as soon as possible to avoid getting yourself into a potential mess which could damage your reputation or inflict harm on others. Remember, safety is the first priority, so if you do not have the right tool or improper modifications are required, do not proceed.

Politics

As I have learned, if you have nothing nice to say, do not say anything at all. In this country, everyone is entitled to their own political views. Always remember to keep an open mind, and remember that political matters are personal to each individual. Aligning yourself with a specific political party may limit you to perspectives that you may not always believe in. Politics and logic, reality, and the truth do not always go hand in hand, which can often lead to frustration.

If you plan on or wish to get into the world of public service, you better make sure that you have a squeaky clean record and reputation; you and all your associations will be put under a powerful microscope where the smallest issue can be quickly and easily magnified out of proportion. Keep your nose clean, and never do or come close to anything that may hurt your reputation or image since appearance often becomes reality. If you do aspire for higher office, start off in smaller local roles and work your way up the ladder. You will also need to become a great salesperson to sell yourself and your platform. Lastly, never step on anyone on the way up since you may wind up falling down or needing their help in the future.

The Internet

The Internet, like any revolutionary force in the world, can be extremely helpful in daily life or could be used for evil purposes. On the positive side, you can instantly learn about any topic you can think of, and some you never thought imaginable. Within seconds, you can find the answer to a complex question or simply uncover the lyrics to a new song. New information becomes available for worldwide distribution in just seconds and has provided whole new categories of career paths for millions of people.

On the other hand, the Internet can have its dark side. Since it is open to just about anyone, you should always double-check the source of the information. Even sites that allow customer feedback or opinions could be the work of a competitor. The Internet is also a breeding ground for computer viruses and other malicious code that can cripple your system as well as infect people that you e-mail or share files with. All types of information, including pornography, is easily available, and therefore children's access to the Internet should be either regulated or supervised at all times. Avoid issues with blogs, chat rooms, and child predators by not allowing them into your house just as you would prevent a stranger from entering. Always check the security of a web site that you are performing transactions with to ensure its validity. Review any page that you are entering information on, ensuring that it begins with https:// or submits to https:// and not http://. Never download or install software from a questionable or unknown source. When in doubt, avoid it altogether. Lastly, always secure your own wireless network (if you are not sure if it is secured or not, chances are it is not, so get help right away), and never simply borrow or hop on someone else's signal since you might as well let them stand over your shoulder and watch you enter your user name and password when logging into your online banking web site.

With the Internet comes the use of e-mail. E-mail can be a great tool to keep in touch with someone as well as aid in distributing information quickly and cheaply. However, there are a few precautions that you will need to take when working with e-mail. First of all, never send personal or sensitive information in the body of an e-mail. Think of an e-mail as a postcard that can be viewed by anyone. Secondly, do not put personal or sensitive information in unencrypted attachments. Next, never open any e-mail or attachment if you do not know the sender; certain file types are more susceptible to having viruses than others. The target of a link in an e-mail or web page can be different from its label so do not be so quick to click on a link that looks legitimate. An authentic web site can be copied with a few mouse clicks, so just because it looks like the real thing, that does not mean it truly is legitimate. Lastly, protect your address book as you would any other piece of personal identity.

There are four key steps you should take to protect your computer, including your identity and personal information, from potential disaster. Even if you never browse the web, you should still follow these easy steps to insulate yourself from trouble. They will only take a few moments every so often, and most can be scheduled to occur automatically. First, make sure that your operating system (Microsoft® Windows for example) is up-to-date with the latest patches and updates. This will help protect the core of your computer but will not provide full coverage. The next important step to take is installing anti-virus software. This will protect your files and downloads from viruses. You should schedule or manually scan your hard drive(s) and download new virus definition profiles on a periodic basis to catch problems before they cause any harm. However, anti-virus software will not do it alone. You should also purchase or download spyware protection software. There are a few good versions available for free, but you should be extra careful since they themselves can contain spyware code. Just as you need to update your anti-virus program for the latest protection, you will need to manually or schedule the download of spyware protection updates. Lastly, you should back up your files on a regular (monthly) basis. You do not need to back-up every file on your computer, just the ones that you have created or saved since installing the programs. To facilitate this, you should create a new main folder or drive called "Data" and save all your files to that folder. This way you will have all the files you need in one central location. To help save space, you should compress and encrypt a copy of the Data folder/drive using a program such as WinZip® or StuffIt® before burning it to CD/DVD or copying to a portable media such as a flash drive. The most important part of creating a back-up is where you store it. Leaving it in a drawer next to your computer is not going to do you any good when there is a fire or robbery. Therefore, treat back-up files as if they were valuable jewelry by storing them in a hidden, bolted down, fireproof house safe. You can also store them outside of the house, but be sure that it is a secured location such as a bank safety deposit box. Lastly, whether available for a small fee or for free, I would not trust the security or reliability of your data to Internet-accessible storage web sites.

Music

Whether you are listening to music or playing a musical instrument, it brings great joy, excitement, and energy. There are so many different genres of music that there is something for everyone. You may not have an appreciation for all types of music, but you should at least expose yourself to each of them once in your life. Your taste in music can also change with age; something that you previously did not care for may become appealing later on in life and vice versa. Music can give you the energy to exercise or the motivation to tackle a difficult challenge or nagging task.

The ability to play a musical instrument is a wonderful talent to possess. You do not have to be predisposed to the gift in order to learn; practice is the key to success. You must be disciplined in dedicating some minimum time to frequent, consistent practice. As with most things in life, it is easier to learn when you are younger, but it is never too late to start trying. Lastly, learning to play an instrument is one of those things in life that you may not fully appreciate until you are older.

Dancing

Knowing how to dance is a skill that can be used for a lifetime. The only thing that dancing requires is music, and it can be done alone, with a partner, or group of people. It is a great form of physical exercise, builds discipline and can help expand your creativity through choreography. Dancing can be as challenging as any sport, as exhilarating as any victory, and as intimate an experience that any two people can have together.

Travel

Getting out to experience the world firsthand is a wonderful way to build on your experiences and education. You should take any opportunity you can to visit historical sites and museums, both close to home and abroad. It is also important to get to know your own country by visiting different landscapes and regions. This will help build pride and patriotism in your country and hopefully help you make a positive impact on society.

You should, however, always consider your personal safety and the stability of the region. If it is too dangerous, for any reason, you should look to make alternative plans. Weather can also play a huge role in your travel plans, so be smart about it. For example, do not plan a cruise to the Caribbean in the middle of hurricane season. Also, make sure that the trip makes an impression on you, but you do not leave your impression on the location. In other words, respect the environment and leave it the way you found it so others can enjoy nature the way it was intended.

Sex

Sex is not something that should be taken lightly or seen as casual. As a general guideline, if your age ends in "teen," you are too young to be engaging in sexual activities of any type. In case you are not certain, yes, oral sex is sex. Between the risk of catching a sexually transmitted disease, potential emotional consequences, and accidentally creating life, sex is not something that should be played with by teenagers. Only if you are a responsible, consulting adult should you be having sex. Make sure that you always take appropriate and adequate measures in protecting against unwanted pregnancy and diseases.

You should never feel pressured into having sex, regardless of the circumstances. Never feel ashamed or less of a person for saying no to someone. If you are raped or forced to have sex, you should immediately report the incident to the police. You should also try to preserve any evidence that could be used later on to prove a case, including skin cells under your nails, fibers, hairs, and bodily fluids such as blood and semen. As terrible of an ordeal as it may be, try to remember any scents such as cologne or deodorants and distinguishing marks such as tattoos, birthmarks, or scars. You should never live in fear of retaliation if you report the rapist to the police, and know that you will have the full support of your family and friends as well as other victims who have gone through a similar experience.

Religion

Religion is always an interesting and often controversial subject. While most people are born into a religion, it is something that is very personal. That is not to say that religion is for everyone; however, you should believe in something to some extent. Part of the purpose of religion is to help you lead a moral life, so if you chose not to believe in a particular religion, at least glean some aspects from all of them and be a good person. Whether you believe religion to be true or just a bunch of fabricated fables that tries to keep people under moral control is up to you to decide and discover on your own. Either life is just a series of connections and coincidences or there is some type of higher power at work.

Aging

As much as we would like to, there is nothing we can do to stop time. Aging does not affect all of us equally, and that is why it is so very important to take care of your mind and body while you are young. There are so many environmental factors that already take aim at us, so try not to add to the damage by voluntarily doing harm to your body with junk food or dangerous substances.

As we get older, our bodies and minds start to slow down. It is perfectly normal to start developing minor aches and pains like arthritis or an intolerance to dairy. However, you do not have to sit back and let nature get the upper hand. Continue to exercise within reason and keep your mind sharp by not becoming a couch potato. Avoid becoming a pharmaceutical company's best customer by taking care of yourself naturally or not letting problems develop in the first place.

Age is definitely a state of mind when it comes to your brain. The minute you stop learning and experiencing life, your mind will start to atrophy just like an unused muscle would. Keep a positive attitude regardless of the situation since you may start to see friends and family members developing illnesses or passing away. Be young at heart and it will be too.

Daily Affirmation

A daily or weekly affirmation can help keep you centered; think of it as a pledge to yourself. With all of life's hectic daily tasks and responsibilities, we can easily lose sight of how fortunate we really are and how many non-materialistic fortunes we own. Do yourself a favor by creating your own affirmation and posting it somewhere that you can see every day such as on your bathroom mirror. It does not have to be long or complex; in fact, it should be just the opposite. Be sure to maintain and update it as you travel through your journey in life. Here is an example of a simple, yet powerful affirmation that I turn to daily:

> I have two happy and healthy children.
> I am healthy, have a good job and a warm home.
> I have a loving family and friends who I can trust and rely upon.
> I lead an honest life on a "straight and narrow" path.
> I always act responsibly, with safety and reliability in mind.

Karma

While the concept of karma has never been scientifically proven, it does have its merits. Basically, it states that what comes around goes around. Karma is a pretty good standard to live by, and hopefully it will keep you in check. It strikes more often than not, so rather than tempting fate, it is best to lead a straight and narrow life... just in case.

Teaching "How to Fish"

There is an old Chinese expression, "Give a man a fish, and you feed him for a day. Teach a man to fish, and you feed him for a lifetime." Empowering someone, or better yet, a group of people to be able to help themselves is probably the single most important impact you can have on society. Successfully teaching others not only frees you up from performing the task yourself, but it also enables others to help themselves. Along with the literal affects of empowering others, you are also providing confidence and inspiration as well. Furthermore, with any luck, they too will pass on the ability to others. However, just as with any other influential force at your disposal, make sure that you are only propagating positive activities and never passing along harmful or destructive abilities.

Maintenance, Repairs, and Improvements

"Only when the horses have escaped do men repair the stable."
– German proverb

The purpose of this section is to give you a sense of what is involved in various types of projects and repairs. It absolutely does not mean that you should tackle a project or repair armed only with the knowledge presented below. Furthermore, no matter how large or small the job, you should always maintain a clean and orderly work site. Place tools you will be working with in one location and the materials in another to promote safety and reduce wasted time caused by searching for a tool or making unnecessary trips. Use a tarp or other type of mat to visually separate the work site from the tool and material areas. In addition, take the necessary steps to protect and secure tools and work materials by covering them with tarps or locking them away to prevent theft. Lastly, secure the site at the end of each day from potential hazards such as open holes/trenches, live wires, and construction debris.

It is always a good idea to purchase extra material, especially those that are inexpensive or will be used in large quantities. It will save you time in the event of a mistake or plan miscalculation and could be used on a future project or potentially returned to the store if unopened/unused. Having an extra two-by-four or pipefitting lying around may actually come in handy in an emergency. Moreover, be sure to clean, wipe down and/or maintain (oil, for example) tools so they remain in good working condition and do not pose a safety concern. Be sure to take the time to remove any unnecessary tools and materials from the site to reduce clutter and enhance safety. Finally, while no one will ever take more pride in your property and efforts than you, never take the "can't see it from my house" approach when working on someone else's home, vehicle, or business.

Vehicle Maintenance

While it is nice to support your local auto mechanic, it can become rather costly in no time. There are a number of minor repairs and replacements that you can perform on your own. They include changing light bulbs, lamps, air filters, and windshield wipers. You should always follow the recommended instructions found in your owner's manual. Always use the correct size and type of replacement parts, whether they are original equipment manufacturer (OEM) or aftermarket, the later of which are typically less expensive. Be careful to know the subtle differences in technologies so that you do not lessen the lifespan of a part. For example, when working with halogen light bulbs, you should never handle them with your bare hands. The oils in your skin can create hot spots which will cause the bulb to break prematurely.

The responsibility of owning a car does not end simply with driving. You should be able to perform light and emergency maintenance without the aid of others. Even though we have cell phones, there may be times when you do not have it with you, it is out of battery, or you cannot get a signal thereby leaving you stranded and on your own. Once you have been shown how to perform the following procedures, there is no reason why you should not be able to help yourself out of a bind.

Without a sound battery your car is nothing more than a two-plus-ton paperweight. A vehicle battery is very much like any regular cell such as AA, C or D. By the way, the accurate use of the term "battery" is when you have more than one cell (AA, AAA, C, D, etc.) together. The term nine-volt battery is used property since it is actually comprised of six 1.5-volt batteries put together in series. Your vehicle battery provides twelve volts of power;

however, the amps are much higher than a smaller battery could deliver. In addition, your car battery contains liquid acid, usually in the form of sulfuric acid, which can cause severe burns if it leaks or explodes. Basically, as long as you do not allow the positive and negative lines to come in contact with each other or allow the battery to become overheated, you should be safe from chemical and electrical risks. While you are working with the battery, you may see and hear little sparks coming from a terminal, which is normal when metal surfaces come in contact with each other.

You should check to make sure your battery is in good condition by visually inspecting it at the beginning of every season. Cold weather, for example, can reduce the chemical potential of your battery just enough to render it unusable. However, you may simply forget to turn off your lights one time, which can drain your battery significantly. Assuming your battery is in good condition, you should be able to jump-start your vehicle using a set of heavy-duty jumper cables and another healthy vehicle (type does not matter). There are a couple of different products on the market that allow you to charge your battery using the cigarette lighter port; however, you may require the heavy-duty capabilities that only jumper cables can offer. If your battery is more than five years old, you should consider replacing it once you get the car started. Follow the steps below to safely jump-start your vehicle.

You can perform the following steps by yourself or with the assistance of another person. However, you should keep anyone not involved in the operation at a safe distance behind the vehicles and away from any traffic.

1. Inspect your battery to ensure the housing is not cracked and no fluid is leaking out. If the battery is in poor condition, do not try to jump start the vehicle and replace it right away. To achieve a good connection between the cable lead and the battery terminal, carefully

clean off any loose debris from the battery leads using a dry paper towel. If you are not able to get a good connection, use a wire brush or sandpaper to remove the inhibitor.

2. Inspect the jumper cables. Ensure that wires are not exposed and the four connectors, known as leads, are firmly attached. The gauge or thickness of the cable should be significant since large currents will be flowing through the wires.

3. Open the hood of the healthy vehicle.

4. Hold the jumper cables so that none of the leads are touching one another. Place one of the positive leads (usually red) to the "good" battery. Both ends of the cable are the same.

5. Connect the other positive lead to the "bad" battery.

6. Connect the negative lead (usually black) of the healthy source to the good battery.

7. Connect the remaining negative lead to a metal part, such as the frame, of the bad vehicle.

8. Start the engine of the healthy vehicle first and then try to start the vehicle with the bad battery. If it does not start right away, give it ten seconds and try again. If repeated attempts do not work, the battery may need to be replaced or the issue is not related to the battery, as in the case of a broken alternator. If the vehicle starts, allow it to run for ten minutes which will give the faulty battery enough time to sufficiently recharge.

9. When you are ready to remove the cables, follow the above steps in reverse order. Be careful as not to let the leads touch each other.

10. After the battery has recharged, shut off both engines. Before the other vehicle leaves the scene, try restarting the engine with the

freshly charged battery to ensure the process was completely successful.

After five years or so, a vehicle battery's usable lifespan starts to come to an end. You may find a lot of powder forming around the positive (red) battery terminal. It will look like a white, yellow, or greenish powder that you should avoid contact with. If you do get some on your hands or skin, wash it off with copious amounts of water. Before you remove the old battery yourself, ensure that the battery housing is not cracked or leaking any fluids. If it is, you should take great care in removing it by wearing thick rubber gloves, or allow a professional to handle it. Never let the battery acid come in contact with any surface other than thick plastic or an absorbent material such as paper towels. Assuming the battery is intact, you will need to remove the positive lead from its terminal first and place it out of contact with any metal surface. Next, remove the negative lead from its terminal and place it to the side ensuring it does not come in contact with the positive lead. Some automobile components, such as airbags, can remain charged for several minutes even when the battery has been disconnect so always respect the electrical system of your vehicle. You can now carefully remove the bolts or other fastening devices that are holding the battery in place. Be careful when lifting the battery out of the vehicle since it can be a little heavy. Lastly, now that you can see the bottom of the battery, inspect it for any damage. Old batteries can be recycled, and you may be able to drop it off at the same store that you purchased the new battery. Never dispose of old or unused batteries in an incinerator or Dumpster[®].

Not all automobile batteries are the same. They come in all sizes and need to be matched by vehicle year, make, and model. Furthermore, depending on price, you can purchase a higher-quality battery that usually has more cranking amps (especially important in cold weather). To install the new battery, follow the aforementioned steps in reverse order. If the new battery is not the same size as the old and the leads do not reach, you may need to safely raise up the battery with a block of dense plastic. Before reattaching the vehicle's positive and negative leads, use a wire brush or sandpaper on them to achieve a clean connection between the lead and the battery terminal. Be sure that you do not reverse the leads; reattach them securely. Once the new battery is in place and all tools and other objects are clear of the engine, you can try starting the car. It should start up without a problem, but you may need to reset your clock and pre-set radio stations.

Antifreeze is the lifeblood of your engine. Without it, you would not get much further than the corner of the block. When used in the correct proportions, typically pre-mixed, it can protect from temperatures well below zero to well above boiling. It is mainly comprised of ethylene glycol, and it may have other additives such as corrosion inhibitors to bolster its durability. Ethylene glycol is poisonous but has a sweet taste which may lead animals or children to drink it. Therefore, you should always treat it as a hazardous material. There are other types of coolant that use propylene glycol as the main component, which is less toxic but is still not a hundred percent safe.

You should inspect the coolant level at the same time that you are inspecting your battery. The proper way to check the level is at the reservoir, not at the radiator. Be sure to check it while the vehicle is cold. Never open the radiator cap when the vehicle is warm or hot. You can be seriously burned by the hot liquid or steam. If necessary, add the proper type of coolant based on your owner's manual recommendations. In general, you should have the system flushed every few years depending on the type of coolant used. The coolant will "wear out" and can cause engine damage when the corrosive inhibitors no longer offer proper protection. Flushing the system should be done by a professional to avoid exposing the toxic coolant to the environment.

There may come an occasion when your cooling system develops a leak; hopefully you notice it before you get on the road. However, if you are already on the road, you should pull over safely as soon as possible to avoid irreversible engine damage. If you notice the engine temperature rising from the dashboard gauge, you can help alleviate a potential problem by turning on the heat. Granted it is the last thing you want to do in the summer time, but it may make the difference between getting stuck in the middle of nowhere and arriving at a reasonable location safely. If you do break down and have water available, do not use it since it will not be able to withstand the high engine temperatures. Do not try to add any foreign substance to the system to plug the hole since it can also plug up the engine as well. Depending on the location of the leak, you may be able to temporarily repair a hose with duct tape, which you should have in your emergency kit.

Knowing how to change a flat tire should be a prerequisite for getting your driver's license. There is no reason why you should have to wait for a tow truck and potentially pay a significant amount of money when you can safely do the job yourself in about ten minutes. Even if you are covered by an automobile club, the longer you are out on the road, the longer you are at risk of being struck by another vehicle or taken advantage of by a stranger.

As with anything you do, you need to approach changing a tire with safety. There are two main safety concerns that are tied to one another: being struck by another vehicle and vehicle stability. You will want to park your vehicle as far away from traffic as possible. However, you will also want to make sure that you have a strong foundation to lift the car upon. Otherwise, if you park your vehicle on a slope or on soft ground, it may fall off the jack, which could cause you major health issues and/or damage to your vehicle.

Furthermore, your safety can be affected by the side of the vehicle that you will be working on. You are at greater risk of being struck by traffic if you need to work on the driver's side of the vehicle if parked on the right shoulder. In either case, as long as it is safe, you may need to park on an angle or turn the car around so that you give yourself some additional protection. These are viable methods as long as the vehicle is not sticking out on the road and you do not have to enter into traffic respectively.

Follow the steps below and you will be on your way before you know it. However, check your owner's manual for details specific to your vehicle.

1. Put your hazard lights on to help prevent any accidents and make sure that no one is within or goes into the vehicle while you are working on the tire. Any passengers should remain off to the side at a safe location.
2. Check that you have a spare tire (and that it is sufficiently inflated), a jack, and lug wrench (also know as a tire iron). Some tires may use a special lug nut that requires an adapter "key" in order to be removed.
3. Remove all the tools and the tire from the vehicle. If your vehicle comes with tire chocks or wedges, use them to help prevent the multiple-ton object from rolling or shifting.
4. Put the emergency brake on to prevent the vehicle from rolling.
5. You may need to pop off a cover plate or hubcap to gain access to the four to six lug nuts. Use the lug wrench to loosen all the nuts halfway. If they are very tight, you can stand on the end of the wrench using one leg and your body weight to loosen them. Remember, righty tighty, lefty lucy.
6. Put the jack in the proper place and begin lifting the vehicle. Make sure that the jack is on solid ground (preferably concrete or asphalt)

and you are making a good connection with the hard-point under the vehicle. You can seriously damage the vehicle or create an unsafe situation if you do not place the jack in the proper location.

7. Lift the vehicle more than is required to remove the old tire since the new tire is fully inflated.

8. Ensure that the jack is stable before completely removing the lug nuts.

9. Remove the old tire and place it on its side halfway under the body of the car just in case the jack fails or becomes unstable.

10. Place the new tire on the vehicle.

11. Hand-tighten the lug nuts in a triangular pattern. This will ensure that the tire seats itself evenly.

12. Remove the old tire from under the body and slowly lower the vehicle.

13. Tighten the lug nuts all the way using the triangular pattern.

14. Replace the cover plate or hubcap if necessary and place all tools and the old tire back in the vehicle. Take a quick look around the vehicle to make sure you have not left anything behind.

Depending on the nature of the flat, you may be able to have it plugged or patched; otherwise the tire will need to be replaced. Any damage to the sidewall of a tire usually means that it will need to be replaced. In addition, if previous repairs have been made to the tire or it is significantly worn, you should replace it. If the spare is a full-sized tire, then you can use it permanently, thereby making the old tire the new spare tire. However, some vehicles have "donut" tires which are only meant to be used for fifty miles or less (enough to get you to a service center), and you will need to keep your speed under fifty-five miles per hour.

Once a season, you should also check liquid levels including windshield wiper fluid, oil, and brake fluid. Simply refill the windshield wiper reservoir to capacity with acceptable fluid. Never use plain water since it is subject to freezing and could potentially crack the transfer lines.

It only takes two minutes to check your oil level and quality. You should not depend strictly on any automated or onboard systems to warn you of dangerous oil levels. When the engine is cool, simply open your hood and locate the oil dipstick. Draw out the stick and wipe it with a clean paper towel. Reinsert it and pull it out again. This time, note the level of oil using the scale at the tip of the stick. Wipe the stick clean before reinserting. You should also notice how clean or dirty the oil is from the paper towel. New oil is a rich amber color, whereas heavily used oil turns dark brown or black. If you need to add oil, locate the cap on or near the engine and add only small amounts at a time. Wait a minute and recheck the level by repeating the above steps as many times as necessary. You never want to overfill your engine oil.

Changing your oil has become relatively inexpensive enough to have it done for you by a trusted local service center. Just be careful when they try to sell you other services or recommend that you replace other parts. In any event, you should have a basic understanding of how an oil change is done, especially if a leak develops. Before you talk about changing your oil, you have to realize that there are two main categories of oil, synthetic and conventional. For decades, conventional oil was used in almost every car. However, with engine enhancements, synthetic oil was developed to handle hotter temperatures and the additional punishment. Furthermore, oil is available in different weight/viscosity, with each vehicle requiring a specific type. The most common are 5W-30, 5W-40, 10W-30, and 10W-40 and a typical vehicle utilizes four to seven quarts per change. Lastly, the frequency of change also depends on overall driving patterns (city versus highway; city being more punishing) as well as the specific vehicle so be sure to check your owner's manual. Your engine's oil lifespan can range from 3,000 to 15,000 miles.

The first step to changing your engine's oil using the traditional gravity draining method is to make sure you have all the required items before you start. It would be a huge pain and waste of time if you had to pour back the old oil into your engine because you forgot something from the store. You will need the following items: the right type, weight, and quantity of oil, a new oil filter, a filter wrench, and a container to catch and temporarily store the old oil. The next step is to ensure that the vehicle is not warm or hot. You can receive serious burns if you come in contact with hot oil or touch hot metal surfaces such as the exhaust system.

Depending on the road clearance of your vehicle, you may have an easy time getting at things from underneath or a more difficult experience. You can use ramps to elevate the front end of your vehicle as long as they are properly rated. The only potential disadvantage to using ramps is that not all the oil may be able to drain due to the incline. In any case, engage the emergency brake to prevent the vehicle from rolling while you are underneath it. Never use the jack to elevate your vehicle or change your oil in a location where other vehicles may come into contact with you. Once you have access to the bottom of the vehicle, you can place the oil basin or container under the plug in the oil pan. With a ratchet and socket or adjustable/standard box wrench, loosen the plug enough so you can remove it by hand. Be careful when the plug finally comes out since the oil will begin to flow right away. Allow the oil to drain for a couple of minutes while you open the hood and remove the oil cap. Next, move the oil basin under the oil filter location and use the wrench to turn it counterclockwise to loosen. It is about the height of a can of soda with approximately double the diameter. Just like the plug, once loose, use your hand to remove it completely. A small amount of oil may also come out from the filter and/or engine.

Set aside the old oil for the moment and begin the process in reverse. Before installing the new oil filter, place a thin layer of new oil on the new filter's gasket. This will help ensure a smooth installation and proper seal. Tighten the new filter with the wrench, paying special attention so as not to over-tighten it. Reinstall the oil pan plug as well. Next, add the proper type and quantity of oil as recommended in your owner's manual. Be careful not to spill any oil on the engine or any other metal since hot surfaces will generate smoke if oil comes in contact with it. After a few moments, confirm the oil's level using the dipstick. Lastly, dispose of the old oil properly and never simply dump it down a storm drain or place in with regular household garbage. Otherwise, you are now set for another few thousand miles.

The brake fluid level can be determined by simply viewing its reservoir, which should have lines designating the proper range. You can simply add the appropriate fluid necessary if it is too low, but you should not have to make any adjustments under normal circumstances. Always add fresh fluid from a sealed, new container since moisture absorbed by the fluid can significantly affect performance. Furthermore, brake fluid is a nasty liquid which can be combustible and corrosive, so handle it with great care. If the level is too low or consistently needing to be refilled, you may have a larger issue such as a hole or leak in the line. Knowing that your brakes are a relatively important part of your vehicle, you will want to get the system inspected immediately if you suspect any problems.

Given the high price of gasoline, anything you can do to save on fuel costs quickly pays off. Tires that are under-inflated can cost you gallons in wasted gasoline a year. You should check the pressure in all four of your tire at least twice a year, if not with every season. Using a simple pressure gauge, you can determine if your tires are under-inflated, over-inflated, or just right. If you do need to add air, just visit your local gas station. They usually offer compressed air for free or for a couple of quarters. Simply press the nozzle against the tire's stem and activate the flow of air from the hose. It only takes a few seconds to inflate a tire, so be careful not to add too much air. You can always deflate a tire slightly by pressing on the pin in the middle of the tire's stem. Keep in mind that every vehicle requires a specific type and size of tire; therefore, tire pressures can vary from brand to brand as well as vehicle make and model. While you are checking the tire pressure, you should also do a quick check of the tire treads. A simple way to tell if you have enough tread left on a tire is to insert a quarter, with Washington's head down, into the tread gap. If you can see all of Washington's head, then it is time to replace the tire. By the way, the traditional method involved a penny, but that leaves too little tread to be safe. Be sure to check all four tires since they can all wear differently, especially front versus rear tires.

If your vehicle has almost any type of malfunction, one of the first areas that you will want to check is the fuse panel. Knowing how to replace a fuse can save you a ton of money in potential towing and mechanic fees. A fuse is typically made out of a strip of metal which will burn out, and therefore disrupt the circuit if there is an electrical surge. They are rated by the number of amps the circuit should not exceed and commonly range from ten to forty-five amps. Obviously the more power a component demands, such as the case with heated seats, the larger the amps required. However, you may be surprised at just how many items require a fuse, ranging from seat belts to the fuel system. A blown fuse may be a sign of a larger issue or may be an isolated incident that requires only simple replacement. Every vehicle is equipped with at least one fuse panel, and the location can vary greatly from model to model. Consult your owner's manual for the location of the panel(s) as well as the map or legend describing the fuse layout. Never try to defeat or use an inappropriately rated fuse when one burns out.

There are a number of miscellaneous fluids and other warning signs to be aware of from a maintenance perspective. Under normal circumstances, you should never need to add brake fluid, power steering fluid, or antifreeze. However, you should inspect their levels on a quarterly basis. You should also inspect your air filter, which can get clogged with dirt and debris and cause a reduction in air flow to your engine. Replacing it is a snap or two, literally. While under the hood, take a quick look at your engine belt, also known as a serpentine belt. Make sure it is not excessively cracked or worn, especially before a long trip. If it does need replacing, take it to a professional. Lastly, check your tires' air pressure on a seasonal basis since under-inflated tires can be a safety hazard as well as take away from gas mileage.

Depending on your vehicle, you may have taillights that are made using typical bulbs or, on newer vehicles, they have been replaced with light emitting diodes (LEDs). LEDs have an extremely long lifespan and you should never need to change them under normal conditions. However, front lights, high beams, and turn signals most likely use the older style bulbs that do burn out once in a while. Following the instructions in your owner's manual, you can quickly and easily replace them in minutes. Also, it does not hurt to have a few extra bulbs in your glove compartment, especially since you can receive a moving violation ticket if your lights are not functioning properly.

One other major and important maintenance item is your vehicle's braking system. The main components which require attention are the brake pads and rotors. The brake pads are designed to wear over time and will require replacing approximately every 30,000 miles under normal conditions. Typically, the front set of brake pads wear quicker due to design and the additional weight and force placed on them. In addition, the rotor or disc, which is what the pads come in contact with to slow down the vehicle, also become worn over time, but at a slower rate than the pads themselves. Rotors are made of durable metal, but the pads will cut into them over time. Therefore, when you change the brake pads, you will probably need to have the rotors cut so they can be balanced and operate properly. However, after some time, you will need to replace the rotors altogether if there is significant wear or damage. If you hear a grinding or metal on metal sound as you brake, you are in serious need of either new brake pads and/or rotors. Do not rely on the vehicle's onboard systems to alert you to a problem since sensors can fail as well. As you would expect, the rotors are more expensive than brake pads. This is another one of those jobs that you should always leave to the professions, even if only the brake pads need to be replaced.

There will probably be many occasions when you will need to transport oversized items in or on your vehicle. Even if you have the largest SUV, you may need to tie an object to the roof rack or secure a door that cannot be fully closed. No matter what you do, you need to transport objects carefully, not only for your own safety but for the safety of all those on the road around you. Be sure to use appropriate cords and straps to secure items, else find another way of getting the object from location to location. Never use tape, twine, or thin string to carry loads or expect them to handle high tensions. In addition, be careful to not allow the load to shift or become affected by head or crosswinds. Furthermore, realize that your vehicle can become top heavy, so take turns wider and slower. For heavy loads, leave more space between you and the vehicle in front of you since you may require longer braking times and distances. Lastly, you should also consider using your hazard lights to warn other motorists of your slow-moving vehicle.

For safety reasons, most, if not all, vehicles have "kill" switches which can cut off fuel lines and electrical power in the event of an accident or sudden jolt. Working in conjunction with the kill switches, your doors may be automatically unlocked to help aid in a potential rescue. It is important to know if your vehicle is equipped with such devices since they may prevent you from driving away from a minor accident. Consult your owner's manual for the location of the reset switches and additional details.

Call Before Digging

Whether you are performing work yourself or have hired a contractor to complete a project, anytime digging is involved, you must have all underground utilities marked out. Regardless of the size of the project, you always need to put the safety of your family and your neighbors first. For example, you may be digging a hole for a mailbox post, planting a tree, installing a sprinkler system, or building a deck. Even if you are working in your backyard, that does not mean that one or more utility lines do not pass through it. Always err on the side of caution since you can be held liable for damages caused by a lack of mark outs. Lastly, do not forget about other lines such as septic, sprinkler, swimming pool and landscaping lighting. It is best to map them out when they are first installed so you have a permanent record of their location.

Requesting a mark out is as simple as dialing 811 or visiting www.call811.com. You will be directed to the local call center, which will handle your request. There is no cost to you for this service, which will be performed by the utility companies themselves or a third-party contractor. Once a request has been filed, they will come out to your property, typically within a week, and using colored spray paint and flags, mark the approximate location of gas/steam/oil (yellow), telephone/cable television (orange), electric (red), sewer (green), and water lines (blue). Only after all the lines have been identified should you begin digging. Lastly, always ensure that you also have any required permits and/or inspections completed as part of the project.

Plumbing

Shortly after you move into a new home, you should locate the main water shut-off valve. Furthermore, you should make everyone in the house aware of its location in the event you are not home and an emergency occurs. It can be located just about anywhere but is typically found in a basement, crawl space, or garage. Once you do find it, you should test it to make sure it seals completely; when a water line breaks is not the time to test it. You may also have other smaller water shut-off valves throughout the house, such as for an icemaker, but they are not generally required by code.

Be sure to insulate any pipes that may be exposed to freezing temperatures. This will prevent pipes from bursting as well as precious natural resources from being wasted. You can quickly and easily purchase and install the pipe insulation yourself. It is typically available in several diameters as pre-shaped foam, complete with adhesive on the open end. Simply cut the insulation to fit the length of pipe and seal by joining the ends together. To insulate fittings, such as elbows and valves, make relief cuts in the insulation to promote proper coverage.

Plumbing is one of the easier types of household projects, but it can be the most frustrating due to pesky leaks. Furthermore, leaks caused by old age, freezing conditions, or poor workmanship can create thousands of dollars in damage quite quickly. Therefore, the secret to a good plumbing job is doing it right the first time, especially since we do not have x-ray vision to see through floors and walls once they have been closed.

In general, there are two types of material you will work with, copper and plastic. Polyvinyl chloride (PVC) and chlorinated polyvinyl chloride (CPVC) are two types of plastic that you can use instead of copper, depending on their application such as hot or cold water supply lines. You may also see or use acrylonitrile butadiene styrene (ABS), which is used mainly on drain, vent, and waste lines but follows the same general principles as PVC and CPVC. Both types of piping are typically available in two types of thickness or schedules. Schedule 40 is the standard thickness whereas schedule 80 has a thicker wall for higher pressure or harsher conditions. You may also use flexible lines when making connections to faucets and toilet bowls. Lastly, you may use parts made of various metals and plastics when making drain connections from sinks, tubs, and showers. However, the in the latter two cases, the connections are all made using standard threaded male and female ends.

Let us begin with the easier of the two materials, plastic. Basically all you will need is a hacksaw, PVC primer, and PVC glue. To make a connection, cut the pipe to length, leaving the appropriate amount of space for the pipe to join the fitting properly. Typical fittings include forty-five or ninety-degree elbows to make turns, couplings to join two pieces of pipe together, tees and crosses to split the flow of water, and plugs and caps to stop the flow of water. Before you start gluing any pieces together, make sure that you dry fit all of them. You may need to cut off a small amount of pipe if things are not fitting or lining up properly. Keep in mind that the dry fit can be a tight one, so avoid getting the pieces stuck in one another. Once you are ready to glue all the pieces, start at one end of the line and work your way to the other end. Using the PVC primer, apply the solvent to the outside end of the pipe as well as the inside of the fitting. Use as much solvent as you need to cover the parts, but be careful as it has a tendency to get everywhere if you are sloppy or rush the job. If the primer is tinted, usually purple, it will stain anything that it comes in contact with, so protect any surfaces you do not want damaged. Do not wait for the solvent to dry. Next apply the PVC glue in the same manner as the primer. You should work at a slightly faster pace with the glue since it dries quickly. Attach the two parts and hold them together for at least ten seconds. They have a tendency to push apart so mild, steady pressure is required until the glue begins to cure. Wipe any excess glue from the new joint. Repeat as many times as necessary to complete the job and wait one to two hours before flowing water through the section of pipe. You can work on a few connections at a time, but be careful not to let the glue dry or allow the fittings to become misaligned. One trick is to use a permanent marker to draw a straight line on both the fitting and the pipe when you are dry fitting them so you can quickly and easily line them up when the primer and glue have been applied. After you are done with the project or repair, be sure to close both the primer and glue containers tightly and store them in a safe, non-flammable location.

Working with copper pipes and fittings is a little more labor-intensive than PVC, though it follows similar procedures. You will need a pipe cutter, sandpaper and/or wire brush, flux, solder, propane cylinder (typically blue in color) with a valve, and a lighter or other ignition source such as a sparker. It is also helpful to have on hand a bucket of water with a cloth towel to quickly cool parts and a small piece of sheet metal to use as a buffer in preventing wood or other materials from catching fire from the torch's flame. If you are adding a section of new pipe to an existing line, you will need to shut off the water supply at the nearest point or at the main shut-off valve in the house if no other local shut-off is available. You will need to drain the line of all water before you try to make a new connection. Otherwise the water in the line will absorb the heat by turning the water into steam, and you will never get a solid seal. It is helpful to open up any faucets at the same level or above the line you are cutting into to purge residual water. Lastly, if you are not able to get all the water to drain from the line, you can temporarily plug the line using white bread (sans crust). It will hold back the water long enough for you to complete the new connection and then it will simply wash away once you open a faucet.

To cut the pipe, you can use a pipe cutter for quick and clean cuts. Technically, you could use a hacksaw, but it will take more time and will not produce a nice clean cut. Next, you will need to clean the surface of the pipe and the inside of the fitting of any oxidation or corrosion. Clean the surface until it is a shiny copper color. Next, apply flux using a small brush to both the outside of the pipe and the inside of the fitting. The flux will help the solder flow around the parts to make a complete seal. Fit the two parts together and ignite the propane torch. Unwind a six to eight-inch length of solder wire and apply the heat to the fitting (not the pipe). It may take ten to twenty seconds or more to sufficiently heat the pieces so that the solder will easily flow into the gap between the parts. Once hot enough, remove the flame from the fitting and touch the solder to the joint. The solder should easily flow into the gap; any excess flux and solder will flow out and could cause burns, so be careful to protect your eyes and skin. Lastly, you can either submerge the parts in a bucket of water or place a wet towel around the area to cool the parts. Unlike plastic, you can flow water through copper pipes immediately.

One minor maintenance task when it comes to plumbing is cleaning out your traps. A trap is the U-shaped part of the drain under a sink, shower, or bathtub. It is designed to hold a small amount of water so that waste gases do not back up into your house. However, due to its shape, it can become clogged easily, especially by long hair or food particles. When you notice water taking longer to drain from a sink, it is probably time to clean the trap. However, you should try to be proactive and clean them out every six months or so; you can use the change in daylight saving time as your guide. If you perform the routine maintenance, you can avoid a clogged drain problem at an inopportune time as well as eliminate the need for harsh chemicals that are neither good for your pipes nor the environment.

Traps are made of either plastic or metal; however, they operate in the same manner. Simply clear out the area under the sink and get a small bucket and towel ready to catch any residual water. Then loosen the two rings at the ends of the trap either by hand or with a large wrench; remember, counterclockwise to loosen, clockwise to tighten (think of the cap on soda bottle). Remove the trap and clean it as best you can. Do not place the debris in the toilet; instead throw it in the garbage. Once clean, reconnect the trap and open the faucet to allow the trap to refill with water. Check for any leaks before you put the cabinet back together. If you find that the drain is still slow, you may need to remove the drain plug arm from under the sink. Sometimes, hair and other debris becomes caught in the small arm that is used to move the drain plug up and down. It only requires loosening one other nut above the trap to remove the arm. Lastly, you can clean out the faucet aerator screen of any debris that might cause the water to flow slowly or in an uneven pattern. Simply unscrew the fitting from the faucet using your hand, special adaptor that came with the faucet, or a pair of pliers. If you use pliers, you should line the teeth with a cloth or paper towel as not to damage the finish of the fitting. Rinse out the screen and replace by screwing it in clockwise.

For stubborn or inaccessible clogs, you may need to use physical means to unblock the drain. A drain snake is a length of coiled metal that you feed through the drain lines to loosen any clogs. They typically come in twenty-five to fifty-foot lengths, which should be sufficient for most applications. In addition, you will most likely have other clean-out ports in your drain system which can be accessed by unscrewing the plug from the drainpipe. They are typically found both between the main drain line and your sinks, tubs, and showers as well as on the main drain line itself.

A common job that you can easily do yourself is connecting an icemaker water line to your refrigerator. Any home improvement store will have the kit that contains all the parts you will need to complete the job. You will not even need to turn off the water to complete the small project. You will only need an adjustable wrench and screwdriver in most cases; however, you may need to drill a couple of small holes to route the tubing from the water source to your refrigerator. In that case, just make sure you use the correct type of drill bit for wood, plastic, masonry, ceramic, or concrete and drill a hole slightly larger than the tubing diameter, which is usually one quarter of an inch.

There are two ends to the water line, the water source and the connection to the icemaker. Start at the refrigerator end and connect the tubing to the fitting. To make the connection you will need three parts. The first to go on the end of the tubing is the nut, which is usually made of brass. The next item to go on the tubing is the ferrule. It is a small plastic washer-like fitting that makes a watertight seal once the nut is tightened. Lastly, insert the small metal tube into the end of the tubing. This will prevent the tubing from begin crushed as you tighten down on the nut and ferrule. Simply screw the nut onto the male end of the refrigerator and tighten firmly but do not over-tighten. As you are tightening the nut, make sure that the tubing does not slip out from the nut. Next, route the plastic tubing as necessary to the water source.

You will be attaching the other end of the tubing to a cold water line, so be sure not to mix things up with a hot water line. You will need to locate a cold supply pipe, typically three-eights to three quarters of an inch in diameter. Then make sure that the valve is completely closed on the new water line saddle. Place it around the pipe and tighten the two screws on either side evenly. As you do so, the metal spear on the saddle will pierce the water supply line. Once you have tightened the two screws completely, you can attach the other end of the plastic tubing to the saddle using the same method as before. Then, simply open the valve on the saddle to let the water flow through. Check for any leaks, but you should have no problems the first time through.

Electricity

For some reason, electricity seems to scare people. Just like anything that you do not know much about, you should respect it but never fear it. You can quickly and safely make a number of minor repairs and changes with ease, all without having to pay an electrician hundreds of dollars. There are two basic concepts that apply to all electrical work. The first is to always work with the power turned off. You can easily shut off the power to the switch, outlet, or fixture you are working on using the correct circuit breaker or fuse. All homes have a circuit breaker or fuse panel, which can be located just about anywhere in the house, including the garage or basement. Breakers/fuses are rated by the number of amps they can withstand. Common values are 15, 20, 30, and 50 amps. They act as shut-off valves for the flow of electricity as well as protecting you from any power surges or overloads. Special breakers known as ground fault interrupters (GFI) are required in wet and outdoor areas and can protect you from accidental shock or worse. If the breakers or fuses are not labeled, you should make it a mini project to map all switches, outlets, and alarms to their corresponding breaker/fuse. Mapping the panel is easiest to do with two people and a couple of cell phones, but it can be done by yourself with the aid of a loud radio. This will not only save you time with the next repair, but it can be a tremendous help in an emergency situation.

The second fundamental electrical concept is: white to white, black to black and ground to ground. It may sound simple, and it basically is. When working with electricity, whether alternating current (AC) or direct current (DC), you need to connect the positive to positive (usually black or sometimes red; also known as hot), negative to negative (usually white and also referred to as neutral) and the ground wire to ground line (usually bare metal or covered in green sheathing). Crossing lines can cause a problem if not stopped by a fuse or circuit breaker. Furthermore, never touch a live line with anything metal, your bare hands or with water, even if a GFI outlet or breaker is in place. Ground wires should always be used and not simply snipped off since they direct surges of electricity, as in the case of a lightning strike, safely down to the earth (hence the name "ground"). If you have any doubts about what you are doing, do not hesitate to ask a trusted and reliable source for advice, including staff at your local hardware or electrical supply store. You can also find additional details in any number of do-it-yourself books or web sites, which usually present multiple scenarios to fit your specific situation.

To replace a regular switch, you will need to first make sure the power is off to that line. When you remove the cover plate, you will probably see two wires screwed into the side of the switch or coming into the switch from the back. There may also be a ground wire attached to the switch. Basically what

246

is happening is the switch is stopping the flow of electricity from either the positive or negative wires but not both. If the switch is a three way, where two switches can control one outlet or fixture, you will have one additional wire. Essentially all you need to do is move the wires one by one from the old switch to the new switch, ensuring a tight connection. When complete, reattach the switch to the box, but do not put the cover plate on until you test your work. Turn the electricity back on at the breaker/fuse panel and confirm that the switch is operating correctly. There should not be any sparks, smell of burning plastic or excessive heat coming from the switch. Also, you can replace a normal switch with a dimmer switch with the same ease. There is only one additional factor to a dimmer switch though. They are rated by the number of watts that it will be connected to it. For example, if you have a fixture that has four sixty-watt lights, you need to make sure that the dimmer is rated for a minimum of 240 watts. Always round up to the next highest rating when purchasing a dimmer switch so in our example a 250-watt or 300-watt dimmer switch would be appropriate. In addition, dimmer switches give off much more heat than a regular switch, so do not be alarmed as long as it is not extremely hot. Lastly, be careful not to arbitrarily break off any metal tabs on the side of the dimmer switch since those are used to safely dissipate heat.

Replacing an outlet takes only a bit more effort than a switch. Instead of only working with a positive or negative wire, you will be working with both. Basically, there is a positive (black) side, a negative (white) side and the ground. Simply replace each wire as you would with a switch. Furthermore, if the outlet is connected to a switch, you can easily have the top outlet always on and the bottom outlet controlled by the switch or vice versa by simply breaking off the small metal connector tab on the hot (black) side of the outlet. The half that is connected to the hot wire will always be on, regardless of the switch's position.

If for some reason a breaker will not reset itself and there are no other known issues, you may need to replace it. It is not a difficult task to perform at all. First you will need to purchase a suitable replacement. It does not need to be the same brand, but it should be the same type including amps, throws, and poles. You can always remove the old one first and bring it with you to the hardware store so you can match it up exactly. To remove a breaker, first shut off the main breaker at the panel. Never work on the main breaker(s) themselves since the lines you are working on will remain energized. Then remove the cover to the panel to fully expose the breakers. A breaker only has one wire, the hot or positive, connected to it. It connects to the neutral or white line by the blade on the panel fitting into the slot on the breaker. Remove the breaker by pulling it towards you from the outer side. Next, loosen the screw to remove the hot wire. Place the hot wire into the new breaker and secure it by tightening down on the screw. Reinstall the breaker into its slot in the panel in the off position. Turn the main breaker on and then turn on the new breaker. Once you have confirmed it is working, reinstall the panel cover.

There may also come a time when you will need to run a new line or tap into an existing line. Both are relatively easy to do, with the biggest issue usually the routing of the wire itself. Depending on the existing load of a circuit, you may be able to tap into a line. The main factors when adding to an existing line include the power demands of the new items, the power demands of the items currently on the line, the amps of the breaker and the gauge of the wire. Wire is rated by how many volts and amps that can safely pass through it. Residential wire is typically made of either aluminum or copper. Copper is preferred since it can carry slightly higher loads when compared to the same gauge of aluminum wire. The gauge or thickness of the wire is very important from a safety point of view. The thicker the wire, the higher the loads it can handle. However, do not get confused since the higher the gauge number, the thinner the wire's diameter. In residential situations, you will commonly find ten, twelve, and fourteen-gauge wire used for most circuits. Wire, including extension cords, should never get hot. If it does, that means that the draw is too much for the wire to handle and the item should be shut off immediately to reduce the risk of fire.

When evaluating the items on the existing circuit, you can quickly get an idea if you can safely add to it. If you have a washer and dryer on a line, then adding to it is not feasible. You should never put anything on circuits that contain heat, smoke, fire, or carbon monoxide detectors. However, if the circuit only has a few low-wattage lights on it, the breaker is rated at fifteen or twenty amps and the additional load is minor such as a light or fan, chances are you can add to it safely. There are a number of ways you can add to a line if all the prerequisites are met; however, always check with your local electrical codes and Engineering Department before performing any work. Depending on the specific conditions, you may be able to start the extension from an existing outlet or splice into the line itself using a junction box. When extending the new line, be sure to use appropriate hardware, the proper gauge wire, and fasten the line where required.

If you are not able to safely add to an existing line, you may need to run a new circuit from the main panel or a sub-panel. The main concern is if you have enough service coming into your house. Depending on the size of the home and if the appliances/utilities run completely on electricity or also use natural gas or propane, the amps coming into the main panel can vary. Typically residential service ranges from 100 to 250 amps, but you can always have the electric company supply more amps to you; just be sure you increase the main breaker amps appropriately. Assuming you are in good shape, you will just need to add a new circuit breaker to the panel. Use the same simple procedures as outlined in the section for replacing a breaker. Then run and secure the new line as needed. Never make sharp turns or allow the sheathing to become ripped or torn, thereby exposing the wire, which can cause a short or fire hazard. Just as when you are adding to an existing circuit, be sure to use the appropriate hardware required, including boxes, covers, and connectors.

Nearly every electronic device these days is either powered or charged using a wall or car adapter. However, just because the plug of one charger fits into another device, that does not mean it is safe to use. There are two important compatibility factors when it comes to chargers. The first is the output voltage, which can have a wide range but is always lower than the input voltage, typically of 120 volts. For example, the output voltage could be designed to match that of what batteries would otherwise generate. The second factor is the number of amps. Amps for typical applications are in the milliamp range. Both values can usually be found on the charger itself, but it is not uncommon for two products from the same manufacture to require different chargers. If you are not sure of either the voltage or amps coming from the charger, then do not use it in another device. Using the inappropriate charger can cause a wide range of problems, including the device not working, permanent damage of the sensitive electronics, and fire.

Natural Gas Lines

Working with natural gas lines can be dangerous but is actually very safe and simple as long as you know what you are doing and follow a few key steps. Relocating or extending an existing gas line is a relatively simple job but could easily cost you hundreds of dollars if performed by a licensed professional. However, you should never work with any utility unless you have been taught by an experienced person and have performed representative tasks under their supervision. Just as with electrical work, always check with your local Engineering Department for all applicable codes and regulations as well as the need for any permits and inspections. Before working on any type of gas line, be sure that the flow of gas has been cut off and will not be inadvertently turned back on while you are working with the line (i.e. lockout/tagout). Clearly, you should never smoke or have any source of sparks or open flames in the general work area. Serious, even fatal results can occur if safety is not made the top priority. If at any time during the project you smell gas, immediately get out of the area and confirm that the gas has not been accidentally turned back on. If at any time you feel the situation getting away from you, dial 9-1-1 so the fire department can stabilize the incident.

Before you break the first connection, you should ensure that there is adequate ventilation to allow the residual gas to purge from the system. Natural gas in its raw form is colorless, odorless, and lighter than air. Suppliers add mercaptan to the gas to give it a detectable scent which smells like rotten cabbage. Residential gas lines are comprised of heavy-walled steel pipe that have threaded ends. Typical diameters are three quarters of an inch but main supply lines are larger. Flexible lines are typically used to connect a rigid line to an appliance such as a water heater, dryer, or fireplace. In addition to straight pipes, fittings and valves are used to make turns and connections and allow you to safely turn on or off the flow of gas respectively.

The basic connection consists of a male threaded end, typically a pipe, and a female threaded end, usually a fitting or valve. In order to reduce the risk of leaks, you should always apply a strip of Teflon® tape or pipe dope formulated specifically for gas lines. Wrap the strip of tape around the male threads in a clockwise manner. Screw the male end into the female end until snug (remember, righty tighty, lefty lucy). Be careful when joining two components as not to cross thread the connection. If this happens, you should immediately discard the parts so they are not accidentally used in the future. Once the two parts have been joined, use two appropriately sized pipe wrenches to completely tighten the connection. Never over-tighten a connection or leave it too loose. Believe it or not, that is pretty much all there is to it. You would simply repeat the connections until you have completed and secured the line. You should also include a shut-off valve if you are adding a new segment of pipe for code and/or convenience reasons.

When you have finished your work and have completed the circuit, you will need to test for leaks. Ensure that the line has been ended properly before turning the gas back on. You should check every connection at least twice with a proper detection agent. Good old soapy water will quickly show any leaks though. If there are any leaks, you should shut the gas off immediately and fix the connection. Repeat the testing procedure until all the connections have been confirmed.

HVAC

When it comes to your home's heating, ventilation and air-conditioning (HVAC) system, there are a few important maintenance items that you should be on top of. The easiest but one of the most important is the air filter. Central heating/cooling air filters typically require changing or cleaning anywhere from once a month to every three months. They are available in various qualities, but I highly recommend spending the extra money to get the best, especially if you have allergies or pets. If you think spending twenty dollars on a filter is expensive just wait and see how much it costs to have all your ducts cleaned. Every unit is slightly different but the filter is usually readily accessible. Before you install the new filter, use a marker to right down the date on which it should be changed in case you forget. If you have a window or wall-mounted air conditioner, simply wash or vacuum out the foam air filter.

If you have central air-conditioning, you may have a condensation pump that discards the humidity pulled out of the air. The small pump tends to become clogged over time, especially if the unit is located in a basement. You should check the pump and transfer lines to make sure it is clean in the beginning, middle, and end of the warm season. You may be surprised at just how much water is in summer air which could quickly cause water damage to the surrounding area if there is a blockage. Conversely, for the dry winter months, you may have a humidifier for central heat. Often dissolved minerals in the water cause the mechanisms to clog, rendering the humidifier useless. Check the unit at the same intervals as you would the condensation pump for optimum efficiency.

In addition to the HVAC system, you should also consider adding to your maintenance list the hot water heater if you have a standalone gas or electric unit. Generally, there is not much maintenance required, but you can help prevent a few mini disasters. First, you should ensure that there is no debris, especially paper or flammable liquids, near the water heater. There could be a sizable open flame in addition to the pilot light at the bottom of the tank, which can act as the source of a major fire. Furthermore, check to make sure that the exhaust vent is not in contact with combustible materials since it can become hot too. If you do not have a whole house water filter in place, at the beginning of every season, you should bleed off some of the water from the bottom of your hot water heater. Otherwise dirt, sand, and other debris can build up at the bottom of the tank, causing hot spots and uneven heating which can lead to the tank cracking or rupturing prematurely. This can become a major problem if you do not catch it immediately as cold supply water will continue to flow all over your basement, first, or second floor until it is shut off. Typically, there is a valve or spicket at the bottom of the hot water heater unit. Simply place a small bucket under the opening and allow the water to flow for a few seconds. Hopefully, any dirt and debris that has accumulated at the bottom of the tank will be flushed out. Be careful not to burn yourself with either the hot water or steam.

Another precaution you can take is to replace the unit before it causes any problems. While there is no specific lifespan for hot water heaters, you can expect that once it reaches its tenth birthday, it may be well worth replacing it early. However, double-check your specific model since some units only have a six or nine-year tank warrantee. Otherwise, water damage can ruin all types of objects, including irreplaceable memories packed in boxes, and even cause potential structural issues. Regardless of the age of your tank, I would greatly advise that you install an automatic shut-off valve on the cold water supply line. For about $100, a sensor will detect water on the floor in the event of a leak which will send a signal to the valve to close until you attend to it. The monitors are even equipped with an audible alarm to notify you of an event. Therefore, at worst, you should only have a flood equal to the water held in the tank, which you can contain by building a small dike using concrete blocks. One of your last options is to have a drain system that can either direct the flow of water into the wastewater system of your home or, if the hot water heater is located in the basement, divert the flow of water into a secondary drain such as a sump pit.

Replacing your hot water heater sounds like a big project but can be done in minutes. You may wish to consider installing a tankless water heater that generates hot water on demand. These units are more expensive initially, but they could save you money on utility bills since water is heated only when called for rather than having to maintain forty or fifty gallons of hot water all the time. Tankless units can also last two to three times longer than conventional water heaters, plus you do not have to worry about a tank rupturing. If you plan on going the tankless route, just make sure that your electrical system can handle the extra demands that the unit will require if not using a gas-powered unit. The main disadvantage of tankless water heaters is the heat transfer mechanism becoming fouled by impurities in the water, such as dissolved minerals, which can greatly reduce the efficiency of the unit. The main steps to changing a tank unit are as follows; just be sure you have all the necessary tools and hardware before beginning the job. Keep in mind that most towns require a permit to replace a hot water heater. First you would need to close the valves for the cold water supply coming into the unit as well as the hot water line leading out. Next, turn off the pilot flame and shut off the gas or electric line that acts as the heating source. Drain the tank of any water and disconnect the gas or electric line. Using a pipe cutter or hacksaw, cut the two water lines below the valves, and unscrew the remaining pipe segments from the old unit, which can be reused on the new one. Move the old unit out of the way and position the new unit into place. Follow the same steps in opposite order to reconnect the unit. The longest step remaining is to install the couplings which will rejoin the two water pipes.

Painting

It seems to be that people are from one of two schools of thought when it comes to painting. They either love it or detest it. However, given the high costs of hiring a professional painter, picking up a paintbrush and roller quickly becomes a reasonable alternative. There are some important factors to keep in mind before beginning any painting project.

Before we talk about painting, we first need to discuss paint itself. Paint comes in various types, and your selection should be based on where and to what it is going to be applied. Most paint is typically available in at least one of three container sizes: quart, one gallon, and five gallon. You may also be able to purchase small samples in case you are not a hundred percent sure of the color you want to use. Some paints may also be available in a spray can for specific types of applications. For interior use, a water-soluble, latex-based paint is appropriate. For outdoor use, you can either use a water or oil-based product which may be a paint or a stain. Stains are available in various opacities ranging from near transparent to completely opaque. Paints are also available in a variety of finishes ranging from flat to very glossy. Available finishes typically include (in order of gloss): flat or matte, eggshell, satin, semi-gloss, gloss, and high gloss.

Most paint actually starts off its life as a white base to which small quantities of tint are added to make any color imaginable. One of the benefits of water-based paints is easy cleanup with little impact on the environment. However, their durability is usually less when compared to oil-based paints. Oil-based paints and enamels require solvents for cleanup and contain higher levels of volatile organic compounds (VOCs) which evaporate to the environment as the paint dries. These compounds can contaminate air, water, and soil and are therefore a less favorable option.

You should always allow yourself enough time to complete a painting project since stopping in the middle or part of the way through is not an option. You should also protect any items you do not want to get paint on, including the floor, by covering them with a tarp. Remove as much extra clutter from the location to give yourself an open and safe area to work in.

Before you even crack open the first can of paint, you should make sure that the walls are smooth and clean of any debris, including flaking paint, dust, dirt, and oils. Take special care when removing any type of paint that may be lead-based. If you do need to remove lead-based paint, be sure to protect yourself with a mask or respirator as well as the surroundings from becoming contaminated. Lastly, patch any holes or other damage with Spackle®. Keep in mind that the glosser the paint finish, the more imperfections will stand out.

Now that you are finally ready to paint, you should determine where to begin. You should try to start in a corner and work your way around. You will need a three-inch brush to paint small areas and the wall or ceiling where the two meet. If you do use masking or painters' tape, be sure to remove it before the paint dries, otherwise you will have a big mess to fix. A smaller one-inch brush comes in handy for tight places, including corners.

You will need a full-sized roller to apply the bulk of the paint. Apply the paint in long, even strokes for maximum distribution and quality results. Use the roller in straight up and down motions to achieve the best finish. Never get too far ahead of yourself with either tool since the cutwork can dry to a different shade than the rest of the wall if not done together. Never go back over half-dry paint with wet paint; if you do, the finished texture and color will be off from the rest of the area.

You should clean up any splattered paint as soon as possible. Extend the life of rollers and brushes as well as help the environment by washing them out promptly and completely. Allow them to dry without being crushed or deformed and store them in a clean, dry location. When it comes to oil-based paints, stains, and urethanes, there is one trick that you can use to save time and help preserve the environment. If you need to apply multiple coats to a surface, you can reuse the same brush without having to clean it with harsh chemical solvents. Simply place the brush in an airtight plastic freezer bag (remove any excess air) and put it in the freezer. When it comes time to apply the next coat or do touch-ups, simply allow the brush to warm up for a few minutes and you will be back in business. By the way, there is another "cool" trick that utilizes the freezer. If you have thin or tapered candles, put them in the freezer a couple of hours before you are going to use them. For some reason, it will prevent the wax from dripping down the candle and getting all over itself, the holders, or the table. To be honest, I do not fully understand why it works, but it does for all types of candles ranging from small birthday cake candles to long dinner candles.

Last but not least, I would highly recommend against painting any type of exterior concrete such as foundation walls. The paint will just not stand up to the elements and will begin to flake off or become unsightly in a very short time. The only time-consuming recourse you would have is to power wash off the paint. Painting interior concrete, such as in a basement walls and floor is safe, but you may want to think twice before painting high traffic floors such as those found in the garage. The wear, heat, and weight of the tires and vehicle can quickly ruin the finish. Dirty snow and ice can also turn your shiny new floor into a mess in no time.

Tiling

Tiling is one of the easiest and most inexpensive home improvement projects that can add significant value and appeal to almost any room. Given the wide availability and selection of tile, marble, and granite, you can quickly turn a plain space into a beautiful oasis. You can tile walls, floors, and surfaces such as countertops. There are only a few basic considerations to successfully complete a tiling project. As always, you need to have the right tools. They include a trowel, tile cutter, adhesive, and grout.

Trowel selection will have a big impact on the quality of your results. You need to use the proper-sized notched trowel to apply the adhesive; otherwise it could lead to cracked or loose tiles. The size of the notches is proportional to the size and location of the tile. Larger square notches should be used for large floor tiles, whereas a smaller triangular notched trowel should be used for smaller wall or countertop tiles. If you cannot decide between two sizes, err on the larger side.

The type of tile cutter that you will need depends on the material that you are installing. There are basically three classifications of cutters. The smallest type of cutter is called a tile nipper. It can be used to take off small amounts of material on ceramic tiles; using a nipper on marble or granite would be next to impossible. The next type of tile cutter is a dry cutter. It is used to score small tiles which can then be snapped to make the break. It too should be primarily used on small ceramic tiles and for straight cuts only. The final type of cutter is a wet saw. It can be used to cut the hardest of materials, including marble and granite. It uses regular re-circulating water to lubricate and cool the saw blade. While a wet saw may not look as dangerous as a circular saw for wood, you have to treat it with the same respect, especially due to the potential for flying bits of tile. Always wear safety goggles and tie back any loose clothing or hair when operating any type of saw or cutter.

The type of adhesive that you use needs to fit the tile purpose and material. You may or may not use the same type of adhesive on a floor as you would on a wall, so be sure to read the label for its specific application. I would recommend the premixed, ready to use adhesive over the type you mix with water or another liquid to remove any guesswork and to save time. The color of the adhesive is usually white, but it makes no difference since it will not be seen anyway.

Grout is available in one of two general types; it will be either sanded or unsanded. Generally, unsanded would be used for small joints that are typically found with marble or granite. Whereas sanded grout is used in most applications with normal grout line thicknesses. Either way, grout is available in a host of colors, shades, and container sizes. They are mostly available as a powder that must be mixed with water. The good thing is that you do not need to have the grout on hand when you install the tiles, so you can get a better sense of what color grout you might want to use after all the tiles are in place.

Before you begin, you need to make sure that the area you wish to tile is clean of any debris. If the substrate is very smooth, like a Formica® countertop, you should scuff the surface to promote a stronger bond. Next, dry fit perpendicular rows of tiles to ensure the best look as well as to avoid the use of small slivers of tile at the end of a row. Spread a layer of adhesive on the surface using the appropriately notched trowel. Work in small area at a time so the adhesive does not cure before you fit the tiles in place. Place the tiles down and use a slight twisting motion in conjunction with firm pressure to ensure good contact and a level tile. You can either use store-bought spacers or your eye to line up the tiles. In general, the distance between tiles, known as the grout line, should be anywhere from an eighth to a quarter of an inch. Do not worry about any minor amounts of adhesive that remain in the grout line. Repeat until the entire surface has been completely covered. Follow the directions on the adhesive container for proper curing times, typically twenty-four hours, and do not walk on or otherwise disturb the tiles.

Once the adhesive has fully cured, you can begin grouting. It is easier to complete with two people but can be done with only one person. In either case, follow the directions for mixing the grout. Only prepare a small amount at a time since it begins to dry rather quickly. Next, prepare a bucket of clean, room temperature water along with a large sponge. Using a float (a trowel with a rubber face), spread the grout perpendicular to the grout lines. Do not worry about getting grout on the tiles, but you should not use more grout than you need to at any one time. Use the sponge to wipe off any excess grout in the same diagonal fashion. Rinse the sponge as often as needed. Place large amounts of any unused grout back in the bucket and add small amounts of water as necessary if it begins to become too thick or harden. Continue to use the sponge until there is only a very thin film on the tiles. Work from one corner to another of the surface until all the grout lines have been filled. Once you have finished all the grout lines, you can go back with a fresh bucket of water and clean sponge to remove the thin film of grout remaining on the tiles. You must get the tiling completely clean at this point or else the film will remain permanently. Allow the grout to dry for the recommended timeframe, which is usually twenty-four hours. Depending on the location and wear that the surface will receive, you may want to use a clear sealer on the grout to prevent it from getting dirty or staining.

Molding

Another quick and easy home improvement project is adding or replacing crown, base, or chair rail molding. It really is amazing how such a small touch can make such a large difference in a room. Molding can be purchased in fixed lengths, typically eight, ten, twelve, and sixteen feet, from nearly any home improvement store. It is available pre-painted white or as natural wood, and it should be painted or stained before you install it. There are only two main tools that are required for installation, a saw and a nail gun. Technically you can use a manual miter saw and hammer with nails; however, I highly recommend using the powered version of the tools, which can even be rented for the day if you do not wish to purchase them.

Installation is a piece of cake but requires sticking to the old adage of measure twice, cut once. You can easily get confused when cutting the molding on a 22.5 or 45-degree angle for corners, so take your time and visualize the end results. Depending on the angles, you may need to flip over or rotate the piece of molding on the saw before you cut it. Just like a hair cut, you can always take off more if you need to, but putting a piece back is not a realistic option. Once the section is cut and dry fits well, simply use the nail gun with appropriate length finishing nails to secure it to the wall. Be sure to nail into a stud, top or bottom plate, and avoid the last two inches of an outside corner as not to hit the metal corner bead. Once all the molding is in place, simply use wood filler or paintable white caulk to seal nail holes, fill in any gaps between sections as well as the gap between the molding and the wall or floor. In the case of a wall being longer than one piece of molding can cover, use a forty-five-degree cut to join two or more pieces together. After a few quick touch ups, the weekend project will soon add years of value and richness to your home.

Wood Flooring

Replacing old carpet with wood flooring not only instantly beautifies your home but it also adds value to it at the same time. Furthermore, wood flooring is also healthier for you since dust, dirt, and pet dander will not accumulate as it does in carpet. There are a variety of flooring types and styles which can all be installed relatively easily. The main factors that will influence your decision will be the location of the flooring, type of foot traffic and your budget.

In general, there are three main categories of wood flooring. The first, easiest and least expensive type of wood flooring is laminate. It can be installed on top of any sub-floor surface, including concrete, which makes it a good selection for basements and houses built on a concrete slab. The boards fit together tightly by snapping into place and do not require any nails or glue (considered a floating floor). Each board end has a tongue side and a groove side to which the other boards fit tightly. Furthermore, each board top and bottom has a tongue and a groove as well. There are a wide variety of colors and styles available for you to select from, and it is a wise choice for high-traffic areas. The boards themselves are only approximately one quarter of an inch thick or less and the pattern is actually a print of wood grain. Laminate flooring cost as little as a couple of dollars per square foot and comes in fixed lengths. The boards are made of small wood fibers which are laminated for a smooth and durable finish. The only downside to laminate flooring is that its composition is not the same throughout the whole thickness of the board, as you would find with hardwood flooring. If you drop a sharp or heavy object, and it penetrates the surface layer of the laminate floor, the dent cannot be sanded out and may ruin the entire board. Otherwise, laminate flooring is very forgiving, and you could always use a tinted wood filler to conceal any damage. Lastly, you will only need to install thin padding as an underlayment which is available in large rolls and is also relatively inexpensive.

The second type of wood flooring, on the complete opposite end of the spectrum, is hardwood. It can be the most costly and difficult to install relatively speaking. Hardwood is available in a great number of types, colors, styles, and finishes. However, I would highly recommend purchasing pre-finished hardwood which has been stained and/or sealed by the manufacturer. Otherwise, after you spend time with the installation, you will have to sand, stain, and seal it. This adds not only to the labor of the project but also the potential for dust and fumes. The factory-applied finish typically comes with a twenty to twenty-five-year warranty, but hardwood floors can be sanded and refinished as many times as necessary since it is solid wood throughout the thickness of the board. Hardwood boards are typically three quarters of an inch in thickness and are solid wood throughout. The width of the boards typically ranges from two inches to five or six inches and they come in random lengths approximately one to six feet. Each board end has a tongue side and a groove side to which the other boards fit tightly. Furthermore, each board top and bottom has a tongue and a groove as well. I would recommend the wider boards, even though they cost more per square foot, since they will save you time, energy, and nails when it comes time for installation. Hardwood flooring cannot be installed on concrete; you would have to use engineered flooring.

The last type of wood flooring is known as engineered flooring. It is a hybrid between hardwood and laminate flooring using a wood veneer layered on a composite base. It can be more durable than hardwood, but unlike hardwood, it can be installed on concrete. It can be installed using nails, glue or no type of fastening device depending on the manufacturer and design. Engineered flooring comes in random board lengths in a variety of colors, styles, widths, and patterns. Just as engineered flooring lays between hardwood and laminate, engineered wood is typically available in three-eighths of an inch thickness but may not require any type of padding underlayment. Each board end has a tongue side and a groove side to which the other boards fit tightly. Furthermore, each board top and bottom has a tongue and a groove as well.

To estimate how much flooring you will need to complete a project, simply measure the length and width of the room in feet and multiple the two together to get the number of square feet. Also, do not forget to include the closets. Then add approximately ten percent to the total for waste (fifteen percent if you plan on installing it on a forty-five-degree angle) before dividing the total area by the number of square feet of flooring per box, rounding up to the nearest box. For example, if the room is ten feet by twenty feet, the total area is 200 square feet. Then add another twenty square feet for waste, which brings the total to 220 square feet. Let us assume that the flooring is available in boxes of twenty-three square feet. You should therefore purchase ten boxes of flooring. If the flooring is a stock item, you should be able to return any unused boxes; however, you should keep at least one near full box for any future repairs. Store unused flooring in a cool, dry location to prevent water damage and on a flat surface to prevent warping.

Before you install any type of flooring, you need to properly prepare the location. This includes removing the floor molding, being careful not to remove the wall paint with it. One trick is to score the joint between the molding and the wall with a utility knife before prying off the molding. You can save and reuse the old molding, but in some cases you may wish to replace it altogether. Next, remove the old carpeting by cutting it into four-foot-wide sections and rolling it up. Use masking tape to bind the rolls. Next, remove the carpet padding in the same manner as the carpet itself. Now you will need to remove any staples and tack strips used to fasten the carpet and padding. Be sure to remove all loose debris so you have a clean, level surface to lay the new wood flooring upon. Lastly, vacuum the entire area to remove any dust and small pieces of debris. Though not structurally necessary, I highly recommend that you fasten the sub-floor to the joists using two-and-a-half-inch, course drywall screws. This will help prevent the sub-floor from squeaking due to house settling as well as seasonal differences in temperature and humidity. Install the screws every foot to one and a half feet into the joists. You can use the existing nail pattern as a guide in finding the floor joists.

Installing each type of flooring follows the same general steps with slight differences along the way. You will need to start at a left corner of the room and run the rows, preferably, along the longest side of the room. Follow the manufacturer's recommendation for the spacing between the floor and walls to allow for expansion and contraction of the floor. The gap can range from a quarter to a half of an inch, depending on the type of wood flooring.

For laminate flooring, be sure that you have installed the thin padding layer following the manufactures instructions for spacing and fastening. Start laying the first row of flooring, with the tongue side facing the wall and butting each end tightly to the previous board. You can purchase an installation kit that contains a metal bar which is useful for making tight joints when you get to the end of a row. The kit will also have a specially designed plastic block that can be used to tap the boards into place. When you start the second row, use a laminated board that has been cut in half so the joins are staggered. With any type of flooring, you do not want to have two seams line up or close to one another. This is not only for ascetic reasons but for structural stability as well. This same principle applies to any material or structure ranging from drywall to a brick wall. Simply interlock the boards by holding the new one at an angle and pressing down into place. The tongue and groove design will pull the boards together, but you can give them a quick tap with the plastic block and a hammer for a tighter fit. Simply repeat the procedure for subsequent rows, making cuts as necessary. The most useful tools to have for making cuts are a power miter saw for end cuts and a jig saw for curved or irregular-shaped cuts.

When installing hardwood and engineered floors that will be nailed in place, you should first examine the quality and thickness of the sub-floor, assuming it is not concrete. You may need to install a layer of three-eighths to half-inch-thick plywood to strengthen the base for the flooring. If the thickness of the sub-floor is less than three quarters of an inch and/or made of oriented strand board (OSB), you should install the additional layer of plywood. This will give the flooring nails a firm substrate to grasp on to. Furthermore, be sure to leave a gap of a quarter of an inch around the perimeter of the room to allow for expansion and contraction of the plywood, though it should be minimal due to the design of plywood. Furthermore, run beads of a strong construction adhesive along the perimeter and inside of the bottom of the plywood sheet before installing. This will help reduce any squeaking that would otherwise occur from the wood sub-floor rubbing on the plywood. Lastly, place a layer of rosin paper, available by the roll, on top of the plywood, which will act similarly to the adhesive in reducing any squeaking. You can use masking tape to joint sheets of the rosin paper together as well as to hold down the ends of the paper to the plywood.

Now that you have finished all the preparation, you can start installing the hardwood or engineered flooring. You can rent or purchase the floor nailer/hammer as well as a cordless nail gun that can be used for face nailing the first row and installing the molding. Start the same way you would for laminate flooring, but you will just need to face nail the first row to hold it in place. The nail holes will be covered by the molding. Be sure to place the first row with the groove side facing the wall and do not count on the wall being perfectly straight. Then install the second row and nail every eight to twelve inches using the floor nailer. It will drive an L or T shaped nail into the tongue end of the board. Do not nail the board too close to the end since it may split the wood. Repeat each row, being sure not to have two seams line up or be within six inches of each other. To minimize waste, you can use the cut end of the previous row to start the next row, as long as the remaining piece is greater than ten inches in length. Repeat until the room is complete. You may not be able to fit the floor nailer in place for the last few rows because of a wall. Instead, you can put the last few rows of boards together and pull them towards you while face nailing the last row in place.

As soon as you turn around, you will have a whole new floor that will last for many decades. The only tasks remaining are to install any transition strips, replace the molding, and trim door bottoms as required using a table saw. You can use tinted wood putty to fill in any gaps or imperfections in the flooring. Be sure to clean your new floor with the recommended solutions and avoid having any water come in contact with or remain on the floor. Water and humidity can quickly cause the wood to swell and buckle or ruin the finish. Lastly, a patina or natural aging of the wood will cause a slight color difference to appear between exposed flooring and those areas covered by furniture or area rugs.

There is no graceful way to repair a damaged wood floorboard, but it can be done regardless of type. Basically you will need to carefully cut out the damaged board using a circular saw with the depth set appropriately. Then you will need to trim off the tongues and groove on three sides (leave the long groove in place) of the replacement board. Dry fit the replacement board but place a piece of thin string or thread under the board to help you get it out. Once you think you have a good fit, you should remove any rosin paper and run a generous bead or two of a strong adhesive on the sub-floor. Install the replacement board and use heavy weights to keep pressure on the board until the adhesive cures. If you need to, you can place a couple of face nails into the hardwood or engineered board if the sub-floor is wooden. Then fill in the face nail divot with tinted wood filler. Otherwise the alternative is to rip out and replace all of the flooring from the end of the room to the damaged piece. Lastly, for pesky squeaks, simply sprinkle some fine saw dust or cornstarch between the boards and wipe away the excess.

Door Locks

Knowing how to change or install a lock and deadbolt not only saves you time and money, but it also promotes safety. There can be any number of reasons why you would need to change your locks. For example, when you move into a new home, one of the first things you should do is change all the exterior locks, even if it is a new construction home. Furthermore, you should change the number and reprogram any garage door openers as well. However, there may come a time when you simply lose your keys. In any event, all it usually takes is a screwdriver and five minutes. Most doorknobs are standard in terms of size and location. The only concern that you might need to pay attention to is if the handle is a lever [and locking] type. In that case, you will just need to purchase the correct version based on if the door swings to the left or to the right.

There are three main parts to any door handle. The first part is the inside and outside handles. They are held in place with two screws from the inside. Simply unscrew them and pull them from the door. The second part is the latch section of the handle. It is held in place with two screws from the edge of the door, and it opens and closes with the turn of the handles. Loosen the screws and remove the part from the door. Next, simply follow the same steps in reverse to install the new handle. Finally, the last and easiest part of a door handle task is the plate where the latch fits into the doorjamb. In some cases, the replacement lock may be the same style and you can just leave the old one in place. Otherwise, all you need to do is remove the two screws from the old plate and replace them with the new version. If the new plate does not fit exactly in place, you can use a sharp utility knife to trim away any excess wood standing in the way. Be sure to test the new doorknob from the inside as well as the new keys.

In my opinion, all exterior doors should have a deadbolt lock in addition to the regular locking door handle. For fire safety concerns, you should not install a deadbolt that uses a key on the interior side of the lock. A deadbolt lock is designed and installed much like a regular doorknob, using the same number and location of screws. If you only have a regular doorknob on your existing door, there are only a few extra steps required to add the holes for the deadbolt lock. Furthermore, you can utilize the same cordless drill that you use to install and remove screws to make the new holes in the door and jamb. Nearly all home improvement stores sell the kit to get the job done quickly, safely, and easily. The kit will contain a jig that provides the proper spacing and location to drill the hole through the front of the door as well as through the edge of the door. The only detail you will need to pay attention to is if your door has a metal or wood face. Be sure to purchase the appropriate kit since a wood hole cutter will not work very well on a metal door. After you have the two holes in the door drilled out, all you need to do is drill the hole in the doorjamb and router out a slot for the plates on the door edge and jamb so they fit flush. Within a half hour, you will have better secured your family and property as well as saved a few bucks in locksmith fees.

Hiring a Contractor

When the time does come to hire someone to provide a service, there are a number of actions you should take to protect yourself and to promote a smooth, successful project. First, you should get at least three estimates from different companies. One of the best ways to develop a list of candidates is to ask friends and family if they know of anyone in the field or would recommend the person who they have used in the past. Otherwise, you may need to open up the phone book yellow pages and make an educated guess.

In addition, stay away from the Internet as your primary means of sourcing companies; however, you can use the web to research information about the companies. Estimates or proposals are typically free so beware of anyone who may want to charge you. Once you receive all the estimates, you will need to carefully review the details of each to ensure you are comparing apples to apples. Be leery of any extremely low or high prices. As you review the estimates, you will want to make sure it is clear on several aspects, including but not limited to who will be supplying the materials, when the job will start, the estimated duration of the effort, the payment schedule, who will be responsible for any cleanup and disposal of wastes and any warrantees on the material and labor. As part of the estimate, be sure to ask for at least three references as well. Do not hesitate in visiting the referrals to get a firsthand view of the contractor's quality. Furthermore, it is extremely helpful if you can inspect work that was performed a number of years ago so you can see if it has withstood the test of time. Next, only work with a contractor, vendor, etc. who is fully insured and certified, licensed and/or bonded. This will help protect you if an accident occurs on your property while the work is performed. Before you sign any contracts, do some research with the Better Business Bureau (www.bbb.org) to see if there have been any complaints, suits, or other legal action taken against the company. Do not hesitate in walking away or turning down any company that gives you a bad feeling.

Typically, a deposit is required to secure your place in the schedule and perhaps to purchase materials. The deposit should not exceed the one third to one half range of the total estimate, and never hand over all the money up front. If the work requires multiple days to complete, you may be asked to provide partial payments. However, you should only provide the final payment once the work is completely finished, no matter what little tasks remain. Otherwise, it may be weeks or months before they return, if at all. Lastly, try to make your payment(s) using a credit card or check so you not only have a record of the transaction but also some level of protection in the event a problem does arise.

Life Events

"After the game, the king and pawn go into the same box."
– *Italian proverb*

Marriage

Marriage can be a wonderful institution but should not be entered into lightly; divorce rates in the United States are almost fifty percent. Considering the level of commitment, you need to be reasonably sure that you are ready to accept the responsibility. Although no one can predict the future, try to be forward thinking since there are a number of factors to consider. Furthermore, keep in mind that marriage is an option and not necessarily for everyone. For those that are very independent and/or largely motivated by non-home life activities, the institution of marriage may be one that, for the sake of everyone concerned, you should not enter into at all.

How compatible are you as a couple? While opposites may initially attract, they may not be able to sustain over time. You will never be a hundred percent compatible or see eye to eye on every issue, but you should have more in common than not. Do your short-term and long-term goals relatively match? For example, do you want kids but they do not? Financially are the two of you compatible? Are you both spenders or is one a saver and one a spender? This is a very key factor in your future relationship since money plays a significant role in every aspect of life. From small purchases to large expenses, you need to be on the same page. It is not only the large decisions in life such as where you live or career paths that are important but daily living and routines should be considered as well. Does one of you prefer an active lifestyle and the other a more homely life? Just as important as being in love, make sure that you consider all the effects of situations that you have control over.

Each of your families is also another important part of your marriage. Do you get along with your potential in-laws? Relatives may not have a large impact right now, but they can play a large role in your relationship, beginning with the wedding itself. People come in all shapes, sizes, races, religious beliefs, and nationalities. Especially in the global world we live in today, it is not uncommon for marriages to have a blend of backgrounds. The most important factor in all of it is how your significant other treats you. If they are a good person and will treat you well, then there is no reason why anyone should have an issue with your intentions.

When the time comes to propose marriage, it is not only a tradition but a sign of respect for the groom-to-be to ask the father of the bride for his blessings. This should be done shortly before the proposal is made to the bride, and if there is not a father in the equation, then the mother is the next appropriate person to sit down with and have a brief discussion.

Just as no two women are alike, neither are engagement rings. Tradition, or should I say the marketing department of the diamond companies, has set the unofficial standard of two to three months salary as the amount of money you should spend on the ring. The two main components of this serious investment include the setting and the diamond. The setting can vary in style, design, and composition and can be designed from scratch or selected from models already created. Some settings have smaller surrounding diamonds known as "begets". However, other settings have only one large diamond in the middle and are known as "solitaires". All diamonds have four main characteristics which determine the quality and therefore cost. Cut, clarity, carats, and color are known as the four Cs of diamonds. The cut refers to the general shape of the diamond and can range from square to round. The cut of the diamond is critical since it has a significant impact on how much light is reflected, which in turn affects its brilliance. The clarity of the diamond refers to any imperfections that may be inside. Since diamonds are nothing more than carbon atoms that were subjected to great heat and pressure, there may be some pockets of carbon or other impurities that result in dark spots. Obviously, the fewer imperfections in the diamond, the better the quality. Diamond weight is measured in carats, but just because a diamond has more carats, that does not mean it is better. Larger diamonds have a greater chance of being lower in clarity; however, near-perfect large diamonds are very expensive. The last characteristic, color, can vary from near colorless to light yellow. The scale used is the letters D through X, where X has the most relative color.

Since the commitment to a ring is a significant one, you may need some help in selecting the right one. Unless you wish to surprise your girlfriend, you may opt to go together to shop for a setting and diamond. Otherwise, you can ask one of her trusted friends or a relative that may be familiar with her taste and style. Depending on the jeweler's policies, you may be able to return the ring within a set number of days if it turns out not to be the right one for her.

Once you have purchased a ring, you should have it appraised by bringing it to a different certified jeweler for their evaluation. The appraisal should cost less than a hundred dollars and should only take a few minutes. Clearly the diamond should appraise for at least the amount you purchased it for, but it will typically be a few dozen percent more. One important thing to remember is not to let the diamond out of your sight both at the time of purchase as well as during the appraisal. Also, do not confuse a diamond certificate for an appraisal. A certificate will detail the physical properties of the diamond, whereas the appraisal places a value on the diamond.

Furthermore, depending on how much you spent on the diamond, you may wish to have it insured. Lastly, you can also have the diamond laser inscribed with a serial number to help identify and safeguard your investment. The inscription will not adversely affect any of the diamond's qualities.

Pregnancy

Expecting a child is one of life's greatest miracles. It is a very exciting time, especially if it is your first child; however, it is perfectly normal for it to be a time filled with many questions and even apprehension since your body is undergoing many changes. Furthermore, as funny as it may sound, the topic of pregnancy is not just for women. Men should be as well informed, if not more so, of what is occurring as well as what to expect, especially in the case of potential complications. In addition, no two pregnancies are the same, so just because you had a good or bad experience the first time, that does not mean that you will have the same in the future. However, there are a number of things to be aware of throughout all pregnancies to make the experience safe, comfortable, and enjoyable.

First, if you are on any form of prescribed birth control, you should give your body a couple of months to purge itself and normalize before conceiving a baby. Next, even before you are pregnant, you should be taking prenatal vitamins. This special formulation is best in the prescription form and you should start taking them a couple of months before you start trying for a baby. The quantity and types of vitamins, such as folic acid, will help in the development of your baby. It is not the end of the world if you do not take them or miss a dose, but you should take advantage of the benefits they provide.

Just as we are all different, so too is conception. For some couples, it happens very quickly and easily. However, for others, it could take a little longer, either due to a medical problem or just due to timing. Stress will certainly not help the matter, so try to be as relaxed as possible and avoid placing additional pressure on the situation. In addition, there are only a few days out of the month that you are most likely to get pregnant. Note that this "rhythm method" should never be used as a means of reliable birth control. The best timeframe in which to try for a baby starts three days before your ovulation peaks. The date of ovulation varies by the length of your menstrual cycle; ovulation tends to occur around the tenth day of a twenty-four-day cycle, for example. You can purchase relatively inexpensive ovulation kits at any pharmacy to test for the beginning of ovulation. You should then skip having sex every other day for a week in order to prevent sperm levels from dropping too low. To further help the matter, you should refrain from having sex five days before you begin trying to allow sperm levels to be at their maximum. If you are not successful that month, do not worry and just try again the following month. The additional stress can only make matters worse, so again, relax and allow nature to take its course.

If you continue to try for a year without getting pregnant, you may want to consult with your Obstetrician/Gynecologist (OB/GYN). There may or may not be an issue with either one of you. Assuming there are no apparent problems, you may want to have a sperm-count test performed to confirm the number and quality. This is a good first option since it is the least invasive way to rule out where the issue may lay. In the event that the test results show no issue, there can be a range of physical reasons why you are not getting pregnant, including none at all. Sometimes the issue can be resolved relatively quickly and easily, as in the case of laparoscopic removal of endometrial tissue which can prevent implantation from occurring. In other cases, it may require more aggressive approaches such as daily injections or in vitro fertilization (IVF). However, before you start down any of those paths, you should sit down and have a very serious and realistic discussion with your spouse. You should also be aware that procedures may be only partially covered by health insurance, or not at all. Furthermore, and more importantly, the road can be a very bumpy one that you will need to mentally prepare for, just as much as you will need to be ready physically.

If you have exhausted all of the options for having your own baby, you do have one option remaining, adoption. Adoption can be as fulfilling of an option as having your own child, and some would argue even more. The adoption process can also be long and difficult, so be sure that you are ready to accept the challenge. Keep in mind that newborn babies are higher in demand, so you may need to consider an older child or one from another country. Either way, be sure to follow all legal procedures and do not take any shortcuts that may jeopardize your chances of adopting.

Once you are pregnant, you have forty weeks ahead of you to eat right and prepare yourself mentally for the big day. Now is the time to treat your body that much more like a temple since everything that you are exposed to can pass to your baby. Never smoke, drink alcohol, or introduce any harmful substance into your body. Steer clear of any environments that may pose a health risk such as secondhand smoke or hazardous work environments. You will even need to pass on normal activities such as donating blood or getting certain vaccinations while you are pregnant.

Before you take any over-the-counter medications, check with your doctor first since they may have an adverse affect on you or the baby. About the only relatively safe medication you can take is Tylenol® and some anti-acids such as Tums®; however, you should check with your doctor first before taking any of them at any time. There are also a number of foods that you will need to limit or refrain from altogether. Do not eat any uncooked foods such as meat, fish, and shellfish. While you would be able to handle getting sick under normal conditions, any type of bacterial poisoning can be harmful to your baby. You should limit your intake of cooked fish such as tuna and salmon since all fish have the potential for high levels of mercury. Also, avoid salty foods that can make you retain water and cause swelling, as well as environments that are above your normal body temperature, including hot tubs.

On the other hand, there are a number of "do's" while pregnant. You should drink plenty of water throughout the day. As a rule of thumb, you should drink half your body weight in ounces on a daily basis. If you feel your calf or leg muscles cramping, it is a clear sign of dehydration. You should also limit demanding physical activities as you get closer to your due date. The best exercise, at any point, is walking. A low impact, brisk walk will help with your breathing and will build up your endurance, which is especially important during labor and delivery. Lastly, try to get as much rest and sleep as possible before you give birth. You will need all your strength and energy to keep up with the around the clock feedings.

If you experience any bleeding and spotting or feel any contractions or cramping in your uterus, you should contact your doctor immediately. In the case of contractions, it may only be a case of Braxton Hicks, which are false labor contractions but, if not, you may need to be hospitalized to stop them unless you are within four weeks of your due date. You should not worry too much about pre-term labor since there are a number of different medications that can be given intravenously, as an injection, or orally in the form of a pill. If you do go into pre-term labor, you should be given a steroid injection, which will help speed up the development of your baby's lungs. There are two different types of corticosteroids that may be given, betamethasone and dexamethasone. They both stimulate the production of surfactants in the fetus' lungs which prevent the tiny air sacks from sticking together and therefore enable easier breathing. Betamethasone is administered in two shots, twenty-four hours apart, whereas dexamethasone is given in four separate shots, twelve hours apart. The risks associated with the medications are relatively low and greatly outweigh the risk of not having received the shots. Depending on their severity as well as how far along you are, you may need to be placed on partial or full bed rest and take a pill every four to eight hours. Hopefully, you are far enough along where it is only for a few weeks, but if not, you need to do whatever it takes for the health and safety of your baby.

Depending on the mother's blood type and the presence of antigens, you may need a special shot at twenty-eight weeks. The RhoGAM shot should be given to you if you have a negative blood type, and if you do not have the antibodies for the Rhesus (Rh) factor. RhoGAM provides temporary immunity against a negative mother's blood from producing antibodies and attacking the baby. If the RhoGAM shot is not given, it can lead to the mother's antibodies attacking the baby's red blood cells, potentially causing jaundice, anemia, or worse. In addition, if your baby has positive blood, you will be given another RhoGAM shot shortly after the baby's birth. The baby will only be a negative blood type if both parents are negative; however, a negative parent and a positive parent could produce a negative blood type in the baby. Furthermore, if you have a miscarriage or an abortion, you will need the RhoGAM shot as well if the fetus had a negative blood type.

During the twenty-eighth week of your pregnancy, you should also be given a blood test to check your sugar levels. It is important to have the test performed since you can develop what is know as gestational diabetes, which can adversely affect the health of the baby. In most cases, the gestational diabetes will go away after you give birth. The test consists of fasting before your blood is drawn to establish a baseline. Then you will be asked to drink a very sugary tasting solution and remain seated for one hour. Another relatively small amount of blood will be drawn at the end of the hour. The results usually take one week to come back from the lab and will be provided to you by your doctor. If you do not pass the first test, you will be asked to repeat the same test but over a three-hour period. If you do not pass the second test, you will be placed on a special diet to regulate your carbohydrate intake. You will also need to monitor your blood sugar levels by testing yourself when you wake up, after each meal and at bedtime. The small meter draws less than a drop of your blood from your hand or arm and will give you a near-instant reading. While the diet and testing may be an inconvenience, it should only be a temporary situation that places your baby's health at the forefront.

Otherwise, take the time to enjoy your pregnancy. Be sure to adjust your schedule and lifestyle so you can keep yourself from becoming run down. Do not be afraid to say no or skip functions if you are not feeling well, especially if it may be stressful or there is a risk of catching a cold or the flu. Perhaps you may want to start a journal of your experiences or prepare a scrapbook for future pictures, starting with the ultrasound images. You can also use the time to consider how you want to decorate the baby's room, especially if you are looking to have more than one child. Regardless, make sure that you and your spouse take the time to bond not only with the new addition but with each other.

Unfortunately, too often women, especially teenagers, become accidentally pregnant. Furthermore, rather than seeking proper medical attention for both themselves and their unborn child, girls hide the pregnancy, deliver the baby themselves, and/or discard the newborn in an unsafe manner. If you or anyone you know ever finds themselves in this situation, you need to do the right thing for both the mother and child. Low fetal weights can cause numerous defects in the baby, the mother can bleed out and die during delivery, and abandoned babies will quickly perish if they do not receive immediate medical treatment. Many states have safe haven laws that allow a girl to drop off their newborn baby at a hospital, police, or manned firehouse without questions or repercussions, as long as they are handed over face to face. Furthermore, laws protect the mother/baby relationship in the event she wants the baby back, as long as it is within a window of time, which is typically two weeks. Please talk to someone, anyone, before allowing a precious soul to become the victim of fear or poor judgment.

Birth

The birth of a baby is probably the single most emotional event in your life. This can be especially true if you are a first-time parent. The range of emotions includes everything from happiness to fear. For those moms who suffer for postpartum, they also add sadness or depression to the mix. Some level of pain usually accompanies every birth as well as days of healing following the big event.

For fathers, there is no physical pain, usually just happiness with a healthy dose of apprehension. However, they should be very sympathetic towards their significant other, who may not only be suffering from the physical pain of giving birth or breast feeding, but also the physiological affects caused by the flood of hormones as they continue to rise and fall. Lack of sleep can also cause both parents to be on edge, so be careful not to snap at one another.

While you are never fully ready to have a baby, planning and preparation can go a long way. There will be so many things to do and take care of when the baby is here (even more so if you have twins or more), so you should try and do as much beforehand as possible. This includes stocking up on food that can be easily reheated or turned into meals and getting ahead on chores. Do not wait until the last minute to pack a bag for the hospital or put the infant seat in the car (you will not be allowed to leave the hospital without one). Make sure that you have all the supplies you will need for the newborn ahead of time so you are not running out to stores on the way home from the hospital.

However, no matter how much you plan or buy, there will always be unexpected events and challenges. The secret to successfully overcoming these challenges is to learn to be flexible and roll with the proverbial punches. Learn to work together and use your teamwork skills to lessen the difficulty level. Sometimes things just happen, and it is no one's fault, so pointing fingers and laying blame is not a positive use of your limited energy. Lastly, learn to think outside of the box when it comes to the challenges of a newborn. For example, if your baby is fed, has a clean diaper, and been burped but continues to cry for no apparent reason, pull out your handheld vacuum. Having it on for a few minutes in the next room will produce white noise that can quickly relax your baby and allow them to fall asleep, assuming the crying is not gas or colic related. White noise is said to mimic the sound your baby hears while in the womb, and you can even make or purchase a CD of white noise which can come in especially handy at bedtime.

You would be hard pressed to find a doctor or nurse that would say that breast milk is not better than formula for your baby. However, there are a host of legitimate reasons why you may not be able to breastfeed. Those reasons include factors from both you and your baby, especially if they are born very early or have other complications which require constant medical attention. As difficult and inconvenient as it may be, you should at least give breastfeeding a chance. It is especially important to try and get your baby the first few days of feedings since colostrum is packed with many key nutrients to help build your baby's immune system as well as vitamins, minerals, and other proteins. If you are unable to breastfeed directly, you can try pumping the milk, which can be frozen and stored for up to three months. If you are experiencing any problems or difficulties, many hospitals have access to a lactation consultant that can help you with techniques, products, and provide words of encouragement. You can also contact the La Leche League or visit their web site at www.llli.org. Lastly, for the time that you are nursing, consider yourself still pregnant. As funny as that may sound, it is for your baby's protection. Everything that you introduce into your body can be transmitted to your baby through your breast milk. Therefore, stay away from certain types of foods such as cabbage, which can give your baby painful gas, and be careful with any medications that you take. If you need to, you can always "pump and dump" the contaminated batch(es) and tap into a supply that you previously collected and froze.

You should never heat breast milk or formula in a microwave since it will destroy key nutrients. Instead, you should warm bottles using warm water and always test the temperature of the liquid before giving it to the baby. Furthermore, breastfeeding can easily save you a couple of thousand dollars in formula costs, help with weight loss, as well as promote a stronger bond between you and your baby. Do not feel bad, defeated, or ashamed if you are not able to feed your baby breast milk. However, the longer you can breastfeed them the better, despite the demanding strains on your day such as working full time. You can try to set a goal of twelve months of breastfeeding, which is the point when they can be switched over to regular whole milk.

There are a number of newborn basics that everyone should be aware of, regardless of whether you are a parent or not. You may visit a newborn or may be asked to watch one for a short time, so be prepared. Many hospitals offer free or low-cost classes which can be taken by both parents before or during your stay. However, never shy away from asking your nurse any questions that come to mind. First, when holding and transferring a newborn, always support their head and neck. A newborn does not yet have the muscle strength to fully support their head so avoid any bobble-head motions. Next, always lay a baby on their back. This will partially help in the prevention of sudden infant death syndrome (SIDS). Furthermore, if the baby spits up, they will not choke on the fluid. Next, it will take the umbilical cord approximately two weeks to fall off. To help keep it clean and dry, you should wipe their belly button with an alcohol swab during every other diaper change at a minimum. Lastly, babies, especially those born before forty weeks, are susceptible to jaundice. Bilirubin is produced as the normal result of red blood cells breaking down. When the liver has not had a chance to fully develop, it cannot adequately filter out the bilirubin. In fewer cases, breast milk and blood group differences can cause jaundice. Either way, the whites of a newborn's eyes and skin will take on a yellowish color the first few days of life, and it can last for one to two weeks. In most cases the jaundice will go away on its own, but your pediatrician may have blood tests run to confirm that the levels of bilirubin are decreasing over time. Otherwise, simple phototherapy treatments at the hospital usually clear up the issue.

When it comes to boys, there are some special handling requirements. First, always use a cloth or the new diaper to cover them since they have a tendency to act like an out of control fire hose. Secondly, if they have been circumcised, you will need to protect the fresh wound from sticking to the diaper as well as from infection. Use a generous amount of petroleum jelly or antibacterial ointment on a three-by-three gauze to cover the tender area.

Children

You are never really a hundred percent prepared to have a baby, but there are some things you can do to help the situation. First, you need to make sure that both of you are mentally, physically, and emotionally stable. If you find that you cannot take care of yourself, there is no way that you will be able to care for someone who requires twenty-four-hour attention. Next, make sure that the relationship between you and your spouse is strong and solid. If you think that having a baby will help your shaky marriage, you are dead wrong. A new baby will test your relationship in every which way, so you need to be at the top of your game. Another important factor is your economic situation. If you can barely take care of yourself, you may need to rethink your plans. Make sure that you have adequate material means to support the new lifestyle. A one-bedroom apartment and a two-seater convertible are not going to make for very baby-friendly conditions.

If you have all the worldly items in line for a child, make sure that you and your spouse are ready for the responsibility of another human being. Raising a child is the single biggest responsibility you can have in life and is not something that you can just wing. You need to do more than a good job in raising them. Your goal should be that they exceed all your good qualities and turn out even better than you.

When the big day does come, you will automatically fall in love with your child. Unless there are postpartum issues, you should have no problems in nurturing your newborn. You will need to make some sacrifices in your own life for your child, but it should not be given a second thought since they are number one in your life forever. Make time to spend with your child and enjoy every moment, as they will grow up faster than you realize. Also, do not forget about the needs and feelings of older siblings when you have additional children. Prepare siblings months ahead of time and get them involved with the new baby as often as you can. One trick is to purchase a few small gifts beforehand so that they can be given to the older brother or sister when friends and relatives bring presents for the new baby. Hopefully, the more your child is a part of the new addition, the less the chances that major feelings of jealousy or rivalry will arise.

As much as we like to think that our children are perfect, there will come times when we need to apply some discipline. Years ago a parent would give their child a quick whack on the butt and that was enough to get the message across. Unfortunately, times are not what they used to be, and if you did the same thing today, whether in public or in your own home, you would probably see someone's cell phone video of it on YouTube and have the Division of Youth and Family Services (DYFS) knocking at your door by dinner time.

You should never take physical action against your child since it not only causes physical and mental harm, but it also promotes violence which could be passed down to their children or affect their attitude towards others including siblings and their future spouses. Instead, employ the popular "timeout" method when your child needs a behavior adjustment (just be sure to first count to three slowly). A timeout consists of removing the child to a non-active environment for a few minutes so that they may calm down and perhaps even reflect on their actions so that they will not be repeated. Try to use a neutral location such as a hallway and not their bedroom, which could have adverse affects. While it may not be as quick and effective as a good smack on the rear, its message usually gets the point across. It is especially affective when enacted before a major incident is allowed to occur and can also be used in any setting, just not at home. This is another good reason to always closely supervise your children and nip any negative behavior in the bud. By the way, you can also apply the timeout technique to an object when two or more children are battling after it. Removing the toy from the equation defuses the situation immediately.

While I previously referred to DYFS in a sarcastic sense, it is a very important service whose main purpose is to protect children from harmful parents/guardians and abusive or neglectful environments. While I highly doubt you will ever need to call upon DYFS for yourself, you never know when a friend or schoolmate may need their assistance. Every state has some form of the program available though it may be known under a different name such as Child Services. No one should ever be afraid to contact them, but likewise their services should never be abused or have false claims reported.

Unfortunately, there is no exact formula for successfully raising a child. What may work for one child may not work for another, even when they are from the same family. However, there are a few general and fundamental methods that can be used to produce a strong young adult. Just as life occurs in a general order, so too do the relative order of the guidelines. First, establish a routine for your child. This does not mean that every minute needs to be scheduled or packed with activity. Instead, it is intended to promote a stable routine, which children tend to do best with; none of us like sudden or constant change, so we should not expect the same of our children. The next core principle is to lead by example. Small children are especially like sponges that absorb and emulate everything from your attitude to your vocabulary. Be your child's first and best role model by providing them with a wholesome environment. One of the single most important elements of parenting is consistency. To avoid confusing your child, as well as to show a unified front, both parents or guardians need to deliver consistent messaging. Communications include everything from development direction to the consequences for breaking the rules. Without strong leadership from the top, your methods, reasoning, and actions may be questioned, vulnerable to attack, and appear to be weak. Next, take an active role in their lives. Again, keeping moderation in mind, you do not want to be in their face twenty-four hours a day, but by the same token, you do not want them raising themselves. The key is to involve them in as many of your regular everyday actions as possible, including your efforts that directly affect them. For example, if they give you a difficult time while trying to brush their hair, let them feel a part of the effort by allowing them to pick out which color hair band they want to wear that day. Natural curiosity dominates their young little world, so take the time to explain why and what you are doing; you, the parent, should show them proper methods and techniques the first time they are exposed to something new, not some stranger.

Whether used to steer children away from a meltdown during the "terrible twos" or using school sports to occupy their free time that might otherwise be consumed by negative influences such as gangs, drugs, and alcohol, the tactic of distraction works at nearly any age. In addition, there are few better feelings in the world than having inspired someone to overcome a challenge or try something for the first time. A healthy outlook coupled with positive actions can easily spread like wildfire and make our journey through life a wonderful experience. This holds especially true for children, who should be continually encouraged and praised for their small yet successful actions. Lastly, function as a family as often as possible. This not only instills family values, but it should also promote strong bonds between you and your children as well as those between siblings long after they have left the nest.

Divorce

Divorce has reached epidemic proportions with approximately fifty percent of all marriages in America ending unsuccessfully. Even if you are not the husband or wife, you may be a child of divorce. In addition, chances are you know of someone who has either been divorced or the friend of a child of divorce. In any case, divorce affects many more than just the direct victims and is never easy. Obviously, the issue may be avoidable from the start with better spousal evaluation and selection. However, you typically do not learn everything about a person for several years, and even then, it may not be until you are living in the same space that habits and traits begin to surface. Try to use your observation skills to gain a better understanding of his or her base characteristics. Always be open and honest about yourself and ask that of the other person as well.

If you do find yourself in a marriage that is not working out, you can seek couples or marriage counseling if both parties are willing and able. As difficult as it may be, try to be amicable about the matter, especially if children are involved. Try a separation or cooling-off period to ensure that the heat of the moment is not blocking access to potential solutions. If at last you find that the situation is hopeless, ensure that both of you are aware of and understand the immediate and long-term effects of a divorce. This includes but is not limited to alimony, child support, division of assets, attorney fees, and custody rights, in addition to the mental and emotional consequences.

If you are a friend of someone going through a divorce, be supportive of them in their difficult time and never poke fun at them. Only give your opinions and advice if asked for and avoid meddling in matters that do not involve you. Your friendship can be greatly damaged if you are not careful with these highly personal and sensitive matters.

Children are hit especially hard by divorce. If you find yourself in the direct line of fire, you need to understand a few concepts. First, you are not the cause of or to blame for the divorce. The matter is an issue between your parents and not a result of any of your actions. Secondly, you will need to prepare yourself for some significant changes in your life, including but not limited to where you may be living, with whom and for how long. In the future, you may be faced with the challenges of a stepparent or step/half brothers and sisters. None of this is easy, so always seek support from anyone when you need it. Do not be shy or afraid to ask for help, whether informal or professional.

Retirement

Years ago, you could work for a single company for twenty-five years and retire with a nice monthly pension and Social Security benefits. Take the exact opposite and that is the state of affairs today. While there are some state and federal careers that still offer those types of opportunities, chances are that starting salaries are much lower and pensions will be cut as budget gaps grow larger. If you do take this route, be sure to try and climb the ladder as high as possible to maximize your total compensation. Otherwise, you can easily work for ten or more companies during the life of your career. Furthermore, the length of your career is also most likely not going to be limited to twenty-five years but thirty, forty, or more years. Pensions have practically become an endangered species, replaced by 401(k) programs, in which companies may or may not match a percentage of your savings. On top of that, retirement plans are often directly tied to the general health of the economy and "the market." Therefore, your hard-earned, planned, and saved nest egg value may be significantly less than what you will need when you look to retire. Social Security was established in the early 1900s when the average life expectancy was much lower than today. There very well may come a time when there is little to no money when it becomes your turn to collect.

The point of this lesson is that if you want to retire at a reasonable age with an adequate income, you need to plan and act by the time you are twenty-one years old. Treat your retirement savings as a bill that must be paid in order to avoid working until the day you die. If your company does have a matching 401(k) plan, try to contribute at least the same percentage amount that your employer gives you. There may also be a minimum period of time that you must be employed in order to keep the matched portion (known as being vested). If your company does not have a 401(k) plan, you should open and continuously feed a private retirement account such as a Roth IRA. When you look at how your savings can grow with the compounded interest, your thousands of dollars in annual contributions can turn into hundreds of thousands over the thirty or forty years. While you may have fun spending all your money today, you could find yourself in serious financial problems when you look to retire. Do not wait until it is too late or you become unable to work due to physical problems to think about your financial future.

Death and Dying

There is no doubt that death and dying is a sad event and topic. Whether it happens suddenly or as a result of a long-term battle, when the day comes, you never seem to be fully prepared. Death has much negative connotation to it, but for your own comfort, try to find the positive in it. Remember the good times, take stock of your own life and learn to appreciate it that much more. Furthermore, you may or may not find the person going through the traditional five steps of grief including denial, anger, bargaining, depression, and finally acceptance.

To help you overcome your loss, there are many things you can do. You can honor the person by picking up the cause that they were a part of or by volunteering your time towards the effort. You can visit and keep in touch with the people they left behind, especially any children. Become a big brother or sister to those who now have a void in their lives. You can also become an organ donor if you have not already. Lastly, live your own life to its fullest as the departed would have if given another chance.

Any adult can and should have a last will and testament and living will (also know as an "advance directive"). A living will is extremely important since it clearly defines your wishes given various situations or conditions. If you do not wish to prepare a formal living will, then you should at least talk to a direct relative (spouse or parent) to give them an idea of your wishes. In addition, talk to all the parties involved to ensure that everyone has the same understanding. The last thing you would want is to place additional stress on your loved ones by forcing them to guess what you would want, causing potential conflicts in an already emotionally charged time. Furthermore, assets can become tied up for months to years in the legal system, as in the case of probate. It is highly recommended that you review and update your affairs shortly after a major life change or event such as marriage or the birth of a child.

The Environment

"The best time to plant a tree was twenty years ago.
The second best time is today."
– Chinese Proverb

Natural versus Artificial

While you might expect that the natural version or path to be better than its artificial counterpart, that is not always the case. Depending on your need and the usage, the selection you make, assuming you have a choice in the matter, could greatly affect the outcome or effectiveness. Cost and availability may also be significant factors in the selection process. For certain items, the natural version is purer than its artificial counterpart. Furthermore, there may not be an artificial equivalent or its potency may be less effective, as in the case of breast milk versus formula. When it comes to foods, natural is always better. This holds especially true for beverages, considering all the additives and sweeteners found in most drinks today. There are also many organically grown or raised alternatives to the products we commonly consume on a daily basis. Lastly, in the medical area, natural remedies have their limitations and should never be a substitute for professional evaluation or prescription medicines.

There are a number of natural or natural-based cleaning supplies that are just as good if not better than the chemical cocktails commercially available. One word of caution: just because an item is natural, that does not mean it is completely safe. Often naturally occurring products can be hazardous, even deadly, if used or taken in excess. Furthermore, combining two or more natural components can produce a poisonous new product. In the case in mixing chlorine (i.e. Clorox®) with ammonia, ammonium chloride gas is produced which is toxic in low dosages. Baking soda is a great alternative when a cleaner with an abrasive is needed. Diluted vinegar can be used in all types of cleaning, especially if you need to cut through grease. In addition, there are a number of "green" cleaning products readily available at your local supermarket. If you are not sure about a product, just read the list of ingredients. If you cannot pronounce what you are reading, leave it on the shelf. Lastly, always consider the entire life cycle of the product, not just the final result.

Take Only What You Need

Whether it is food at a buffet or a free paper, only take an appropriate amount so other people can enjoy it too. This concept applies to nature and the environment as well. If you are out in nature, only use what you need and always leave the rest the way you found it. If you have no intention of using something, do not take it just because it is free. Take a page from the American Indians, who use every part of the animal they hunt and kill.

Gardening

Gardening is an excellent way for you to learn patience and get closer to Mother Earth. You do not need acres of land to garden either; a few square feet or pots of soil will do the trick. It can be a very soothing hobby and used as a relaxing escape from the daily grind. You can also share the experience with a child as a hands-on learning tool. Growing your own fruits and vegetables gives you a greater appreciation for the amazing power of nature. In fact, during World War I and II, many people had "victory gardens" in which the common citizen could bolster local moral while relieving the strain on food demands during the war. You will not only learn more about the foods you commonly consume, but it will show you the importance of organic growing methods. Try using natural forms of pesticides as well as organic fertilizers which you probably have on hand and do not even realize it.

Conservation

Conservation can take many forms, but it typically refers to natural resources and electricity. The major resources include water, fossil fuels, wood, and paper. The basic idea is to use only what is minimally required. Conservation could be as simple as turning the lights out when you leave a room or not letting the water run while brushing your teeth. There are many new products, such as compact florescent light bulbs, that consume a fraction of the energy when compared to their predecessors. Just be careful with some of the alternative products since they may have drawbacks. Using the compact florescent light bulb example again, they contain small amounts of mercury, which means you need to dispose of them properly and be careful not to break them as well.

You can easily save gasoline by driving a hybrid vehicle or by carpooling. Tons of chlorine can be saved by curbing your misuse of water. There are also seasonal changes you can make to lower your utility bills. For example, you should close blinds and drapes in the summer months to reduce room warming due to the greenhouse effect. The opposite works well in the winter to reduce heating bills, assuming you do not have any major drafts. Another seasonal trick is to close forced hot air/air-conditioning registers in rooms that are not occupied. You can also help conserve natural resources by slightly altering your daily activities. For example, cut showering time down by a couple of minutes, unplug chargers when they are not in use since they consume electricity even when they are not actively recharging electronics, run dishwashers and washing machines during evening hours and only when they are at full capacity, lower the temperature setting on hot water heaters, and install a digital thermostat. Digital thermostats can be easily installed and programmed to automatically lower and raise temperatures while you are not home, thereby adding comfort, saving hundreds of dollars a year, and reducing overall consumption. Furthermore, take full advantage of the digital world we live in by suppressing paper statements for such things as banking, insurance, and any other monthly bills. Suppressing extraneous postal mail also has the natural benefit of reducing the risk of identity theft. Lastly, upgrade any old, energy-hogging appliances including air conditioners, heating systems, refrigerators, dishwashers, clothes washers and dryers. Newer models will pay for themselves in no time at all while saving natural gas, electricity, water, and detergents. Make a conscious effort to limit your consumption and before long it will become a natural part of your daily life.

Conservation also has a built-in benefit; the less you use, the more money you save. Depending on the state you live in as well as your utility company, you may be able to shop around for electric and gas suppliers. You should at least look into the option and make sure that you are comparing apples to apples. Be sure to ask question regarding the agreement, including the length of the contract, additional charges or restrictions, penalties for early termination, and price locks. In addition to saving money, you can also help the environment by selecting a supplier that generates the energy in the "greenest" manner. However, we have to keep in mind that conservation is not just for dollars and cents sake but to ensure that future generations have resources available to them as well.

Another benefit of conservation is the reduction in the amount of toxic or harmful byproducts generated. You can directly reduce the generation of carbon dioxide and other unwanted emissions by reducing your energy consumption. However, the ultimate solution is to use the natural resources around you to your advantage. For example, depending on the location and position of your home, you may be able to install solar panels or use the power of the wind to generate electricity. If it is a plausible option, you should have them installed as soon as you can to maximize on your investment. In fact, you may become completely self-sufficient and/or able to sell surplus power back to the utility company for a profit. The whole point is to try and leave as little of an impact on the environment as possible; leave it the way you found it OR BETTER!

Reuse

Any time that you can safely reuse an item, you save yourself time and money, all while helping to preserve the environment. This should be the second option when conservation is not possible. Many objects can be reused multiple times without any health or safety risks. Prior to reusing an item, perform a quick inspection to ensure it is clean and still in sound or working condition. While some items can be reused in their original capacity, others may have outlived their intended purpose but can be still used in other creative ways. For example, plastic containers and cardboard boxes can be reused multiple ways and multiple times.

One of the best examples of reuse in action is Freecycle™ (www.freecycle.org). After you locate your local group and register, you can begin giving and receiving nearly anything for free through e-mail-based posts. The non-profit, volunteer-policed organization has millions of members throughout the world. This simple yet amazing resource keeps tons of usable items out of landfills every day.

Recycling

Recycling is the last option for preserving our environment. If you cannot conserve or reuse an item, hopefully you can recycle it. You should always recycle common items like paper, plastics, and glass. However, there are a whole host of other objects that can be recycled ranging from old computers to building materials. Even old car tires can be ground up and used in playground padding/mulch. Make sure that you dispose of hazardous materials that cannot be recycled properly, including old paint, oil, gasoline, antifreeze, and batteries. Many town municipalities have annual or semi-annual household hazardous waste days where you can drop off old or unused products. In fact, entire businesses have flourished on recycling just a single product. Remember, one person's garbage is another person's treasure.

Final Thoughts

Hannah and Andrew, as you can probably tell by now, a great amount of time, energy, devotion, and love has gone into ensuring that you have all the tools and skills to lead a happy, healthy and successful life. I continue to pledge my undivided attention to helping you build a strong foundation. As you will learn, nothing worthwhile in life comes with great ease. Therefore, at a minimum, keep my version of the Ten Commandments close to your heads and hearts, and I assure you that there is nothing that will stand in your way.

1. Your health and safety are everything; without them, everything else is meaningless.
2. Honor and respect yourself, others, and the environment around you.
3. Always try your hardest, and give everything you do an honest effort to the very end.
4. Always keep your eyes and ears open; the power of observation is critical in all aspects of life.
5. Education is not optional; experience is crucial, but no replacement for an education.
6. Everything in moderation.
7. Be proactive and not reactive.
8. You are a product of your environment; surround yourself with quality.
9. Experience life and what it has to offer.
10. Be positive and have a healthy, flexible outlook.

Regardless of what may lie ahead on your journeys through life, I will always be proud of you, and will support you in everything you choose to do. Remember that you are only human; mistakes will happen, and imperfections are not the end of the world. It is completely normal and understandable just as long as you make a pledge to yourself to learn from the mistake, and continue to improve your quality. Never stop asking me questions on any topic, and know that you can always confide in me. No matter how tough the situation may be, know that you can always count on me being there for you, day or night, whether you are three or fifty-three.

Oh, and by the way, do you know the reason for the title "From an Oak to His Acorns" other than the obvious? In fact, oak trees cannot produce offspring (acorns) until they are at least twenty to twenty-five years old. I told you nature was smarter than us!

Essential Safety Skills Checklist

By the time you are able to drive a car, if not sooner, you should be able to perform the following actions flawlessly and without hesitation. Review and reacquaint yourself with each on an annual basis if necessary. The difference in knowing and not knowing could be a matter of life or death.

❑ Perform the Heimlich maneuver on a baby, adult, a pet, and yourself

❑ Contact Poison Control

❑ Basic First Aid

❑ Infant, child, and adult CPR

❑ Basic usage of an automated external defibrillator

❑ Operate A, B, C, and ABC class fire extinguishers

❑ Start a fire without matches or accelerant

❑ Read a map and determine north, south, east, and west at any time

❑ Change a flat tire

❑ How to swim

❑ Defend yourself without the aid of any weapons

❑ Safely handle a handgun, rifle, and knife

Important Information

The only thing constant in life is change. Therefore, use a pencil when completing the information in this section.

Our Family Name: _____

Street Address: _____

City: _____

State: _____

Zip Code: _____

Home Phone: _____

Parents/Guardians

Name: _____

Cell Phone: _____

Work Phone: _____

Name: _____

Cell Phone: _____

Work Phone: _____

EMERGENCIES: 9-1-1

DOMESTIC VIOLENCE HELP: 800-799-SAFE or ndvh.org

SUICIDE PREVENTION LIFELINE: 800-273-TALK (8255)

POISON CONTROL: 800-222-1222

ANIMAL EMERGENCIES: www.vetlocator.org

NORMAL HUMAN BODY TEMPERATURE: 98.6 °F (37 °C)

Medical Information

Key Health Indicators

	Value	Last Checked
Blood Pressure	_____	_____
LDL	_____	_____
HDL	_____	_____
Triglycerides	_____	_____
Total Cholesterol	_____	_____

Insurance Information

Type	Provider	ID Number	Coverage/Co-pay
_____	_____	_____	_____
_____	_____	_____	_____
_____	_____	_____	_____
_____	_____	_____	_____
_____	_____	_____	_____

Pharmacy Information

Name: _____

Address: _____

_____

Phone: _____

Fax: _____

Medical Information

Physician Information

Name: _____

Address: _____

_____

Phone: _____

Fax: _____

Name: _____

Address: _____

_____

Phone: _____

Fax: _____

Name: _____

Address: _____

_____

Phone: _____

Fax: _____

Name: _____

Address: _____

_____

Phone: _____

Fax: _____

Family Information

Name	Birth Date	Blood Type	Allergies

Our Heritage and Religion

Heritage: _____

_____

_____

_____

_____

_____

Religion: _____

House of Worship

Name: _____

Address: _____

_____

Phone: _____

Fax: _____

Primary Spiritual Leader

Name: _____

Address: _____

_____

Phone: _____

Cell: _____

Fax: _____

Our Family Lineage

Use the space on these two pages to diagram your family's lineage.

Our Family Lineage

Be sure to include any major medical issues such as cancer and heart disease that may have an effect your own health.

Important Dates

Date	Event
2nd Sunday in March; 2 a.m.	U.S. Daylight Saving Time Begins* Spring ahead (lose one hour)
1st Sunday in November; 2 a.m.	U.S. Daylight Saving Time Ends* Fall back (gain one hour)
_____	Smoke alarm batteries last changed
_____	Hazardous household waste pick-up/drop-off
_____	Recycling pick-up
_____	_____
_____	_____
_____	_____
_____	_____
_____	_____
_____	_____
_____	_____
_____	_____
_____	_____
_____	_____
_____	_____

* Not all areas in the U.S. participate in DST. They include: American Samoa, Arizona (except the Navajo Indian Reservation), the Commonwealth of Northern Mariana Islands, Guam, Hawaii, Puerto Rico, and Virgin Islands.

Important Contact Numbers

Number   **Contact**

_____   _____

_____   _____

_____   _____

_____   _____

_____   _____

_____   _____

_____   _____

_____   _____

_____   _____

_____   _____

_____   _____

_____   _____

_____   _____

_____   _____

_____   _____

_____   _____

_____   _____

_____   _____

_____   _____

_____   _____

Our Neighbors

Name: _____

Address: _____

Phone: _____

Cell: _____

Other: _____

_____

_____

Name: _____

Address: _____

Phone: _____

Cell: _____

Other: _____

_____

_____

Name: _____

Address: _____

Phone: _____

Cell: _____

Other: _____

_____

_____

Useful Conversion Factors

1 Pound (lb)	=	16 Ounces (oz)
1 Pound (lb)	=	454 Grams (g)
1 Kilogram (kg)	=	2.2 Pounds
1 Ton	=	2,000 Pounds
1 Gallon of Water	=	8.33 Pounds
1 Cubic Centimeter (cc)	=	1 Milliliter (ml)
1 Tablespoon (tbs)	=	3 Teaspoons (tps)
1 Quart	=	4 Cups
1 Gallon	=	4 Quarts
1 Gallon	=	128 Ounces
1 Gallon	=	3.8 Liters
1 Centimeter (cm)	=	10 Millimeters (mm)
1 Inch (in)	=	2.54 Centimeters
1 Yard (yd)	=	3 Feet (ft)
1 Meter (m)	=	3.3 Feet (39.4 inches)
1 Mile (mi)	=	5,280 Feet
0° Celsius (C)	=	32° Fahrenheit (F)
100° Celsius	=	212° Fahrenheit

*Family Recipe for*_____

Serves: _____

Preparation Time: _____   **Cooking/Baking Time:** _____

Pasted Down By: _____

Ingredients: _____

_____

_____

_____

_____

_____

_____

_____

_____

Instructions:

_____

_____

_____

_____

_____

_____

_____

_____

_____

_____

_____

_____

_____

_____

*Family Recipe for*_____

Serves: _____

Preparation Time: _____   **Cooking/Baking Time:** _____

Pasted Down By: _____

Ingredients: _____

_____

_____

_____

_____

_____

_____

_____

Instructions:

_____

_____

_____

_____

_____

_____

_____

_____

_____

_____

_____

_____

*Family Recipe for*_____

Serves: _____

Preparation Time: _____   **Cooking/Baking Time:** _____

Pasted Down By: _____

Ingredients: _____

_____

_____

_____

_____

_____

_____

_____

Instructions:

_____

_____

_____

_____

_____

_____

_____

_____

_____

_____

_____

*Family Recipe for*_____

Serves: _____

Preparation Time: _____   **Cooking/Baking Time:** _____

Pasted Down By: _____

Ingredients: _____

_____

_____

_____

_____

_____

_____

_____

_____

Instructions:

_____

_____

_____

_____

_____

_____

_____

_____

_____

_____

_____

_____

_____

About Pediatric Cancer Research Foundation

The Pediatric Cancer Research Foundation, a 501(c)(3) non-profit organization, was founded in 1982 to improve the care, quality of life and survival rate of children with malignant diseases.

Since its inception, PCRF has raised over twenty million dollars to fund cutting-edge research that leads to medically sound treatment protocols for childhood cancers. Research funded by PCRF has led to survivors in all fifty states and in many countries around the world. Through these types of research supported efforts, children's cancer survival rates have risen faster than for any other type of cancer. Survival rates were ten to fifteen percent twenty-five years ago, whereas today the survival rate is approximately seventy-five percent. But the battle is far from over – cancer continues to afflict more children under eighteen years of age each year than any other disease; about thirty-five kids per day are diagnosed with cancer in the United States alone.

PCRF is privately supported through donations from individuals, charitable foundations, and businesses that recognize the urgent need to improve treatment and cure childhood cancers. All contributions to PCRF are tax deductible.

Dedicated volunteers support the foundation, enabling over eighty percent of every dollar raised to go directly to research. The foundation raises funds through gifts from individuals, special giving programs, events, corporate sponsorships, grants, and the sale of holiday cards drawn by children fighting cancer. For more information, vistit www.pcrf-kids.org.

PCRF | Pediatric Cancer Research Foundation

Notes